Living
To
Play

Living TO Play

From Soccer Slaves to Socceratti – A Social History of the Professionals

John Harding
with Gordon Taylor

ROBSON BOOKS

First published in Great Britain in 20023 by Robson Books, 64 Brewery Road, London, N7 9NT

A member of **Chrysalis** Books plc

British Library Cataloguing in Publication Data
A catalogue record for this title is available from the British Library.

ISBN 1 86105 560 9

Printed in Great Britain by St Edmundsbury Press, Bury St Edmunds, Suffolk.

Contents

Acknowledgements

I would like to thank the following people for their help and support in the writing of and research for *Living To Play*:

Tony Barker
Harry Berry
Claire Beswick
Micky Burns
Rosy Canter
Andy Cowie
Mike Davige
Fred Eyre
Ted Farmer
Sir Tom Finney
Ed Furniss
Peter Gilpin
Mrs Ronni Harding
George and Jennifer Hardwick
William Hodgson
Duncan Holly
Brian Horsnell
Simon Inglis
Paul Joannou
Tony Matthews
Philip Paul
Jeremy Robson
Dr JK Rowlands
David Sullivan
Tony Tams

Janet Unwin
Alf and Dorothy Walton
Andy Ward
John Weir
Tony Whelan
Charlie and Janice Williams
Gerry Wolstenholme
At the PFA: Carol Brown, Karen Chapman and Louise Pearson
At Robson: Mike Flynn, Anthea Matthison, and Jane Donovan and Richard Mason (in particular).

Foreword

Gordon Taylor MA

Chief Executive, Professional Footballers'
Association. President, Fifpro.

While the origins of football could well go back to the ancient
Roman and Chinese civilisations, professional football, as we know
it today, was founded and organised through the English public
school system. Not surprisingly, it mirrored the class system in
England and the first men paid to play the game had great difficulty in establishing both their status as professionals and their normal
rights as working men. In fact, the general perception of players by
club owners could be best summed up in the writer J B Priestley's
words. 'Professional footballers,' he wrote, were considered,
'hirelings, merely paid to kick a ball.'

A myth developed in those early days was that professional footballers were so desperate to play and felt so privileged to be allowed
to do so by the club owners that they gratefully accepted conditions
and terms akin to those once enjoyed by medieval serfs. The establishment of the PFA in 1907 (originally called the Players' Union)
gives a lie to that myth. Edwardian football stars like Billy Meredith
of Manchester United and Wales, took up the baton handed on
by their Victorian forebears to organise professionals in order
to improve their lot significantly. The early Players' Union was

dedicated to improving the working conditions of every pro foot-baller, not just those at the top level. The modern PFA still believes in and is guided by that principle.

The problems pro players faced for much of the last century cannot be understated. Many players were not considered by government civil servants to have an entitlement to basic workmen's compensation and insurance rights. This affected their pensions and their unemployment pay. When they were injured, they often found their insurance premiums didn't cover the costs of treatment. Their earnings were restricted by a strict maximum wage ceiling and their freedom of movement was hampered by a transfer system that kept even the greatest players tied to a particular club for life – if the club directors so decided. Sir Tom Finney, that wonderful player for Preston North End and England after the Second World War, was scandalously denied a fabulous opportunity to play in Italy by his directors, who refused even to discuss it with him! Wilf Mannion, another gifted England international of the 1950s, staged a virtual one-man strike in a vain attempt to break free from Middlesborough. The effort almost broke his health. They, like so many other great players, wondered why they should only be able to obtain a maximum of £20 per week when comparable stars of stage and screen were earning salaries of five times that and more.

With football having become the global game it is now, and with the Premier League providing more players for the World Cup than any league in the world, it is interesting to see how, in earlier years, so many British players looked across the seas in attempts to break free from their 'chains'. From the 1920s on, there were concerted attempts by players to establish alternative careers with clubs in North America, in France and in Colombia, where opportunities temporarily seemed to be much brighter. The FA in England treated such men as if they were fugitives from justice, giving credence to Players' Union Chairman Jimmy Guthrie's claim, when speaking at the TUC Congress in the early 1950s, that professionals in this country were no better than 'soccer slaves'.

It's also interesting to note, particularly with so many foreign players now earning their living in England, that the first professionals were not English at all, but Scottish. For some years in the 1880s, the Scottish FA refused to allow professionalism and, in the decade that followed, Scottish players flocked across the border, much to the concern of some English commentators, who felt the English game was being damaged. By contrast, English players looked upon the arriving Scottish 'professors' as simply fellow tradesmen, looking to make a living. Just as with today's foreign imports, the Scots brought with them skills and ideas that only made the home game more attractive. Everyone benefited.

The belief of men like Billy Meredith that if pro players were granted proper status and accorded employment rights similar to those enjoyed by other professional tradesmen, then the wider game itself would benefit accordingly, has proved more than justified. The early unionists understood that the correlation between good working conditions and a balance of power between players and bosses would lead to an improvement in the status and popularity of the game, as well as to an improvement in their own performances and prospects. Their struggles in those early, difficult days set in motion the changes that led to the establishment of the conditions that footballers enjoy today. The removal in 1961 of the maximum wage restriction, the right to freedom of movement won in 1978 and confirmed by the Bosman decision in 1995, have at last allowed players the freedom to capitalise on their abilities and thus encourage greater talent into the game. With satellite television bringing football into every home on a regular basis, it has never been more popular. As a result, top football players are earning more than the equivalent pop stars. At the same time, the base of the football pyramid has been maintained with more amateur players active than ever before. Once again, everyone benefits.

Living To Play, the first book to provide a comprehensive social history of professional football through the eyes of the players themselves, illustrates that, for so many years, the more things changed the more they stayed the same. Colin Veitch, a star player for Newcastle United and England in the decade before the First World War and a prominent Union man, was convinced that his two elder brothers were just as capable as he of becoming successful professional footballers. However, they were prevented from entering the profession by parents concerned that it was a precarious way to earn a living and not socially acceptable. Veitch felt sad that his brothers had lost a golden chance to fulfil their boyhood dreams. He, by contrast, struggled through college bearing the stigma of 'professionalism'. He even played for a time under a pseudonym in order to avoid being 'tainted'.

When I started playing in 1960, I had no need of an 'alias', but my parents were just as concerned about my future as Veitch's had been about his. Before I joined Bolton Wanderers as an apprentice, they insisted that I carry on with my education in the afternoons, which was difficult for me but ultimately worthwhile. The stigma attached to professional football may, at that time, have disappeared to some extent, but the notion of the pro game as being insecure and something of a gamble remained. Even today, when the image of the profession has altered so dramatically and when the likes of David Beckham have achieved iconic status, three out of four youngsters who join the game at age sixteen are out of it by the time they are twenty-one.

A young man starting out in the game today will receive the same warnings both Colin Veitch and I did as to its dangers and the likelihood of failure. However, he will now find that education for life after football as well as a proper grounding in the skills and knowledge of the game itself are positively encouraged. There is no longer a social stigma attached to being a pro player. Likewise, within the game itself, it is no longer considered irrelevant and somehow suspicious to study for qualifications that can help transform an individual's quality of life, whether he is successful as a player or not.

One thing will remain constant, however. It can safely be said of heroes past and present, as well as of the many thousands of paid players who have graced our football pitches down the years, that not one of them would have swapped their football career for any other and that nothing in their lives since football has ever quite lived up to the thrill of being a player. I can vouch for that myself. In the words of Robert Louis Stevenson: 'If a man loves the labour of his trade, then regardless of any question of success or fame, the gods have called him.'

Introduction

Living To Play looks at soccer players' lives away from the playing arena. In many ways, it is a companion to *For the Good of the Game*, the history of the Professional Footballers' Association written in 1991. That book revealed the struggle of professional players to establish themselves and their Union as a meaningful presence in the running of the game. They wanted better pay and the same freedom to move from workplace to workplace as other working men (and women) possessed. It also demonstrated how aware players' representatives have always been of the necessity for reform of the game and the dangers inherent in neglecting the education and welfare of young men choosing football as a profession.

The decade since *For The Good Of The Game* has seen enormous changes take place in professional soccer. The Bosman ruling liberated players from the restrictions of an outmoded and discredited contract system. TV revenues have helped create scores of soccer millionaires whose faces and day-to-day lives are as familiar as those of rock and film stars. New stadia, new competitions, a National Football Museum, as well as the arrival of scores of talented foreign players have raised the game from being a national preoccupation to a virtual obsession.

Inevitably, the profession of football had to change radically. Increasing demands on players' bodies and minds necessitated rapid overhauls of coaching and fitness-training, of injury treatment and tactical awareness. The accompanying social demands resulted in more enlightened education programmes for younger players and crash-courses in lifestyle-management for established stars. In essence, the profession has become truly professional at last.

Leading the transformation from the front has been Gordon Taylor's PFA. Significantly, among many PFA initiatives in education, playing contracts, the Community Programme and drug awareness, Taylor himself is most proud of the Association's anti-racism programmes and the successful assimilation of more foreign players than any other country in the world.

Once the poor relation of the game, the Professional Footballers' Association now stands at its heart, reflecting perfectly the way in which the professional player himself, once the hired hand, is now in full control of his own destiny. *Living To Play* illustrates how things were and the distance the paid player has travelled since professionalism was recognised back in 1888.

In the writing of this book, I am indebted, once again, to Gordon Taylor for his own professionalism and the considerable practical help and encouragement he has given me in charting this journey. He has always been keenly interested in the history of the game. At the PFA in Manchester, he has assembled an unrivalled collection of football memorabilia, including that archetypal football painting, 'Going to the Match' by LS Lowry. His knowledge of the game is unrivalled and his interest in its history is as keen now as it was when he first entered the old Union offices at Hanging Ditch as a delegate back in 1971.

John Harding

Chapter 1

The First Professionals

'How glibly some people talk of football slavery! But how many of them would walk up to the members of a League team and tell them they are slaves? No, my friends, I'm not a slave.'

Albert Iremonger Leng's Football Handbook, 1913–14

In 1900, a waxwork figure of a professional footballer appeared on show at Madame Tussauds in London. Not, as cynics might today suggest, in the Chamber of Horrors, but right alongside sporting greats such as the cricketer WG Grace, the jockey Fred Archer and the yachtsman Tommy Lipton. The proprietors of Tussauds, one of the country's first major tourist attractions, had noticed that Cup Final weekend provided them with a significant boost in attendance figures.

Arthur Turner of Southampton, the player chosen to represent the booming working-class obsession was not, however, in the same league as Grace and Archer. Although subsequently an England international and a two-time cup finalist, he had finished with the game by 1905, and would vanish into the obscurity of running his father's business in Farnborough.

Prominent footballers of the period such as Steve Bloomer, John Goodall and Dan Doyle had none of the national stature of Grace or Archer. The latter earned their money in sports that were long established with solid middle-class, even royal, approval. The professional Association game, by contrast, was seen as a parochial, northern phenomenon, its 'stars' mainly local men whose appeal was limited. While the Cup Final was, by then, a fixture in the national sporting calendar, the game and its followers were regarded with either suspicion or amusement by opinion formers and social commentators.

Intellectuals did, however, occasionally comment on the new phenomenon. In October 1892, Charles Edwardes, novelist, travel-writer, translator of the Italian statesman Garibaldi, wrote a sympathetic survey of the professional game in the journal *The 19th Century* entitled 'The New Football Mania'. He was particularly taken with the players themselves:

'In their respective neighbourhoods they are the objects of the popular adoration. They are better known than the local members of parliament. Their photographs are in several shops, individually and grouped. The newspaper gives woodcuts of them and brief appreciative biographical sketches. Even in their workaday dress they cannot move in their native streets without receiving ovations enough to turn the head of a prime minister.'

Despite the attention, Edwardes felt the players handled things well: 'Their honest heads are not easily turned. They are marketable goods and they are not ashamed. Why, it may be asked, need they be ashamed of it? Every man has his price, we are told by great authority.'

In this respect, Edwardes differed from many middle-class commentators who were disturbed if not downright offended by the very idea of paying soccer players. Edwardes, however, went straight to the point:

'It, football, is something else as well as a passion. It is a profession. In other professions, if a man is bent on pre-eminence, with its various rewards of lucre and public estimation, he must strive hard to attain it. Nor is it different in football. It depends upon the vigour, craft and strength of the player whether he earns £2, £3 or £4 a week during eight months of the year.'

The arguments about whether men should be paid to play the game are linked to the class origins of the majority of team games in England. Association Football had been codified in the 19th century by an upper-class elite as a means of improving the mental and physical health of public schoolboys and, later, as a means of instilling concepts such as fair play, combination and camaraderie – necessary attributes for a colonial administrative class.

Having played a useful part in reforming the nation's public schools and their inmates, the same games had then been employed by social reformers and 'muscular' Christians to divert working-class youth from drink and sloth. When soccer was subsequently appropriated by industrial entrepreneurs and turned into a commercialised form of mass entertainment, there was a struggle. Clubs employing professionals were thrown out of the FA Cup by the game's governing body, the Football Association. When more and more clubs pressed to be allowed to pay players, however, the Association relented, but only after much heart-searching and no little regret.

In the course of the long, sometimes acrimonious, debate, professionalism had been called by its opponents an 'accursed weed', a 'serious evil', and a 'wicked' thing that would ruin the game utterly if allowed to 'run riot'. As a consequence, strict rules had been imposed on paid players so that, by the time

Arthur Turner was being hoisted into place at Madame Tussauds, the profession he represented consisted of men who could only leave their place of employment with express permission from their employers, who could, on occasion, be 'sold' against their wishes to another employer, who could be excluded from playing altogether if they caused any trouble and – most controversial of all – could earn no more than £4 a week.

Ironically, the harsh and inflexible regulations concerning pay and movement under which players were labouring by 1900, and which they felt so degraded them, suited the commercial clubs that comprised the Football League. 'Free Trade' did not exist in the topsy-turvy economic world of professional football. Players either accepted the terms offered them, or they ceased to be players at all.

Meanwhile, amateur players were considered to be superior to their professional brothers because amateurs continued to uphold the moral values that had been invested in team games by their public school creators. Richard Holt, sports historian, has written: 'The term "amateur" has come to mean anyone who does not play for pay, but the original meaning was more subtle. Amateurs were gentlemen of the middle and upper classes who played sports that were often enjoyed by the common people – athletics, rowing, or cricket, for example – but who played these and other games in a special way. For the gentlemen amateur, it was how you played the game that was important.'

Don Cunliffe:
Portsmouth and
England, c. 1906.

The implication being that if you were being paid, there was little chance that you would stick to the rules because you were striving to win at all costs, which a professional must do. This was to miss the whole point of the game. Amateurs played for the sheer joy of it. It was a spiritual thing.

It would prove a stubborn prejudice to overcome, however, and would cast a cloud over the profession for many years to come. Colin Veitch, a star forward for Newcastle United and England in the first decade of the century, was college educated and one of the most articulate players of his day. As a man of many talents, including music and the writing of fiction, Veitch expressed his dismay in 1910 at the distress his decision to become a paid player had caused his family. 'I recollect as though the occurrence was yesterday how many months of agony I had to go through before I could finally admit to the monstrous truth that I had signed a professional form for Newcastle United.'

Odious comparisons with amateur players would continue to have an adverse affect on the development of the pro-game over the course of the coming century. But there were other objections raised to the new 'trade'. First, in the very early days, to the nationality of the professionals, and second, to their bad social habits.

In 1905, one of the early 'greats' of the game, John Goodall, complained in his book, *Men Famous In Football*, that, 'the assaults made on professional football have been quite uncompromisingly bitter'. The men responsible for the attacks often held positions of responsibility within the FA and they ought, Goodall felt, to have known better. Pro footballers were not 'hired footpads' or 'kicking ruffians' simply because they found they could earn a living from 'utilising the skill with their toes'. Rather, he felt, they were merely 'strong-limbed youngsters of the middle and work-ing class with a passion for the game.'

John Goodall's anger at the 'rantings' of these highly placed men may have had something to do with his own ancestry. He was born in Westminster, and thus eligible to play for England, although his parents were Scottish. Although his football career began in Kilmarnock, he later moved to Great Lever, near Bolton, in 1883, and thence on to play for Preston North End in 1885–6. Similar journeys were taken by many hundreds of Scotsmen in the 1880s and 1890s because the first professionals were, to a man, Scottish. In fact, some five years after 'legalisation', it was estimated that no fewer than 230 Scottish pros were registered in England. Thus, to attack profession-als in these early days was to attack, albeit indirectly, Scotsmen.

The Scottish players had been welcomed across the border because of their specific skills: the mastery of the dribbling arts being a characteristic of the Scottish game. Club directorates in England were increasingly aware that crowds came along to be entertained and Scottish 'stars', from the very beginning, proved to be a big draw. With the rapid expansion of the Football League following the lifting of the ban on paying players, English clubs needed as many players of talent and accomplishment as they could find to entertain the patrons.

This mass transfer of talent, though greatly resented in Scotland, was prompted by economic circumstances. First, the Scottish FA

Rob Barr, Third Lanark, c. 1906.

refused to follow their English counterparts in allowing the payment of players for a number of years. Thus, Scotsmen with football talent had nowhere else to go but south if they wanted to exploit it.

Second, most Scottish players hailed from industrial districts in severe economic decline. They could thus be tempted south by the offer of a job from the various prosperous industrialists who were then bankrolling the new English professional football clubs. Their football wage was regarded as an attractive supplement to their 'main' wage as working men.

Exactly who the first professionals to play in England were is open to debate. According to Jimmy Catton, a celebrated journalist and commentator on the game at the turn of the century, the main candidates were Peter Andrews and James J Lang, who came to Sheffield to play for the Heeley club towards the end of 1876 or early in 1877.

'They had been "rolling stones" in their own country and Peter Andrews, after playing for Glasgow against Sheffield, settled down with the Heeley club in the metropolis of the cutlery trade. What induced him to do so? What could persuade him to reside in a town with which he had no ties of home or friendship, but Saxon silver?'

In 1922, in the *Sunday Dispatch*, James Lang dismissed Andrews' case for being the first soccer professional, citing the authority of Charles Clegg, one of the most prominent football administrators of the time:

'Peter didn't go to play football. He was sent to Leeds on business by his firm and after being there for some months became connected with the Heeley club. Later he took his wife and family south.' Lang continued, 'I joined Sheffield Wednesday in the autumn of 1876 and I played my first match for them on the first Saturday of October of that year. I am not going to say that I crossed the border to play for nothing because you wouldn't believe me if I did.'

Catton was always somewhat sceptical about the claim that the men worked at trades outside football and he would tell the tale of two other pioneers with claims to being the first professionals, James Love and Fergus Suter. The two men were playing for Partick Thistle FC in 1876 when Thistle had visited the Darwen club in Lancashire for a friendly match. Love had stayed behind when the team returned north but, 'after Love had been in the "peaceful valley" [of Darwen] a little while, Mr Hindle [Darwen's secretary] received a letter from Suter saying that he was a stonemason and that he was out of work. If employment could be found for him he would come south, follow his occupation [as a stone mason] and assist the club.'

A job was found but Suter, 'soon complained that the stone was much harder than he had been accustomed to in Scotland, that his hands and arms were swelling and that he must have a rest'. During his leisure the members of the club contributed to a little fund each week to keep him in necessaries as they probably had done for Love. Suter at length resumed the mallet and chisel but the stone was too stubborn for the poor fellow and he gave up in despair. Then he was permanently thrown on the club.'

Suter was worth the money the club paid, apparently: John Lewis, a famous referee of the period, described him as, 'Prepossessing in appearance and a striking figure on the field. Standing around 5ft 9ins, he was well built and his dark complexion was crowned with a fine head of hair. In the height of his fame he was regarded as one of the best backs in the kingdom. It was an education to watch him play. He had studied the art of defence which he had reduced to a science...' and there's an argument to be made that Suter and his Scottish colleagues helped raise the general level of play in England. But there were also many complaints from within the game's hierarchy that their presence was damaging English football. 'The little

stream had swollen into a mighty rushing river, flooding the country and doing incalculable injury to purely English football,' wrote one commentator. NL Jackson, a famous amateur footballer and avowed enemy of professionalism, felt that local interest in teams 'as between fellow townsmen, which was a healthy parti-sanship in the old days, has entirely disappeared'.

With fewer English players being picked for top League sides, it was felt that the national team was in danger of being undermined. It's an argument voiced today, as a new influx of talented foreigners has come to dominate the Premier League. However, just as today's home-grown professionals appear unmoved by the situation, so in the 1890s, 'local' professionals appeared quite sanguine.

Bob Holmes played in the same Preston North End side as John Goodall between 1884 and 1901 and won most of the games honours and in 1910 he recalled: 'We local chaps didn't know what the imported Scots were earning. My first professional fee was at the rate of ten shillings a week. Not a princely sum you will say yet we never expressed dissatisfaction. Of course, we continued at our respective trades or professions all the time, but it was different with the men from the North. They were brought to Preston for the sole purpose of playing football and what their wages were I have never been able to find out, but it was pretty obvious that they made a "fat" living out of the pastime.'

In time, such financial differentials between English and Scottish players would disappear. Good players, from wherever they hailed, would earn the top wages, while the transfer of English players between League clubs would rapidly dilute the 'local' nature of professionalism.

There was, however, one further objection raised by the oppo-nents of professionalism that the players themselves found hard to rebut: that they drank too much alcohol, and that such behaviour encouraged the fans who so admired them to do likewise.

Drink and its associated dangers were controversial subjects in general in the late 1880s and 1890s. Temperance Societies were at their strongest; the ruin that alcohol had caused millions of working people's lives was very much to the fore. Many Football Association officials, amateurs to a man, took an active role in fighting the scourge. Lord Kinnaird, the FA president, was head of the YMCA, Charles Clegg, FA Council Chairman, was President of the Band of Hope, and John Lewis, a top referee and FA official, was an enthusiastic advocate of the Sunday Football movement designed specifically to keep men out of public houses.

There were conflicting opinions about the professional game's effect on supporters where alcohol consumption was concerned. John Goodall denied that it encouraged supporters to drink. In fact, he felt that football and footballers helped to keep people out of public houses by providing them with a healthy diversion on their free Saturday afternoon. A couple of years later, interviewed in *The Red Letter*, Bob Crompton, another English international and no less a player than Goodall, made the same point. When asked about the charge 'that football was an incentive to drinking amongst its myriad followers,' he replied, 'The idea is simply preposterous. What happens during the season? They drop in and have one drink after their work on a Saturday afternoon. Then they go off to watch a match, every one of them invigorated by the open air all the time.'

However, NL Jackson wrote in 1900: 'The oft quoted plea in favour of professional football, that it keeps men from the public house, is not supported by facts. Only recently an old Scottish international player protested against the growing influence of publicans in football management. He declaimed vigorously against the practice of employing well-known footballers to serve in public houses on Saturday nights.' And it is true that a growing number of prominent professional footballers did become publicans, Fergus Suter among them. Local brewers, aware of the attractiveness of such men, were only too glad to give them a start in a tied house, and the large increase in business which usually followed such an appointment demonstrated how many of the spectators adjourned to 'football pubs' after a match.

Where the question of the drinking habits of the players themselves was concerned, however, there was much less disagreement. Sadly, too many of the early Scottish pioneers who flocked across the border in search of cash and jobs hadn't helped matters with their generally riotous behaviour. By the early 1900s, however, players were claiming that such carousing was a thing of the past.

Harry Reason, a pro with Clapham Orient, admitted in *The Red Letter* in 1909: 'We aren't abstainers by any means but we find that we can enjoy a quiet chat just as well over that beverage as over any other, and know that it will not have a counter-acting effect on our training. Speaking for myself I say strongly that, although I am not a teetotaller, I prefer the dry ginger ale to anything else I can get.'

Reason explained that there were few places a young man could sit quietly and chat about football other than a public house. A number of prominent players tried to explain the unusual pressures they faced, talking of the temptations laid before players. Bill Appleyard of Newcastle United, writing in *Thomsons Weekly News* in February 1909 asked, 'Is the life of a footballer full of temptation? Candidly, I must confess it is.' And one of the most popular pitfalls was drink. Fans, Appleyard explained, took great satisfaction from buying players drinks. 'It sounds like egotism on my part, and insanity on the part of the type of individual I speak of, but nevertheless it is true.'

Albert Shepherd of Bolton Wanderers went further and pointed out that the 'boys' were always made welcome at bar parlours, and that if he visited a certain 'house' his photograph was soon given a prominent place. 'This, of course, with the idea of attracting people to have a quick sing-song and chat. I have some big friends in the business and I never hesitated to give them a "look-in",' he admitted.

John Cameron, the one-time secretary of the old Players' Union, writing in *Spalding's Football Guide* in 1906 to young would-be players, felt obliged to warn them:

'The worst temptation the beginner has got to face is that of drink. When you become a popular pet your admirers think that they can best show their appreciation of you by buying you beer and Scotch-and-soda. To many of your fatuous admirers it seems an honour to be allowed to pay for your drinks at the "Pig and Whistle". Beware of such admirers.' Old players were even worse. 'The beginner is only too apt to be led by the old stager. Tread warily when you first join the professional ranks.'

Professionals at all levels of the game would continue to suffer from the effects of drinking too much and too often, the alcohol-related death in 1908 of Jimmy Crabtree of Aston Villa and England fame being one of the more high profile examples before the First World War. One hundred years on, the antics of drunken footballers have provided newspapers with more copy than they can use, with prominent players like Jimmy Greaves, Tony Adams, Paul Gascoigne and Paul Merson regularly 'coming out' as alcoholics.

Thus, the profession of football had a troublesome beginning, and many of its early problems continue to dog it to this present day. The heavy, controlling hand of the amateur, which was always resented, prevented professionals from taking responsibility for themselves at many levels, not least the financial one. So much so that even as stern a critic of professionalism as NL Jackson admitted to feeling pity for the paid player, especially in his dealings with employers and administrators who, 'bind him hand and foot', preventing the player from, 'obtaining the advantageous terms which his skill might command and making his transfer a matter of sale and barter'. There were, he thought, many fine men among the professionals, which made it all the more strange that they should submit to 'such servile conditions as those which their masters, by the aid of the Football Association, impose upon them'.

His conclusion continues to reverberate down the ages: 'The paid player is as a rule a good fellow, and as good a sportsman as the demands of his employers, the exhortation of his supporters and the exigencies of his position will allow.'

Chapter **2**

Paying for Play

1. The hard facts

'There we were, sitting in Sunday school, when our teacher asked each member of the class in turn, "What would you like to be when you grow up?" It came to my turn, and I told him outright, "I'm going to be a footballer". He was not impressed. "That is no career. There may be some money in it for a few lucky ones, but, you know, footballers take up the game professionally only when they cannot earn their livings at a better job."'

Len Shackleton, Clown Prince of Soccer, 1956

Establishing a broad overview of what players have earned down the years is extremely difficult. The football industry has always been very secretive about exactly what players have earned. Players themselves have usually kept quiet about the terms of their individual contracts and the dearth of paperwork where

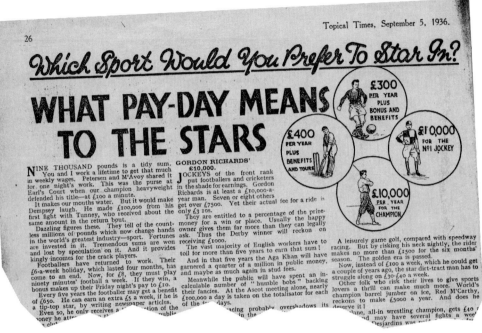

Topical Times, September 5, 1936.

26

Which Sport Would You Prefer To Star In?

WHAT PAY-DAY MEANS TO THE STARS

£300 PER YEAR PLUS BONUS AND BENEFITS

£400 PER YEAR PLUS BENEFITS AND TOURS

£10,000 FOR THE No1 JOCKEY

£10,000 PER YEAR FOR THE CHAMPION

NINE THOUSAND pounds is a tidy sum. You and I work a lifetime to get that much in weekly wages. Petersen and M'Avoy shared it for one night's work. This was the purse at Earl's Court when our champion heavyweight defended his title—at £100 a minute.

It makes our mouths water. But it would make Dempsey laugh. He made £100,000 from his first fight with Tunney, who received about the same amount in the return bout.

Dazzling figures these. They tell of the countless millions of pounds which now change hands in the world's greatest industry—sport. Fortunes are invested in it. Tremendous sums are won and lost by speculation on it. And it provides kingly incomes for the crack players.

Footballers have returned to work. Their £6-a-week holiday, which lasted four months, has come to an end. Now, for £8, they must play ninety minutes' football a week. If they win, a bonus makes up their Friday night's pay to £10. Every five years the footballer may get a benefit of £650. He can earn an extra £5 a week, if he is a tip-top star, by writing newspaper articles. Even so, he only receives a ... tion of the ... money he att...

GORDON RICHARDS' £10,000.

JOCKEYS of the front rank put footballers and cricketers in the shade for earnings. Gordon Richards is at least a £10,000-a-year man. Seven or eight others get over £7500. Yet their actual fee for a ride is only £3 10s.

They are entitled to a percentage of the prize-money for a win or place. Usually the happy owner gives them far more than they can legally ask. Thus the Derby winner will reckon on receiving £1000.

The vast majority of English workers have to toil for more than five years to earn that sum! And in that five years the Aga Khan will have garnered a quarter of a million in public money, and maybe as much again in stud fees.

Meanwhile the public will have spent an incalculable number of "humble bobs" backing their fancies. At the Ascot meeting alone, nearly £100,000 a day is taken on the totalisator for each of the f... days.

...acing probably overshadows its ...

A leisurely game golf, compared with speedway racing. But by risking his neck nightly, the rider makes no more than £1500 for the six months' season. The golden era is passed.

Now, instead of £100 a week, which he could get a couple of years ago, the star dirt-tract man has to struggle along on £30-£40 a week. Other folk who risk their lives to give sports lovers a thrill can make much more. World's champion barrel jumper on ice, Red M'Carthy, reckons to make £5000 a year. And does he deserve it!

...lane, all-in wrestling champion, gets £40 ... and may have several fights a wee... ...desjardins was ...

---

professional football is concerned means that there's little by way of primary sources to consult. But it's necessary to try, however, in order to put into perspective the sense of injustice and sometimes even paranoia that has been a defining characteristic of the professional game where money is concerned.

From the very beginning of organised professional soccer, the payment of players has caused problems. The acceptance in principle of professionalism was traumatic enough for the controllers of the game. The actual amounts paid to players, particularly when the League system was introduced in the late 1880s, appeared to confirm many of their worst fears.

Controlling such payments and limiting the weekly wages of the top players, in particular, was soon mooted and within a decade the 'boom years' for professionals were over. From 1900 on, the Maximum Wage, that artificial 'lid' on the can of financial worms, gave administrators and club owners a method of keeping some kind of control over the game's finances, but players were never able to accept such an arbitrary curb on their rights as working men. For the next 60 years, the 'Maximum' distorted and disfigured the professional game, leading to subterfuge and secrecy, jealousy and resentment. In some respects, the game has probably only just recovered from the damage it caused.

Where the payment of players is concerned, there are four iden-tifiable eras: from the late 1870s to 1901, when clubs were free to pay whatever they liked; 1901 to 1961, when a strict wages 'cap' (the 'maximum') was implemented; 1961 to 1995, when wage freedom existed alongside a gradually crumbling retain-and-transfer system; and post-1995, when players were free once again to negotiate new contracts after their original contracts had expired.

In the late nineteenth century, prior to the implementation of the 'Maximum', football wages moved rapidly from being mere addi-tions to a wage earned in another full-time job to being the sole income for many top-line performers. They earned anything from 10s a match, to £7 or even £8 a week, with hefty signing-on fees into the bargain. The reason for such wage 'inflation' was the suc-cessful establishment of the Football League. Almost overnight, clubs needed anything upwards of 25 players on the club roll, because if they failed to produce full teams each week, as had been the case in the early days, they were heftily fined.

In the scramble for players, the directors of many large clubs opened their purses and set in motion various 'bidding wars'. The men, naturally, played the field, and were often roundly condemned in the press for doing so. Upon learning that Sunderland were pay-ing a player at the rate of £5 per match, a journalist calculated, 'That's a shilling a minute for playing football, and ten bob [shillings] to spend afterwards. Sunderland people seem mighty fond of chucking their money about.'

Despairing of the widespread 'poaching' and the subsequent wages spiral, another writer lamented, 'This is truly the golden har-vest for football professionals. When a second-rate forward receives a genuine offer of £4. 10s a week and others even more, we may well ask what are we coming to?'

But hard evidence was difficult to obtain and often contradictory. In 1893, the *Athletic News Annual* stated that the average wage paid to all pro-fessionals was £3 a week during the playing season and £2 during the summer. Two Derby players had been signed on in that year for £3 a week, and received signing-on fees of £75 and £50. However, two years earlier, a number of top players had been receiving a similar figure, one being George Davie of Arsenal. Players for a top side such as Sunderland were definitely receiving £3 a week by 1893, but some three years later Aston Villa's first team were reportedly being offered…£3 a week!

Lancashire Daily Post,

c. 1900.

Mr. Football Legislator:—"You'll have to come down; this one is quite high enough for you."

By 1900, however, these figures were being comfortably superseded by men such as Billy Beats and Tom Baddelly at Wolverhampton Wanderers, who were on £7 a week all the year round, while the top Aston Villa players were receiving £6.10s.

The 'headline' figures would always be large, however, helping create the drama and controversy upon which football and its media partners have traditionally fed. The spectre of ruinous player 'greed' has usually served as a convenient myth, one that football fans have proved all too prepared to accept.

The fact that football writer Percy Young can claim that most players were earning between thirty and forty shillings during these 'boom years' suggests that, as ever, the bulk of paid players had little bargaining power and little option but to accept gladly whatever they were offered. Even at mighty Aston Villa during the late 1890s, some second team players were guaranteed no more than 15s to £1, with possible increases if they were picked for the first eleven.

However, in the 1890s, there were many instances of unresolved disagreements between players and management committees over contract terms. In 1896, after noting that Aston Villa were 'experiencing a little difficulty in arranging terms with Jimmy Crabtree,' the *Athletic News* reported that the Villa management had cautioned him to be 'satisfied with a reasonable wage'.

In order to impose some kind of overall regulation, the maximum wage was introduced in 1901. This quelled both the moral outrage felt by the more traditional football legislators and the growing exasperation felt by some of the top clubs. Smaller clubs could now rest assured that they would not be priced out of business. Needless to say, the players were not consulted, their Union, rather inconveniently, having just at that moment collapsed.

After this imposition, things become a little clearer, though not much. The majority of top players were awarded the 'Maximum' (and probably for some years were being paid far more than that, under the counter). For the bulk of the profession, however, there was a wide variety of payments, with some clubs offering £4 a week to some players, but certainly not all. By 1910 only 573 professionals out of an estimated 6,800 were receiving the maximum wage, a proportion that probably varied only slightly down the years.

In 1908, the newly formed Players' Union tried to get rid of the maximum wage. It managed to lead the players to the brink of a nationwide strike on the issue in 1909, but failed to convince the Football Association that financial freedom would prove beneficial to the game. What's more, instead of gaining sympathy, the Union's efforts only hardened attitudes on behalf of club managements.

There were changes, however, in the complicated world of football finance in the wake of the 1909 strike. The weekly wage wasn't all a player might earn. After 1910, various bonus payments were allowed to be offered by clubs to players. Thus, after four years as a pro, men in the Football League could earn two further 10s additions to the weekly wage, which ultimately created a new elite band of men on £5 a week.

In the 1920s, a 'sliding pay scale' concept was introduced. New players might be started on £5 a week and earn annual rises of £1 a week over four years. Thus, a new maximum wage of £468 a year had been created. Two years later, however, global economic circumstances (a worldwide slump and mass unemployment) led to it being reduced to £8 a week during the 37-week season and £6 a week during the 15-week close season.

The sliding scale gave club managements flexibility in dealing with players, and many used it as a device to intensify competition between men in the same club. During the 1930s, Grimsby and Sheffield Wednesday pioneered an incentive scheme in which the best players were guaranteed a weekly wage of £6 a week with £2 extra if they kept their first team place. Thus, you could only earn the 'Maximum' if you were a first team player. Being dropped meant a significant loss of wages.

By 1939, according to the Players' Union, fewer than ten per cent of players were in the top bracket, a figure not dissimilar to that achieved in 1910. Second and Third Division players never saw the Maximum, and there were many examples of even the best men earning no more than £7 in season and £4 in summer.

However, players' wages have never been based solely on a flat-rate weekly sum. The peculiar nature of their trade raised questions – was the player a workman or an artist, a servant or a celebrity? This gave rise to various financial additions that clubs might offer. For instance, during the 1909 dispute, top players argued that their special skills were not sufficiently rewarded, that journeymen pros, less talented and less committed men, earned as much as they did. Their 'star' status, clearly a major factor in attracting the crowds, was not reflected in their wage packet. As a consequence, a simple form of 'talent money' was introduced in 1910.

From 1920 the figures for talent money were £2 for a win and £1 for a draw in League and Cup matches. There was more on offer for an FA Cup Semi and Final, but such extras were once again restricted to first team members. Incredibly, these sums remained exactly the same for the next thirty years! So much for box-office appeal.

Beyond the business of pounds, shillings and pence, however, the most significant aspect of a player's employment was that he was prevented from moving to another club even when his contract had expired. The retain-and-transfer system, as it was called, meant that if a man wanted to leave and play elsewhere, he needed permission from the club holding his registration. If the 'holding' club offered him terms similar to those in his previous contract, the player had two choices: to sign or to leave the game entirely. Only if the club decided it was worth selling a player was he allowed to leave. If the player was no longer of any use at all, if he was too old, or too injured, then the club could 'release' him. Only then was the player free to search for another club.

Freedom of contract had been a burning issue in the 1909 dispute; it would remain so until the twenty-first century. In theory, however, this peculiar aspect of a pro player's career – the 'loyalty' factor – was also reflected in the weekly pay packet in the form of what was termed the 'accrued benefit'.

From 1901, a player could, towards the end of his career, look forward to receiving a 'benefit' in the form of the proceeds from a particular match – usually chosen by the player in consultation with the club management. A first benefit was allowed after five years' continuous service, with a second benefit awarded after ten years if the player was still active.

After the First World War, a specific sum was guaranteed rather than a particular match and the payment evolved into a contractual right rather than a 'gift', with specific sums added to the player's weekly wage. The downside where this arrangement was concerned was that, for many years, this 'gift' was taxed.

The sums players might earn depended on each man's worth, in terms of the affection fans felt for him, and the relative power of the club. Clearly, a top club could pay top benefits. Before 1914, the typical amount paid out by the two Sheffield clubs could be anything between £150 and £250. At Aston Villa it was between £300 to £450, rising to £500 for a player like Joe Bache. Billy Meredith, however, at Manchester United, reaped over £1,000 in 1912.

Soon after the First World War, one of the top benefits received was that by George Utley, who walked away from Sheffield United with £1,100. This caused unpleasant disagreements with his fellow players, however, and the FA decided to limit the amount anyone could receive to £500. This was increased to £650 in 1924 but, just as with the talent money, the ceiling figure would remain almost the same for the next thirty years.

Incidentally, the benefit was discretionary. It's clear, however, that a significant proportion of players did receive benefits, most of £400 or above. What's more, if a player was transferred before the five-year period was up, he could be granted an 'accrued share' of what he would have earned – if the club wanted to pay it, and if the player had been wise enough to have such an agreement included in his contract.

One thing every player received, however, was a 'signing-on fee'. Whether you were a youngster putting your signature to your very first contract, or a top international player being transferred to the league champions for a record transfer fee, you were allowed the grand total of £10. Needless to say, this figure, granted by the FA before the start of the twentieth century, went up by not one penny for almost 100 years!

The signing-on fee, however, was understood by all in the game to be little more than a nominal gesture to cover something more substantial. Players weren't free to move of their own accord, but if they didn't want to be transferred, they could refuse. Clearly, all concerned understood that, with wages theoretically the same at whichever club you moved to, a little 'persuasion' might be needed on behalf of the buying club to induce a player to sign. Whatever the two parties worked out in private between themselves was their business. The selling club would receive the agreed fee and so had no reason to complain if the player was being tempted by 'under-the-counter' inducements. So widespread was this practice that, when a player was punished by the FA for asking the buying club for something extra, it came as a big shock.

In 1909, significantly the year of the player's strike, George Parsonage of Fulham was accused of asking for £50 rather than accepting the stipulated £10 signing-on fee. According to Parsonage, the request hadn't been serious: he just didn't want to move to Chesterfield, the club pursuing him and, 'Becoming tired of [the manager] Mr Swift's endeavours, I asked him in what I regarded as a jocular mood, and only with the idea of getting rid of the matter, for £50. That, I thought, had settled the whole thing.' But Chesterfield reported Parsonage to the FA who promptly suspended him from football for life.

A year later, with the football strike dispute settled, the Players' Union tamed, and compromise being the order of the day, Parsonage was granted an amnesty. Billy Meredith wrote in his *Thomson's Weekly News* column in 1910, 'For asking for £50 he has suffered terribly, whereas men who actually receive hundreds [of pounds] have probably never been touched. Of course, no one can blame a professional for being tempted to accept money offered to him.'

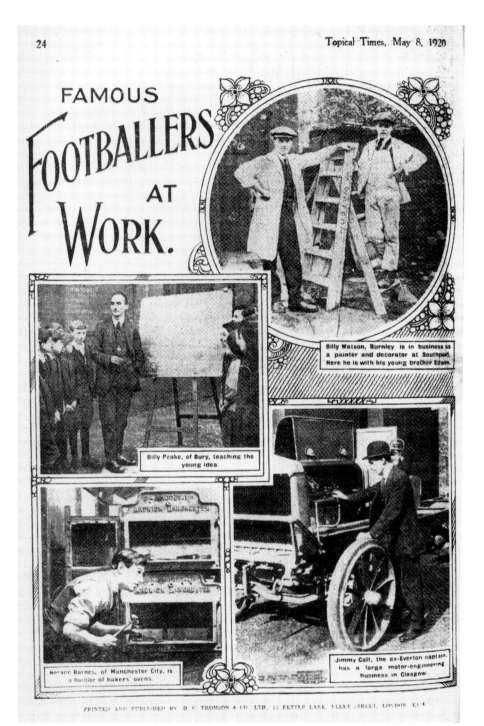

FAMOUS FOOTBALLERS AT WORK.

Billy Watson, Burnley is in business as a painter and decorator at Southport. Here he is with his young brother Edwin.

Billy Peake, of Bury, teaching the young idea.

Horace Barnes, of Manchester City, is a builder of bakers' ovens.

Jimmy Galt, the ex-Everton captain, has a large motor-engineering business in Glasgow.

PRINTED AND PUBLISHED BY D. C. THOMSON & CO. LTD. 12 FETTER LANE. FLEET STREET, LONDON E.C.4.

Because the Players' Union was weak and generated little sense of group solidarity, footballers take-home pay moved upward exceedingly slowly. By the mid-1950s, players were earning a maximum of £15 a week but, as we have seen, many of their 'extras' hadn't altered significantly for decades. The benefit had gone up to £750, but in the meantime, taxes and inflation had also increased considerably. When top players looked at the enormous transfer fees clubs were ever willing to pay, and then considered the £10 signing-on fee that formed their share of the bargain, one might have forgiven them for feeling resentful.

Nevertheless, a peep into a top player's wage packet for 1957 will demonstrate the possibilities then available for the very best players. Roger Byrne, between 1 July 1956 and 30 June 1957, led Manchester United to the brink of a Cup and League Double. (They won the League but missed out in the Cup Final, losing to Aston Villa at Wembley.) Byrne also captained England and played in an Inter-League match, as well as reaching the European Cup semi-final. His year's salary was made up thus: wages from the club £744; League match bonuses £72; League talent money £45 5s 8d; European Cup bonuses £60; accrued benefit £150. Total: £1,071 5s 8d. Add to this his Provident Fund credit of £80 6s 11d, FA Cup bonus £56, FA Cup talent money £50, international match fees £400, and finally an Inter-League match fee £20. Thus a grand total of £1,677 12s 7d.

At the other end of the scale was Charlie Williams of Doncaster Rovers, who left the full-time game in 1960. Earning £20 a week when in the first team, his 'extras' were few. 'I had two benefits at Doncaster. The first one, a reserve team one, brought in £350, out of which I got £240 after tax. If it had been a testimonial match it would have been tax free. That one word made the difference of £110. In my tenth year I got a full benefit which raised £750, out of which I drew £504. So after ten years I didn't get a thousand quid in benefits.'

Things would start to change in 1961, however, when the League, faced with growing player militancy and anger (not to mention an indignant public) finally relented and removed the cap on wages. Before that there would be much struggle, argument, tears and turmoil.

2. Arguments and comparisons

'There is amazing ignorance on the part of the public about this, and they talk as if the majority of players had £4 a week. Why, when I signed on for Notts County, with whom I [played for] eight years, I had 15s a week and gradually advanced until the limit was approached. I am afraid in some clubs the men who get the maximum are in a vast minority...'

Walter Bull, The Red Letter, 1909

For most of the twentieth century, efforts by players to improve their lot were largely fruitless. Earlier prejudices against the idea of men being paid to play, allied to the fact that players appeared to be being paid healthy salaries compared to their working-class counterparts, conspired to leave the professionals perpetually dissatisfied, misunderstood and at a financial disadvantage.

Players did attempt, on occasions, via the popular press, to explain to the fans exactly how and why the wages they received, though seemingly generous, were hardly that at all. In 1909, in an interview in *The Red Letter*, Peter McWilliam of Newcastle United outlined his case in terms that would be echoed down the years by countless players, rich and poor:

'It's like this. I say that a player's life at the longest is a short one, and he is giving the best of his life for the benefit of the public. Four pounds [a week] is really not sufficient for the time he is able to play. We give the vital part of our lives to the game and we should be paid proportionately. Take my own case. I came to Newcastle as a shorthand writer and typist. At that time I did about 120 words a minute. You know what shorthand is? Now I question if I could manage sixty! There you are! I gave up office work and am following a precarious enough profession and all I am entitled to is four pounds a week!

'What's more,' he continued, 'why should a man who once received £8, say (and some got more than that before the rule was passed), now be playing for the same salary as an inferior man who is worth no more than his £4?'

As for the transfer fee, McWilliam thought it ought to be abolished altogether: 'In my opinion, by the time a club comes to transfer a man, they have had their money's worth out of him, and I do not think it is right that they should make any more.'

Walter Bull, a Union activist and Tottenham Hotspur player writing in the same magazine, was scathing of those who felt that players were being greedy. Bull cited a well-known socialist politician who had declared that no man was worth more than £400 a year, but who had not turned down a minister's salary when it was offered to him. Bull felt a minimum wage would be better. 'It is not right that boys should be signed on for a few shillings per week, as I happen to know has been the case with some clubs. If a paid player is worth having I am quite sure he cannot live on less than thirty shillings a week, for he may be married and certainly must have good plain food if he is to keep up his strength and give forth his very best.'

As for the men at the top: 'It seems to me that we are in the position of a comedian who caters for the pleasure of the public. This class may get anything from £10 to £50 a week and surely we, who also give of our skill to please the people, are in much the same position.'

In other professions, Bull explained, workers received a life pension at the end of it, whereas, 'A footballer embarks on his business knowing that he is only engaged for a year at a time and, also, that in ten years at the most his career will be over. Even supposing during all this period he had the £4 a week, he would only have received £2,400, out of which he and a family have to live, and he cannot possibly save enough on which to retire.'

E Charlton of Fulham thought a bonus system would be the answer and, like Bull, cited entertainers as suitable yardsticks for comparison. 'Why do music-hall managers pay Harry Lauder £800 a week and Harold Played-out thirty shillings? Simply because outside the football grounds the best men are best paid and let me tell you the system pays!'

There were, however, contrary arguments made. Many observers inside and outside the game believed that League professionals were well paid. They tended to compare footballers' earnings to the monies earned by men of a similar class in industry – from whence most footballers had come and to where the majority of them would certainly be returning.

In the opinion of John Lewis, a director of Blackburn Rovers and vice-president of the Football League, 'a man who gets £4 a week for five years and then a £350 benefit, followed by another after five years, does uncommonly well for himself, and makes a far better start in life than ninety-nine hundredths of those in a similar station.'

In a similar vein, William Pickford, a top referee, felt that most footballers were 'in a position of financial soundness that might not be attained [in] a labouring or mechanical trade.' Even William Bassett, a former England international, believed that, 'Professional footballers are a handsomely remunerated set of men, and call for the commiseration of no one,' although by the time he made the remark he was on the board at West Bromwich Albion.

And compared to other working-class, even lower middle-class occupations, professional football did offer substantial remuneration. The basic earnings of a First or Second Division footballer on the maximum wage – excluding benefits or other extra payments – easily outstripped the average salary of clerks, skilled or semi-skilled workers, or even supervisors and foremen throughout the period.

However, a star footballer's remuneration came nowhere near the £50 a week which actors in the upper range could earn before 1914. Even stage workers earned £20 a week. By 1914, the wages of variety artistes also ranged widely from £3 to over £100 a week. The majority of theatre managers, some operating a minimum wage, ensured that earnings commenced at £3–£5 per week, an arrangement which meant that even many less established acts fell within the contemporary lower-middle-class pay bracket. Middle-ranking acts earning £10 to £40 weekly were closer to the upper-middle-class category, while star act pay was at a similar level to that of barristers or even cabinet ministers.

Where other professional sports were concerned, some of their big stars certainly earned more than top footballers. Cricketer Learie Constantine apparently earned £800 in 1938 for playing twenty weeks as a professional with Rochdale in the Central Lancashire League. In Rugby League, Billy Batten was earning £14 a match before the First World War, but there were few men in his category.

However, it was across the Atlantic that players began to look with longing, where professional sports stars at the top earned film-star wages. Baseball players earned an average salary of $3,000 in 1910 (£617) but this rose to $5000 (£1,091) in 1923 and reached $7,500 (£1,543) six years later. These incomes compared favourably to those of dentists, doctors, lawyers, professors and other upper-middle-class occupations. Star players earned far more. Pittsburgh's Honus Wagner was paid $18,000 (£3,703) in 1911 and Detroit's Ty Cobb made at least $20,000 (£4,201) in 1915. It was reported in Thomson's *Weekly News* that he was earning £40 a month rising to £100 ($9,000) for six months or £1,800 plus six months' holiday with a Cadillac car included.

However, although Babe Ruth could command a salary of $80,000 (£16,460) by the end of the 1920s, there were many low earners in baseball. In Ruth's team, some men were earning $2,500 (£514) a year.

Ironically, it would be to the United States that many disgruntled players looked in the years following the First World War, in the first of a series of vain attempts to earn the sort of money they felt they deserved.

3. The grass is always greener: the USA

'There are a lot of people who have an idea that all footballers get the maximum wage and roll in wealth. Now it is not so by any means.'

The 'Sentinal', Topical Times, August 1928

In 1921, the FA banned professionals from writing in the press on anything but the most anodyne of topics, and so the open debate about earnings and contracts faded away. The Players' Union, though energetic in pursuing legal claims on behalf of individual players, had no muscle for a full-scale industrial confrontation with the League and no media platform from which to counter the club management propaganda.

Professional players found themselves talked about, mulled over, bought and sold but rarely, if ever, consulted. Those eery, wax-like images so familiar from the ubiquitous cigarette cards of the 1920s and 1930s, all fixed smiles and slicked-back hair, seemed to sum them up. Though apparently happy with their lot, especially during the long years of the Depression and the economic uncertainty that characterised the 1920s and 1930s, certain men did try to escape the system in search of something better.

SPORTS PICTURES
and
FOOTBALL MIRROR

December 27, 1924.

THE PIONEERS.

Ideal Xmas Gift.
RUGBY FOOTBALL
By W. J. A. DAVIES.
Booksellers, **10/6** *net.*

Gift that Delights.
EDUCATED EVANS
By EDGAR WALLACE.
Booksellers **3/6** *Bookstalls.*

(T)   Scottish football circles were much perturbed when some of its best-known players succumbed to the blandishments of agents of the Almighty Dollar, and went off to join Boston, U.S.A. Any English or Scottish League club would be pleased to have this trio for their half-back line (left to right) : Jock M'Intyre (late Greenock Morton), Mick Hamil (Irish international and once of both Manchester League clubs) and Tom Muirhead (Scottish international and late of Glasgow Rangers). These players are the pioneers of a movement which looks like rivalling baseball in the States.

RACING & FOOTBALL OUTLOOK
The Largest Circulation of any Sporting Weekly.

BEST
RACING NEWS

AUTHORITATIVE

INFORMATIVE

WINNERS
EVERY WEEK

2D. Tuesday   *ON SALE EVERYWHERE.*   Tuesday **2**D.

Published by WEBSTER'S PUBLICATIONS, LTD., at 70, Temple Chambers, London, E.C. 4, and printed by W. SPEAIGHT & SONS, LTD., 98-99, Fetter-lane, E.C. 4.—Dec. 27, 1924.

The trump card for football's authorities had always been that beyond the British Isles, there was nowhere else for footballers to turn. No foreign leagues could offer alternative employment. However, as professional football began to take root abroad, opportunities did start to present themselves.

The USA had, even before the First World War, tried to entice Football League players to the various clubs scattered along the Eastern Sea Board, and a number of men had broken their contracts in the mid-1890s to go. The venture did not succeed. In the 1920s, however, news came of 'raids' on British clubs for players to perform in the new American Soccer League. Headlines such as 'US Agents on the Prowl' and 'American Football Menace' set the subsequent tone, although few star players seemed ready to take the risk.

Sports Pictures in December 1924 did show three notable Scottish captures sitting dressed in the colours of the Boston club: Jock McIntyre (ex-Greenock Morton), Micky Hamill (ex-Manchester City and United), and Tom Muirhead (late of Glasgow Rangers). Muirhead was reported to have signed a two-year contract on double the wages he was offered from Rangers, the highest-paying club in Scotland. Apparently the Rangers manager had been dumbfounded when Muirhead announced his decision: 'Apart from the loss of a talented player, the club gets no consolation in the shape of a transfer fee, which, as prices go, would mean £5,000 or more.'

It was chiefly Scottish players being tempted at this juncture, because wage cuts and the disbandment of reserve teams in Scotland were reducing the opportunities for players to earn a living. Later, with the news that English players might also be on their way to America, a certain unease spread among clubs. Charles Sutcliffe, an FA councillor writing in *Topical Times*, was dismissive of the scare stories, considering that most players would find it difficult to settle abroad and few would find the money on offer as substantial as rumoured.

He did, however, make suggestions as to how to 'reward loyalty and continual service', perhaps by offering players more than the single-year contracts that were then standard. He conceded that job security might persuade men that breaking their contracts was not worth it. There was also the worry that, if American football did succeed, players in Britain might use it as a lever to extract better terms from British clubs.

In 1925, Tommy Croft, an Irish international, revealed just how many British players were making the trip across the Atlantic. He had a contract with the Falls River club and told readers of the *Weekly News*: 'I found I wasn't alone in Falls River Club as far as United Kingdom footballers were concerned, for I had as club mates such well-known players as B McPherson (Morton), H Brittain (Chelsea), T Raeside (Dumbarton), B Fryar (Barnsley), F Morley (Blackpool and Reading) – in fact, the entire Falls River team was composed of first-class English and Scottish players, one or two of whom had "jumped their contracts" with their clubs at home.'

He also revealed that players were offered more than simple wages to play: 'Brittain, the Chelsea player referred to, has been appointed assistant to the manager of the Chamber of Commerce in Massachusetts – a fine post – which gives one an idea of the possibilities which are in the States for a good job.'

In December 1926, however, *Topical Times* published an article by Mick O'Brien, the Derby County and Irish international player who had left his former club, Hull City, to play for Brooklyn Wanderers. 'American Football Methods Exposed' was the headline, with O'Brien promising to provide 'a warning to other players in this country thinking of going to the land where they worship the "Almighty Dollar". The conditions in America, he reported, were 'primitive'. 'The grounds are poor; the referees are extremely ignorant; and the dressing rooms are wretched.' The players had to wear knee-pads because the grounds were so hard and scattered with bottle-tops; the play was non-stop and lacked positional play or close-passing. The referees were rarely in control and fights were commonplace. At the end of the article, however, O'Brien revealed that he had in fact been suspended by the club owner and fined $50 for breaking his contract and 'insubordination'.

Other players returning from the States told a different story. Tom Edwards, an ex-Morton goalie declared, 'I am quite satisfied with my contract in Bethlehem [Steel Corporation team], whose terms are better both for playing and close season than any I could get here. I am returning in August or September and taking my wife and child with me, the club paying all the expenses. I have nothing but good to say for American conditions, but if a man plays badly and is dropped, he has nothing good to say of the club. The same thing happens at home.'

A year later, the veteran ex-Evertonian, Sam Chedgzoy, also playing in America, wrote to correct impressions given, particularly by O'Brien, whose comments he declared, 'gave the boys over here a good laugh'. As to the 'roughness' of the play: 'I will say that the game is just what the players make of it and 95 per cent of the players are from the Old Country…'

Alec Jackson, later to become a star with Chelsea and a famous 'rebel', also went to America during this period and played for Bethlehem Steel Corporation's team. His own treatment by the team owners was a revelation. 'They not only offered to send me to university and presented me with a motor car, but took me on many sightseeing tours…' He turned down the university offer but studied metallurgy at a 'prep' school, sent £4 a week home to his mother and enjoyed himself immensely.

The real bombshell came, however, when Dixie Dean, probably Britain's best-known player at that time, was offered £25 a week to play for the New York Giants. Dean had just made football history, scoring 60 goals in a season, 100 goals in all competitions, and was arguably the world's most famous soccer player.

Needless to say, Sutcliffe, in the *Topical Times*, dismissed the idea. 'They think £25 sounds a big sum to we poor Britons, yet we know too well its value in the States. As Dixie is very happy at Everton and is well on the way to qualify for a benefit, I don't think that DixieLand will be any attraction for him.' Although another correspondent admitted that the offer to Dean 'has created something like panic in certain quarters'. Dean's biographer, Nick Walsh, stated some years later that the offer (£120 down and £20 a week) had been turned down by Dean because 'he had no intention of leaving Everton at any price…' This was no doubt true, but it's hard to know exactly what Dean was offered and how it was presented to him as the great man was never asked directly for his version of events.

The American 'raids' revealed frustrations prevalent among professional players that football's authorities preferred to ignore or deny. It wouldn't be long, however, before the gradually expanding football world brought new temptations and reasons for men to kick against the traces.

4. The grass is always greener: France

'About this French business. Let me say at once, that it deserves much more serious attention than it is getting in some quarters.'

Alex James, Sunday Graphic, April 1932

In 1931, France decided to accept professionalism. The French FA followed the English example and set a maximum wage: 2,000 francs a month, or about £20 a month, which was less than the then English ceiling (£8 a week, or £32 a month). This was not particularly tempting, perhaps, to top English players.

However, in April 1931, newspaper headlines announced that a French club, Nimes, had bid for two famous Chelsea players,

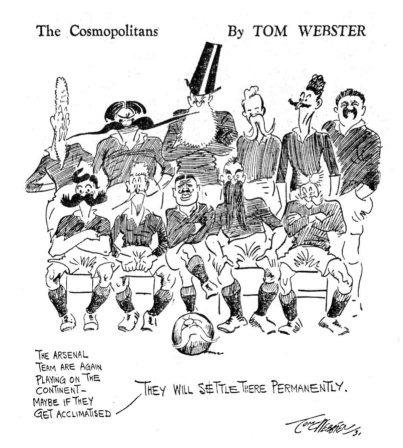

The Cosmopolitans   By TOM WEBSTER

THE ARSENAL TEAM ARE AGAIN PLAYING ON THE CONTINENT— MAYBE IF THEY GET ACCLIMATISED

THEY WILL SETTLE THERE PERMANENTLY.

Daily Mail,
November 1931.

Hughie Gallacher and Tommy Law. The French had offered the two men £18 a week to act as player coaches. As the *Daily Mail* put it, 'The offer which has been made to the two Chelsea players creates a disturbing and rather alarming situation for British clubs'. Though the money offered would appear to be less than tempting, 'It is evident that already a way has been discovered to get round and over the fixed £20 a month maximum by engaging a man to fill a dual position of player-coach.'

The FA's response was to bemoan the fact that it had been too lenient towards players such as Ted Harper, the Arsenal goal keeper, who had gone to the USA and then petitioned to come back again. The FA had agreed, but only after Harper had paid a £10 fine. The next such 'rebel' would never be allowed to play in Britain again.

The day after the *Daily Mail* report, the manager of the Nimes club issued a statement denying that he was about to sign top English/Scots players. The French, he said, couldn't afford them. There followed much behind-the-scenes diplomatic bridge-building, with assurances from the French that they wouldn't break international agreements on the registration of players. Once again, as with the American episode a few years earlier, the reaction of League officials was aggressive and even a little hysterical.

CE Sutcliffe, under a *Topical Times* headline 'Grapple with the French Menace Now!' spelled out the registration rule present in every player's contract, with emphasis on the retention clause. He had apparently been made aware of approaches being made to David Jack and Alex James of Arsenal. The French, he told his readers, ought to be warned. A ban on all English clubs visiting France ought to be considered as a possible punishment. He added, 'Don't worry about the French clubs. They dare not persist in taking players wanted by our clubs, and if they get others it will be at wages much less than most players could command if they remained here. And may I remind the players that France is not the Garden of Eden and their playing fields are not Wembleys? Better be careful or there will soon be empty pockets, sore heads and sore feet.'

Clearly his warnings weren't being heeded by the Players' Union. In August 1932, at its Annual General Meeting, a statement was made suggesting: 'A full list of the French clubs, who turned to professionalism, with all particulars sent to the members seeking information, and recently French agents visited England trying to obtain players for certain positions. Through the efforts of the Union several players had crossed to France for a month's trial, with satisfactory terms. If they are a success they will be offered an agreement which I can assure you will be acceptable to them.'

A number of players did make the leap, and one of them reported back to _Topical Times_ in the summer of 1932. Bill Fraser had been with Southampton but had been put on the transfer list for £750. Few clubs wanted to pay that sum. 'Then one day I was surprised to get a wire from France asking me to sign up with a French team.' Charlie Bell, ex-Arsenal and Queens Park Rangers, was the manager of Marseilles and Fraser was offered good terms: £8 and £6 a week plus bonuses for good play. There he met up with ex-Fulham players Bragg and Pritchard. Fraser, cautiously only signing for a month, said, 'The snags were few. The climate is delightful. The ground is firm and easy to play on. The ball is smaller than over here which also, I think, helps to improve the standard of football.'

He then got word that Fulham wanted to buy him and that Southampton were demanding he return forthwith. The French offered even better terms, but 'this time it became necessary for me to decide to make England my home for family reasons as well'. In fact, the only 'snag' about French football that Fraser could identify was that the English FA wouldn't have allowed him back into this country had he defected to France.

One or two prominent players did take the risk and sign up, however, one being Chelsea star Alec Cheyne. In 1948, in _The People_ newspaper, Cheyne explained that when the club had tried to cut his wages in 1931, 'I objected and took the only step I could to show my disapproval. I went to Nimes in France and took over a job as player-coach. In France I was making about £1,000 a year; and this was at a time when that was real money.' He stayed for two years.

Once again it had taken a 'foreign menace' to reveal the extent to which professional players were, if not quite as persecuted as Cheyne had claimed ('I sold myself into bondage as severe as any suffered by the darkies in the Deep South'), then certainly in a very peculiar position. CE Sutcliffe had asked, rhetorically, why some top players bothered to delay signing contracts offered to them by their clubs, his inference being that they had no choice. One prominent player during the early 1930s, however, made a point of publicising his situation and teasing the authorities.

In the summer of 1932, Alex James, in his column in the *Sunday Graphic*, explained: 'Am I going to sign on for another season with Arsenal? After I had been asked that seventeen times in three days I told the eighteenth enquirer – a taxi driver – that I was through with football for good. That I had always had a secret passion for chickens; that I was going to accept a partnership in a flourishing poultry farm in Lincolnshire; that this was a deep secret and he mustn't tell the other lads on the rank, or it might get about.' He then went on to tell his readers, somewhat tongue-in-cheek, how he was planning to maintain his annual income: 'My summer offers include: (1) a vaudeville engagement; (2) an exhibition and lecture tour in the States; (3) a coaching job at a summer "school" for footballers – new idea this; (4) an engagement at a popular seaside resort giving "ball demonstrations" and keeping goal against all-comers; (5) coaching offers from Germany, Austria, Spain, the Argentine, Denmark and (of course) France. Then there is a wonderful scheme of taking an all-star Alex James team for a continental tour with millions of francs, lire, doubloons, roubles and pesetas for the boys in the grand share-out on settling day.'

Topical Times, October 31, 1936.

23

EXPERIENCES OF A FOOTBALL TRAVELLER

I WENT ABROAD TO MAKE GOOD

By
LESLIE MILLER
('Spurs Outside-Left)

James explained that professionalism, 'will spread like a prairie fire throughout the Continent in due course and supposing the time arrives when the star players are tempted and fall in serious numbers. You see, we are professionals not amateurs. The game is our only livelihood. How long does it take the average professional footballer (married) with an income of less than £8 a week to save £1,000? A good deal longer than the average footballer's career, believe me. Supposing, then, someone comes along with £1,000 in cold cash and says, "Yours, if you sign". Well, not many players are going to refuse that temptation.'

He concluded, somewhat enigmatically, 'No, I'm not saying the French "menace" has arrived, but it's on its way. And no one has so far said a word about where the big bid for English players is really going to come from. It is not France.'

Perhaps James was thinking of Spain. Jimmy Hogan, a British coach who worked on the continent during the inter-war years, revealed in *Topical Times* in June 1929 that professional football had been in existence for a number of years on the Continent, with many clubs paying their players even though professionalism hadn't been officially introduced. The pay was especially good in Spain. 'There is no player in England or Scotland – not even the very best – who can command a salary like the famous Spanish players, Zomorra, Samitier, Pierra, Sagi, Plattko, Rugio and others,' wrote Hogan. 'It is not considered extraordinary for these men to earn so much money.' On the contrary, after an excellent display of goal-keeping by Zomorra, a leading sporting newspaper wrote: 'It is quite just that Zomorra has a salary of 160 pounds per month, but for a player of his ability we consider that double of this amount is insufficient.' While ordinary players earned from £16 to £32 a month a top player could earn from £95 to £160. Considerably more than in England.

The American and French experiences, and the situation that Alex James and other top stars found themselves in did little for the image of professional football as a career. As working conditions in society in general improved and as wage levels rose, professional footballers seemed to be slipping further and further down the ladder.

In November 1935, William McDevitt, manager of Exeter City, pondered in the *Topical Times* on the dramatic rise in transfer fees and attributed it in part to the unavailability of top-quality players. There were also better opportunities for young men to earn a decent living.

'A lot of young players are not so keen to become professional footballers as they used to be. They know that the career is a short one, and very hazardous at the best of times. The absolute maximum income from fifteen years of first-class conditions is £8,000. That is not really much money when one considers the expenses and pitfalls of a footballer's life. The fear of injury and subsequent invaliding out of the game is a big deterrent. Wages for young people have increased generally and young men consider a permanent job at three or four pounds a week to be better than a few years at ten pounds a week, followed by uncertainty. You see, football for ninety-five per cent of the players is a dead end occupation.'

5. Post-war: Bogota, Mannion and Finney

'Imagine Rex Harrison appearing in My Fair Lady at the Theatre Royal Drury Lane for £20 a week maximum wages (winter of course!). Ridiculous, of course it is. Yet Stanley Matthews, in his own field, is as great a star as Rex Harrison and he should be paid accordingly.'

Tom Finney, Finney on Football, 1958

In February 1948, a Sunday newspaper revealed that, after having asked for a transfer before reluctantly re-signing, Wilf Mannion, Middlesborough's 'Golden Boy', was having his new house furnished by the club's fans. A local social club was raising money for a 'wedding present' for the superbly talented England inside forward, who had just moved into a new house, rent paid by the club. According to Alan Hoby of the *Sunday People*, however, it was nothing less than a 'full-blown public subscription fund open to everyone in the town'.

Hoby felt it revealed the 'humbug' of the game, where subterfuges such as 'wedding gifts' had to be used to pay top players something approaching their true worth. The following season, however, Mannion again refused to re-sign and requested a transfer. This time, there was no social club fund; instead,

the club issued him a blank refusal. They wouldn't let him go –
at any price.

The saga that unfolded, and which dragged on for the next six
months or so, was a strange one. Mannion, it transpired, wanted to
move to Oldham, where he'd been offered a good job outside football. Middlesborough, although declaring they wouldn't let him
go, did the next best thing by putting a £25,000 price tag on
his head, which they hoped would frighten other clubs away. It
didn't, and both Arsenal and Celtic were to make realistic, if incon-
venient, offers for him.

Whether Middlesborough would have accepted the offers
became academic when Mannion declared that he wouldn't be
transferred to any club outside of a 20-mile radius around Oldham.
He followed this up by announcing that he wouldn't sign for any
club that had to pay more than £12,000 for him because he felt the
transfer system was a sham. He held out for five months. Legal
action was threatened and he was said to have almost signed for
Arsenal when a Middlesborough director turned up on his
doorstep with a blank contract – which Mannion, to everyone's
surprise, signed.

It was said that he was at the end of his tether. He had a chroni-
cally ill wife and a new-born child and, in psychological terms, he
never really recovered, being a shy and humble man by nature and
certainly not one of soccer's 'awkward squad'.

The Mannion case was more about a player's freedom to move
than it was about money, although the latter obviously came into it.
Mannion was looking to the future and trying to secure a good job
that would relieve him of financial worries. The tenacity of the
club's directorate in refusing point blank in the face of almost uni-
versal criticism to allow Mannion the right to such a choice,
demonstrated how far the system of player control had warped the
judgements of those involved in football politics.

It also illustrated other difficult circumstances under which professional footballers laboured. Many Middlesborough fans resented
Mannion's decision to ask for a transfer and called him greedy and
a 'traitor'. He had been 'disloyal'.

In 1950, within a year of the Mannion case, yet more top players were attempting to break out of the camp. Colombia, temporarily outside the jurisdiction of the world governing body of football,

FIFA, was keen to establish a professional league, and had taken to luring foreign nationals to its footballing shores. In 1950, some of that country's top clubs approached England and no fewer than seven top British internationals, among them Trevor Ford, Neil Franklyn and Roy Paul, were tempted to investigate what were, by any standards, lucrative terms.

They flew out, in farcically secretive fashion, in some cases without even telling their families, but most found the conditions not to their liking and rapidly returned home. Only Charlie Mitten, who had left a Manchester United touring party in America to go to Colombia, decided to stay for a complete season. Most of the players received periods of suspension for their presumption and were transferred by their clubs on their return.

The story has been recounted many times but, from any angle, it was a pathetic event. Professional men scurrying to and fro across the world like boarding-school boys breaking out of the dorm for a midnight feast and having to face the headmaster the following morning. In the event, they all took their 'six-of-the-best' and shook the hand of the head prefect administering the blows.

However, perhaps the most startling of all the furores that preceded the lifting of the wage cap in 1961 was the offer made to Preston North End's Tom Finney a couple of years later in 1952. The England team were on a tour of Italy and Tom Finney, then 30 years old but still considered one of the finest wingers of all time, was made an incredible offer.

Prince Roberto Lanza di Trabia, millionaire president of the Sicilian team Palermo, asked to see Finney after a 1–1 draw with Italy. Finney was sharing a room with Ivor Broadis and it was there that the prince outlined the terms: £7,000 personal signing-on fee; £130 a month in wages; bonuses for results of between £30 and £100; a villa in the Mediterranean; a new, top-of-the-range, continental car; and free travel to Italy for his family.

'I'll never forget Ivor's face when the prince made the offer,' Finney recalled. 'He went white and kept repeating over and over again that it was a dream and all too good to be true. We talked about nothing else that night, but when the prince came back again the following morning, I knew it was more than just pie in the sky. I must admit that the offer began to dominate my thoughts and I remember promising to put the offer to my directors on returning home…'

The Preston North End board of directors refused to consider the offer, even though Palermo offered a £30,000 transfer fee. The board did issue a statement, however, in which the chairman reported that, 'T Finney had approached him regarding an offer received from an Italian club for his services. Unanimously agreed that the player be informed that we could not accede to this request. This player has been retained with the FA and was expected to re-sign for season 1952–53 on his return from holiday.'

Finney later told his biographer: 'To be quite honest I didn't expect North End to react any other way so I accepted the decision without too much fuss and decided that the best thing to do was to try and put the whole business out of my mind.' He went on holiday to Blackpool with his family.

Finney has had many years to think over the affair. He has never criticised the board and has even gone so far as to say, 'perhaps I was lucky in some respects that the decision was never really mine to take'. He now thinks that he would probably not have gone, citing his strong family ties in Preston, and his affection for Preston North End.

It would certainly have been a pioneering move. At that stage, only three players from England had played or were still playing in Italy; none of them were of the stature of Finney. It would be another couple of years before Eddie Firmani left Charlton Athletic for the Sampdoria club to become the first truly successful 'English' player (he was a South African of Italian descent) to make a mark in Italy. John Charles would follow in 1957 and become a huge success with Juventus. Finney would have been very much on his own.

However, Finney has also commented: 'I must admit that the Palermo business has drifted across my mind more than once and the more I think back the more astonished I become about the sheer magnitude of the offer. It would have taken me the best part of a decade to earn what Prince Roberto was prepared to pay me for simply signing on the dotted line. I knew what the English wages were all about, having earned just £5 for a 46-hour week as a plumber just after the war and £14 a week as a professional foot-baller. In many ways I would have liked to have gone across to Italy and given it a whirl. Apart from the obvious attraction of financial security and the prospects of making myself a wealthy young fellow, it was an intriguing and exciting thought. I have often wondered how I would have fared in the continental game.'

His own declared beliefs concerning the payment of players, especially star players, would also appear to point to his going, had he been offered the chance. He told his biographer, 'What is wrong with a free market place? I remember saying years ago that, while I thought Preston North End was the greatest club in the world, if Newcastle United had come in to double my wage I would certainly have signed.'

The fact is, most club chairmen, including those at Preston, knew that the retain-and-transfer system would not stand scrutiny in a court of law. In other words, what they were doing was illegal. Here was a family man with a business of his own, admired throughout the world for his fantastic ability on the field, for his fairness and his honesty. Here was a football 'legend', still celebrated at the club he has always professed to love. Supporters perform plays about him; there is a stand named after him. He later became a Justice of the Peace and is now on the board of the club. In his role as a professional footballer, however, he was considered little more than a piece of property with no right even to an opinion.

One is tempted to suggest that the term 'slavery', so regularly and lightly used by players objecting to their contractual plight, might actually be appropriate where this particular episode is concerned, simply because Finney accepted without demur that he could not even consider the offer. Was this nobility? Or loyalty? Or the mindset of a man whose profession had bred in him such a low opinion of his own capacity to act independently that he was actually pleased not to have the option? Was Finney to be admired or pitied?

Finney is the most decent of men and certainly felt an affinity with, and a responsibility for, those who paid their money to come and watch him play; he never liked letting them down. Aged 80, he has talked of his disappointment at not winning the FA Cup Final with Preston in 1954. His had been a wretched display, largely because he was struggling with an injury. But he recalled: 'It would have been nice to collect a winner's medal like Stan Matthews but it wasn't to be. However, even greater than any sense of personal loss was the feeling I'd let the people of Preston down; that's what broke my heart, looking at the thousands of supporters in their scarves, hats and rosettes at the final whistle...'

Finney retired in April 1960, the very same month in which the Professional Footballers' Association (the old Players' Union) drew up demands that would, by January 1961, result in the removal of the wage cap. Two years later, George Eastham, supported by Cliff Lloyd of the PFA, made a significant dent in the retain-and-transfer system by winning a case in London's High Court against Newcastle United, his former employers. From that day on, the employment prospects for professional footballers would gradually improve.

6. The New Deal: 1961 and beyond

'There was a time not long ago when fans would support their idols in their battle against greedy club bosses. Not any longer…what we are now witnessing in football has nothing to do with the rights of footballers but every-thing to do with excessive greed.'

Charlie Whelan, Daily Telegraph, 2001

In 1960, when clubs became free to pay their players what they wanted, the maximum wage for a professional footballer over the age of 20 in England and Wales stood at £20 a week during the season and £17 a week during the summer. For a 17-year-old signing his first contract, the maximum was £10 and £9; at eighteen it rose to £12 10s and £11; while at nineteen he could earn £15 and £13.

Across Europe at this time few other countries were able to offer as much as most were still only able to support part-time professionalism. There were wide variations in basic salaries. For instance, in Yugoslavia part-timers might earn up to £18 a month, although the top players might get £60 a month.

In Belgium, which had just started a full-time league in 1960, players might earn £12 and £7 a week; whereas in Holland a top international could expect only around £900 a year. In Sweden, where, again, most men were part-timers and didn't even have club contracts, professionals could earn a maximum of £4 a game.

In Portugal a married player might be offered £12 a week while a single man could expect £10. In Denmark, meanwhile, there were some players on £1,400 a year.

As ever, the top stars earned the top money. In Spain, in 1961, Alfredo Di Stefano lived in a £20,000 house in a Madrid suburb, was paid £300 a match, and for a European Cup Final appearance he received £900 in bonuses. He also received a personal share of his transfer fee of £14,000. He was a peseta millionaire.

It would be a long time before players in England could expect such riches, however. Tommy Trinder, the Fulham chairman, famously paid his captain Johnny Haynes £100 a week, but most other players found that clubs continued to operate their own private maximum schemes. At first, £30 a week was the unofficial maximum. George Cohen, playing for Fulham and a future England World Cup winner, revealed, 'When they abolished the maximum wage in 1961, I was on about £45, which was three times what my father was earning as a gas-fitter. And when I made the England squad in the 1963–64 season, my wages went up to £80 a week, which was far more than the basic wage Nobby (Stiles) was getting at Manchester United, for instance. Where we were worse off at Fulham was in terms of bonuses.'

Gradually, however, top players began to earn money commensurate

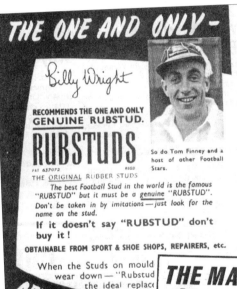

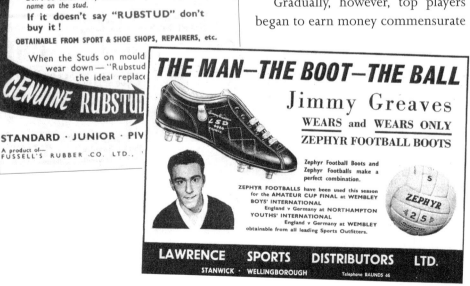

with their popularity and celebrity status, and a gap as wide as that between the Continent's top and bottom earners began to open up. George Best was said to be paid the equivalent of £2,000 a week in 1970, and earned considerably more from endorsements and bonuses. However, a government report in 1973 revealed that 45.5 per cent of the old Fourth Division players and 43 per cent of Third Division men were receiving basic wages of less than £45 a week. Part-time professionalism was very much a reality in lower league football, and during the 1970s things got progressively worse as the British economy went into recession.

However, comparison of the annual earnings of Tottenham Hotspur centre-halves over five decades also reveals how footballers at the very top were beginning to outstrip their counterparts in the wider employment world (the national average wage at that time is included in brackets after each player's annual earnings). Thus, Maurice Norman, Spurs' centre-half was paid £1,040 (£780) per annum in the early 1960s; Mike England, in the early 1970s, was earning about £1,560 (£1,040). By the 1980s, Paul Miller was earning £27,000 a year (£7,000) while Gary Mabbutt in the early 1990s was paid around £120,000 per annum (£14,500). The acceleration rate for those at the very top was soon to increase dramatically, however.

Almost one hundred years after the Football League imposed the retain-and-transfer system on professional players, the right to move on once a contract had ended was re-established in the European Court of Justice by Belgian Jean Marc Bosman. In 1995, the court decided that Bosman, who was out of contract with his club, RFC Liege, should be able to join a new club without a transfer fee being paid.

In many ways we are now back in the 1880s. The European court's ruling appears to have loaded the system in favour of contracted players. With out-of-contract players available for no transfer fee, the battleground has become player's wages, with clubs offering more and more to sign star names. Bosman-style transfers have been rising steadily. In 2000 more than a quarter of top players were contemplating them. Salaries in general, boosted by the huge influx of television revenue following the establishment of the Premiership in 1992, have risen significantly at all levels.

A survey of professional footballers carried out in the early part of 2000 by the *Independent* newspaper, in conjunction with the Professional Footballers' Association, revealed some impressive-looking figures.

In the year 2000, basic pay for top players over 20 years of age rose above £400,000 per annum (nearly £8,000 a week). Thirty-six per cent of players in the same age bracket earned more than £500,000 and nine per cent earned more than £1m a year. Thus, in the year 2000 there were about one hundred Premiership players earning £1 million or more per year.

The highest earners were the 27–28-year-olds, making £572,000 a year on average. Sixteen per cent of these earned more than £1 million. At the other end of the scale, young players and trainees aged between 17 and 20 were being paid between £19,000 and £45,000 a year on average.

Senior First Division players were said to be on an average of £128,000; their counterparts in the Second and Third Divisions earning £52,000 and £37,000 respectively.

Players interviewed in the wake of the report's publication, however, claimed not to be earning as much as stated: Chester City players in ninety-first place denied earning the average £37,000 a year. Nigel Gibbs, the long-serving Watford defender, said his pay didn't approach the £409,000 average suggested for his division. 'Nowhere near,' he said. Gibbs, who had started on £90 a week in 1982 was, nevertheless, all in favour of players earning whatever they could. 'Good luck to them. If the clubs are willing to pay it, the players should try to get it – they only have short careers. The clubs can always say "no", anyway.'

The reaction to the report echoed the sentiments of popular press back in the 1890s. A headline in the *Independent* declared: 'A spiral of huge wage rises at the top threatens the whole national game,' while Dario Gradi, a much respected manager, issued a 'Doomsday' warning. *The Sun*, predictably, was simply exultant: 'Come on you Wads!'

The *Daily Mail* ran an emotive piece beneath a headline 'Footballers who have struck gold': 'While supporters are aware that elite players such as David Beckham and Alan Shearer pick up more than £1m a year, they may be alarmed to learn that even those of comparatively modest ability are on a basic salary of

£409,000 – or £8,000 a week. When win bonuses and sponsor-ship deals are added on, the figure tops £500,000, compared with Tony Blair's income of £107,179…'

Fans of lower league clubs were quoted: 'It's perhaps easier to accept if you support a successful club like [Manchester] United but fans of clubs which are staring at relegation will be less than impressed to hear that the journeyman players who are going out and losing week after week are averaging more than £400,000.'

Jeff Powell of the *Daily Mail* was even more condemnatory. He linked the reputed wage levels with players' general behaviour or, as he saw it, their lack of talent as compared to players of the 'Golden Age' and with that traditional characteristic of the professional foot-baller: 'greed'.

'Spoilt millionaires with egos bigger than their salaries,' was the headline beneath which Powell attacked the modern player. 'Now no one in his right mind would advocate a return to the maximum wage, a slavery by which football club directors grew fat on the exploitation of such heroes as Sir Stanley Matthews, Sir Tom Finney and every other nobleman of the cloth cap era. It has come to a sorry pass when players with two left feet and half a football brain are being paid ten times as much as the Prime Minister and twen-ty times more than a neurosurgeon. It is not their fault. Most of them are children. They can hardly be blamed for grasping at the candy bars shoved in their faces by the club directors and their television paymasters.'

Once again, players' representatives were forced to fight back and reiterate what their forebears had tried to explain in the early 1900s. Barry Horne, PFA Chairman, pointed out that it was a short career, that top men were not paid as much as top golfers or racing drivers, that 'lesser' players didn't earn anything like the stars, and most con-tracts were geared to playing and winning. 'People,' he opined, 'have a perception of footballers earning fortunes and it just isn't true.'

It was pointed out that freedom of contract cut both ways. A player might be able to negotiate a better deal, but if he is injured there is no one to pay his medical and other bills. The obligations towards a player on behalf of the clubs holding his registration have now disappeared. What's more, there are no guarantees that a 'free' player would find work, as clubs are also free to choose from a pool of players with no fees involved.

To the suggestion that player's wages were threatening to undermine the game, that 'the game' couldn't afford to lose so much wealth, PFA chief executive Gordon Taylor replied: 'I wouldn't say money was going out of the game when it's going into players' pockets. The players are the game.'

He added that wages in the Premiership, ironically, 'are considerably less than figures seen in salary-capped US sports, which are usually capped at around 50 to 60 per cent of turnover. In the Premiership it is around 35 to 50 per cent usually. Income from gates, TV, sponsorship and other activities far outweigh wages.'

In 2000, top players' earnings on the Continent were still far ahead of equivalent British players' deals. Roy Keane of Manchester United might have brokered a record-breaking contract guaranteeing him £2.7 million a year, but French international Zinedine Zidane was paid £8m a year with Juventus, Gabriel Batistuta was paid £6m a year at Roma while Brazilian star Ronaldo was getting £5.2m from InterMilan.

Across the Atlantic, meanwhile, Derek Jeter, a 25-year-old New York Yankees baseball player had signed a contract in 2000 guaranteeing him $118.5m over seven years, which was more than £10m a year. Kevin Garnett of basketball's Minnesota Timberwolves signed a six-year deal in 1997 worth £79m and Michael Jordon got $33m for 1997–8 alone.

Inevitably, perhaps, players' agents were blamed by many for negotiating many of the lucrative deals. Jon Smith of First Artists, which represented eighty players, including Sunderland and England striker Kevin Phillips and Chelsea's Marcel Desailly, hit back:

'I find it strange no one objects to the millions Victoria Beckham is earning, yet her husband is arguably a bigger star and people moan that he is paid too much. David Beckham performs every week, but I can't remember the last time his wife performed in public... Footballers generate a huge amount of income for their clubs and so it is only fair that they should share in it. The market will decide how much a player is worth. We have some players earning more than £50,000 a week at the moment and it's possible that we will see the £100,000-a-week player before long.

'I accept that some of the less talented players' wages are dragged upwards because of the earnings of those around them, but then again there must be a lot of pop groups' musicians who earn a huge amount just because the singer is talented.'

Professionals at the lower end of the pay scale, however, seem less concerned by the huge differentials than commentators outside the game. Kevin Keen of Third Division Macclesfield Town, when contemplating a forthcoming FA Cup tie with Premiership club West Ham in January 2002, felt that the Premiership 'is a different world with the money, media, television and the way top players are not just players but modern icons for the public'. When considering the enormous gap in wages – the younger Macclesfield players on £250 a week, while the top West Ham star would be earning one hundred times as much – he declared: 'There is no jealousy. There are a few [in our dressing room] who would love to be in the Premiership. When they are not trying hard enough, I tell the players: "If you work hard, you could be earning thousands a week and have women chasing you".'

It seems that perspective has always been in short supply where football players and money are concerned. This may be because, in Britain at least, the suspicion remains at some subliminal level that paying men to play a game is immoral. It embarrasses us in some way, and righteous indignation seems the appropriate response when salaries start rising beyond what we deem acceptable.

Perhaps not surprisingly, those 'noblemen of the cloth cap era' rarely join the outraged chorus. As Tom Finny commented when told that Roy Keane earned as much in a week as he had earned throughout his whole career: 'Had the revolution come before the war then it might well have been I who stood to benefit. On the other hand, had I played today, then there is no way I would have had a guilty conscience about accepting a huge wage. To say anything less would be hypocritical of me.'

7. Reality bites

'We pay our players far too much and that has got to end. This season there are going to be no pay rises. Clubs have been over extending themselves, every club is facing serious financial pressure.'

Peter Hill-Wood, Chairman of Arsenal, March 2002

In March 2002, the collapse of ITV Digital and the subsequent loss to the Football League of a £315m deal to televise live games from the First, Second and Third Divisions caused panic in the game. Suddenly, the precarious financial situation of so many clubs was revealed for all to see and respected figures in the game starting to talk openly about player redundancies and clubs going out of business.

Even before the ITV Digital debacle, the 72 Football League clubs had been considering a bleak summer when they would cut wages, impose a salary cap and sack up to a third of their playing staff with as many as 900 of the 2,800 full-time pros in the three divisions facing the dole.

Many saw players' wages as the root cause of the problem. For instance, Ipswich Town in November 2002 reported a £3.3m loss even though TV income had increased by £1m. The reason? Wages had risen from £17.6m to £24.2m, and were accounting for almost two-thirds of the club's overall turnover.

John Bowler, Chairman of Crewe, felt that, though it was right that the top players earned good wages, 'the problem is that this has escalated down the divisions, so the average wage has gone up everywhere. There should be no correlation between what David Beckham gets and what a Third Division player receives – there has to be a halt to that.'

At Brentford, Chairman Ron Noades felt that many clubs would face serious problems without the forthcoming ITV revenue they had budgeted for, and 'offloading players' would be the only possible escape from extinction. 'The only way we can reduce our outgoings is to reduce the number of players we employ. But if you reduce the quality of your squad you wouldn't be getting anybody coming to watch. Everybody's going to be looking to offload everything, but it won't be a question of selling them. You'll just be looking, when the contracts run out, not to offer new terms.'

Bradford City, meanwhile, which had been a Premiership club in the year 2000, declared itself bankrupt soon after the ITV Digital deal collapsed. The administrators immediately cut the squad by nearly half, releasing 19 players. Benito Carbone, halfway through a four-year contract worth £40,000 per week, was the highest profile casualty. The administrators calculated that the action would save the club £20,000 per day and possibly their future. Gary Walsh, David Wetherall and Danny Cadamarteri were faced with finding new clubs immediately. Stuart McCall, Gunnar Halle and Gareth Whalley found that their contracts would not be renewed when they expired in the summer.

Mick McGuire, the Professional Footballers' Association deputy chief executive called the Bradford decision 'disgraceful'. 'We are talking about players with mortgages.' While football agent Phil Smith felt the situation created by the ITV failure would be '…potentially catastrophic for smaller clubs. For those preaching part-time football it will be fodder. Some of the contracts of Division One players we are negotiating are far below the levels the public believe. I think everyone is aware of how catastrophic this could be.'

Since then, Barnsley, Leicester and Notts County have followed Bradford into administration, unable to pay their immediate debts, not to mention players' wages. There are many others teetering on the brink. Wage ceilings and performance-related pay, hitherto unheard of, are now becoming a reality. In November 2002, the FA and Premiership were considering launching a £20m rescue package for poverty-stricken FL clubs, diverting money from the Football Stadia Improvement Fund to help clubs make ends meet.

Even at European super-club level, a wage ceiling is now being seriously considered, with penalties for clubs who breach them, while Premiership clubs such as 'Double' winners Arsenal are planning to let go of players. Denis Hill Wood predicted: 'The top half dozen players are going to get more. The rest of them, even in the Premiership, will not. I don't know how the clubs can go on paying what they are paying. Arsenal are spending more on wages than ever before but we're not bust. I read in the papers Alex Feguson may want to get rid of players, but if they're on a million a year it isn't easy to get another club to take them on. There aren't enough clubs around the world with money to buy.'

Suddenly, it seems, the lot of the average professional footballer appears less than glamorous, particularly when it was revealed that Pro-Star, an Agency based in Glasgow, was arranging live trials of players in search of work in front of managers and scouts. At Luton's Kenilworth Road ground, forty-four players – all but five from outside the country – ran, passed and scored in an effort to impress would-be buyers. Representatives came from clubs such as Chelsea, Birmingham, Millwall and Ipswich to run the rule over players who were prepared to hawk their wares in a 'human cattle market'.

It seemed perturbing to some that, with anything up to 600 players, many of whom would be English, shortly to find themselves out of work, yet more foreign players were paying for the privilege (£200 each) of placing themselves in the shop window. Pro-Star, which had to turn away more than forty players eager to take part, stressed that the players on view wouldn't be signed up overnight: 'It's a terrible time for players to be out of contract.' The trials, the agency felt, gave some men hope. Tottenham's Jamie Quilter, a £150-a-week third-year trainee from Essex, agreed: 'Tottenham were not going to offer me another contract so I am just hoping for as couple of offers. Even a trial would be nice.'

For many hundreds of men, their once-lucrative careers now look exceedingly precarious. In the wider football world, the prospect of bleaker times ahead was having an effect on players. Central defender Dean Smith of Leyton Orient admitted that players had become more insecure about their jobs in recent years. 'Squads are getting smaller again and it's getting harder and harder for players released at the end of the season to find another club, whereas in seasons before it was quite easy. Players are having to go into non-League football, go part-time, and get another job while more players are on short-term deals.' There was, as ever, no sense of bitterness concerning the wide differences in pay packets:

'There isn't really a great deal of resentment within squads over different wage levels. Ultimately we're all footballers and everyone has the same understanding – if you're offered extra money, and you can get a deal you're happy with, you take it. If you're not, then don't sign. It's a short career and you've just got to try to do as well as you can.'

Chapter 3

Footballers Are Not Made

1. Rules of engagement

'Football was my ambition, the aim of my life. Like seventy-five per cent of my chums, I played morning, noon and night, my only regret being that it grew dark.'

Jimmy Seed, Soccer from the Inside, 1947

In the very early years of the professional game, it was often the player who found the club rather than the other way around. A football secretary would place an advertisement in a sporting newspaper, usually the *Athletic News*, and suitable candidates applied. For many decades afterwards, players themselves placed adverts in sporting papers, offering themselves for employment. Many of the first professionals arrived in England from Scotland via such a route. The player was then given a trial and, if suitable, signed on. As we have seen, despite Jimmy Catton's little jibe, there was often a job outside football attached, as an additional non-footballing trade was usually necessary, though not crucial.

Gradually, as more and more pro clubs entered the market for players, football agents were employed. The manager or secretary might be in need of a certain type of forward or defender (left or right footed, experienced or a young player just starting out). The agent might have such a player on his books or would seek to find a suitable candidate. Agents were quite influential for a period in the late nineteenth century, until clubs established their own scouting networks and, later still, developed youth policies and even football 'nursery' clubs. Whichever route was chosen, however, most of the early professionals possessed, if not a trade, then usually some years' experience in manual work. The reason for this was that the school leaving age during most of the twentieth century was 14 and later 15 years of age. From both a legal as well as a physical point of view a young boy couldn't hope to be signed on as a professional player for at least a couple of years and with no youth teams and no 'apprentice' schemes, the time would be spent earning a living. This was a vital necessity as most aspiring pro players were working-class boys, without the means to support themselves.

Topical Times, November 12, 1938.

A NEW STAR TELLS YOU—

WHAT A YOUNG FELLOW FACES IN BIG FOOTBALL

15

THE BIG PAY ENVELOPE · KNOCKS THAT MAY CRIPPLE · DROPPED! · STIFF TRAINING · GLOWING PRESS REPORTS · SELFISHNESS

By WILF MANNION
Middlesbrough Inside-Forward

OVERAWED by the glamour of big time football, full of dreams about it like any other youngster fresh from school, I started my soccer career with a lot of wrong ideas.

They've been walloped out of me, now I know what this business is really like, and I feel a lot better for it.

There are so many snags the young player must bump into before he can really start to feel his way around. One of the biggest is that sudden possession of a lot of money.

Coming from a factory and small pay I felt like a millionaire when I got a professional footballer's wage. It was bigger money than I thought I'd get for years, but it was also a pile of temptation. The hangers-on of big soccer are always on the spot to catch the young player, teach him all the ways to spend money, quick and ...

They get sour, start losing interest. Before they know what has happened their love of the game has gone and their skill with it.

I know of one young player like that. He has all the makings of a star, but if he doesn't find some patience, try to realise it's all for his own good he'll never get any farther than he is now.

Middlesbrough treated me differently. Instead of dropping me they only made me train two days a week. And that was certainly enough.

TRAINING GAVE ME A SHOCK.

I GOT the fright of my life when I first started training. I could hardly walk, my leg muscles stiffened up, I thought I was finished.

Then my trainer told me that my running pumps were the cause of the trouble. I wasn't used to them, and every time I stopped running I strained my leg muscles. I was gradually broken in with sand shoes. Now everything is all right.

I found that a full league game was better training than running round the ground. I was happy with a ball at my feet, I still got the exercise, but it was fun.

When I first made big soccer after a spell in the North-Eastern League I felt that I'd never make good. The game was so fast, the tackling so quick, that I was beaten before I had a chance to move. I didn't know what ...

In the next game against Sunderland I felt like a giant. I wanted more goals. The ball came to me near the wing, I thought it was my big chance, but that's because I was selfish. I cut in from the wing, saw Jack Milne unmarked five yards from goal. I knew he couldn't miss if I passed. But I didn't pass. I shot—and missed. And we were losing at the time in a game like a cup-tie, with the crowd yelling their heads off, sitting on the touchlines. It was my first home game.

Perhaps I was enthusiastic, perhaps I wanted to show off. That didn't matter, nor did the fact that later I scored the winning goal.

I felt I'd let the boys down even though they didn't blame me. Their generosity made me feel worse, but it taught me one of the biggest lessons I'll ever get in football. I'll never forget again that it takes eleven men to make a team.

That master of halves, Alf Young, Huddersfield stalwart, gave me some tuition, too. We had a home game with them last year when we were in the running for the championship. We lost, although we played super football that day.

But there was Alf in the middle, stopping every attack as soon as it started. He beat us by himself. I couldn't figure out why my speed didn't leave him ...

A regular feature during the inter-war years in *Topical Times* was to take a look at what players 'might have been', which usually meant what they had been doing before they became footballers. The occupations varied from steel worker to stevedore, granite cutter to baker's assistant, with scores of miners featuring. Thus, for most of the twentieth century, men entering the pro game were men, rather than boys. They also possessed an alternative working identity.

Topical Times, September 5, 1936.

P. GLOVER.   J. MILNE.   E. RIMMER.   H. BARTON.   R. JOHN.

BEFORE THEY BECAME
WHAT THEY WERE   STARS   *By Kenneth Wheeler*

Bob Holmes wanted to be an engine driver and was serving an apprenticeship when he was signed on as a professional: 'Wherever possible I think every footballer should have some business interest outside of the game itself. It relieves the monotony and is the unceasing enemy of listlessness, the most insidious of football microbes.'

But for those who had attractive alternatives, deciding to become a professional footballer was something of a struggle. Charles Buchan had dreams of becoming a schoolteacher. Aged 17 during the 1909–10 season, he played four times for Woolwich Arsenal as a reserve but when he asked for some expenses, the club secretary refused him. Buchan walked out.

He then signed as an amateur for Northfleet, a Kent League side, but professional clubs remained hot on his trail. Bury offered him £3 a week to turn professional but Buchan again refused. ('It was really a wonderful offer when you consider that the wages of a fully-trained engineer, fitter and turner, or a carpenter, were 37s 6d.

They also had to serve a five-year apprenticeship before they got it. There were many young men of my age earning less than £1 for a week's hard work. I did not accept the offer because, at the time, I still wanted to be a schoolteacher.')

He was persuaded to talk to Fulham, who offered him £1.50 a week plus a job, which would have allowed him to continue training to be a teacher, but Buchan asked for £2. They refused. Finally, Leyton Orient offered £3 a week and agreed to him continuing to live at home while training at Leyton three or four days a week. They also offered him an immediate place in the first team. Buchan signed in May 1910. In the event, despite all his manoeuvring, Buchan never completed his teacher training. He had to make the choice.

Jimmy Seed's progress to becoming a professional was more typical and encapsulates all the longings and dreams of what becoming a professional footballer has meant to working-class boys for over a century. His tale also illustrates the hit-and-miss methods the football industry has always employed in discovering raw talent.

Seed had actually watched Charles Buchan from the terraces when Buchan joined Sunderland later in his career. Ironically, Seed's parents had also wanted their son to be a teacher. Seed had other ideas and when he showed no inclination to continue his schooling beyond the age of 14, his parents 'gave up the idea of making me a school teacher. All my pals worked at the pit which, although arduous, ensured them time off and the weekends free. So to the pit I went.'

Seed signed on for a local team and was eventually spotted by Arthur Bridgett, an earlier Newcastle United 'great' then managing South Shields, who asked him for a trial. 'Arthur lived at Whitburn, within a stone's throw of my house. One evening he sent along for me to have a little game in his garden. He acted as goal-keeper and had me dribbling round sticks and generally demonstrating my stuff. Even then I didn't realise what was at the back of his mind. Over a cup of tea in his house we first began to talk of football and the subject led him to fix me for a trial.'

Jimmy, however, failed to impress and heard no more from Bridgett, but soon after he heard that Sunderland were interested. He waited and then, 'one day, fiction became truth. I was in the bath after a night shift when Bob Bawn, one of the Whitburn club, called. He had a card from Sunderland offering me a trial as centre-forward in a North Eastern League match against Darlington.'

Jimmy failed to impress again but got a second chance when a local councillor wrote on his behalf to the club. The second trial proved a success and Seed was called into the boardroom. A contract was put before him and he signed. He had reached the promised land: 'No more pit. No more drudgery with a heart's desire unfulfilled; no more coal dust and the monotony that accompanied it in the bowels of the earth. Just think what that means to a Durham lad with football in his blood.'

There have always been certain rudimentary guidelines laid down by the Football Association concerning the signing-up of young men by football clubs. Quite simply, before 1960, professional clubs could not sign a boy on as a full-time professional until he was 17 years old. He might, in exceptional circumstances, play before that for a professional team if good enough, but only as an amateur.

Between the two world wars, however, there was created what was termed the 'ground-staff' option, whereby a boy might leave school at 15 and be 'attached' to a club working in the club office, or with the groundsman. The groundstaff opportunity was offered to highly prized youngsters for whom there would probably be much competition. It had been devised by the FA as an attempt to eliminate the inevitable 'under-the-counter' financial offers made to promising youngsters or, rather, to their parents.

The boy was allowed to attend the club for training on two evenings a week. He normally signed amateur forms for the club concerned, a seemingly innocuous move that was actually as binding as signing a professional contract, though few youngsters realised it. In effect, it gave the club that had first spotted the boy some quasi-legal hold over him. It 'ring-fenced' him.

Albert Geldard who played alongside Dixie Dean at Everton in the 1930s is the classic 'ground-staff' case. Born in April 1914, Albert was spotted when he was only 12 years old by Claude Ingram, the Bradford Park Avenue secretary-manager. With the permission of Geldard's father and his local school teacher, Albert trained at Park Avenue before making his debut with the reserves against Northern Nomads on 9 March 1929, aged 14 years and 11 months.

The local press raved over Albert's Park Avenue performance in the following season's practice match, declaring they'd, 'not seen a more promising footballer for a long time, wonderfully strong for his age, runs like a true athlete, combines well with his half-back

Sports Budget, November 5th, 1938

250 MORE FOOTBALLS TO BE WON !

SPORTS BUDGET

2^D

VOL 8. Nº192
NOV. 5th 1938
EVERY THURSDAY

PROS FROM THE PIT *See Inside*

and uses the ball to good purpose'. He made his League debut in September 1929, aged 15 years and 5 months – for many years a League record.

While still ostensibly an 'amateur', a club supporter got him a job with a firm of dyers. He then had a job in the club office until, on his seventeenth birthday, he signed professional forms. Even then, however, the forms had been illegally signed some months earlier as Charlton Athletic had shown an interest and the club were anxious not to lose him.

Tommy Lawton was another celebrated 'office boy'. When he turned 14 years of age, he was wooed by Bolton Wanderers, his local team. They offered him a choice between two jobs while he served as an amateur, one paying 10s, another as a butcher's delivery boy at 7s/6d a week. His grandfather and a friend were advising him and they turned it down. Liverpool then offered him a job but that fell through, to be followed soon after by Sheffield Wednesday, who offered free lodgings, 10s a week pocket money and a job to follow. Lawton's mother, however, wouldn't let him travel so far from home. Finally, Burnley, though only a Second Division club, made him an 'assistant club secretary' on a wage of £2 10s (£2.50) a week as well as employing his grandfather as assistant groundsman on £3 10s. A year or so later, the club found the whole family a house in Burnley. Lawton was just 15 and a half years old.

The sequel is instructive. In October 1936, when Lawton turned 17 years, he signed full-time professional forms. In December 1936, Burnley promptly sold him to Everton for £6,500 as understudy to Dixie Dean. Burnley would seem to have invested wisely in Lawton and reaped a rich reward. As we have seen, a young player would usually have received no more than a £10 signing-on fee. Grandfather Lawton's job, however, was the sort of 'under-the- counter' compensation clubs had long since become adept at devising. But the ground-staff route would not be followed by many players; clubs were only allowed to offer a limited number of such opportunities. In 1960, however, an apprenticeship scheme was formalised. Clubs could now take on up to fifteen boys without having to disguise what they were doing. In the years following the introduction of the scheme, the ratio of apprentices to full-time pros increased significantly. However, when we see what the boys were actually doing during their 'apprentice-ships', the reason for the increase will be clear.

The ability of clubs to secure youngsters was extended further in the 1970s by the introduction of the Schoolboy Apprentice system. This allowed boys aged between 13 and 15 to be 'attached' to a club and (their school permitting) to come in and train for three evenings a week. They might even play for a junior club team, once again, the school permitting.

Until the introduction of the Youth Training Schemes in the early 1980s, that was all the game demanded of young men in terms of qualifications. There were no formal examinations to be taken in footballing skills, fitness or even knowledge of the rules. Neither was there any obligation placed on a young player to gain qualifications outside the game as preparation for possible failure later on.

In the early 1980s, however, with economic recession and falling attendances forcing clubs to cut costs, there was a dramatic drop in the number of young men being signed on as apprentices. In 1983, the twenty-four clubs comprising the old Fourth Division had only thirty-three apprentices between them.

The introduction by the Conservative Government of the Youth Training Scheme in 1984, though derided as a gimmick by the trade union movement in general, proved to be anything but for football. Clubs received money for engaging boys on the scheme, which involved releasing them on certain days to attend local colleges. There, they were expected to study a trade or to take O-levels.

By 1989, most professional clubs had between ten and fifteen boys attached as apprentices and the tendency for clubs to 'produce their own' rather than buying or recruiting the ready-made article elsewhere has continued apace. Today, the chances of a young man becoming a professional increase substantially if he is part of a club's youth scheme. In the season 1995–6, of 2,289 professional players in English League clubs, 1,559 had graduated from youth training schemes.

However, becoming a professional has never been about what a player actually knew or could even demonstrate he knew about the game; it has always been about what others thought they saw in the player, his potential. From the very early years, the football industry has employed a rudimentary army of head-hunters whose job it was to scour the playing fields and backyards of industrial Britain in an endless search for new blood.

2. Scouting for glory

'He was persuasive, good in company and always charmed the mothers. He always recognised that the mother was the key figure to win over.'

Manchester United Chief Scout Joe Armstrong's son, 1999

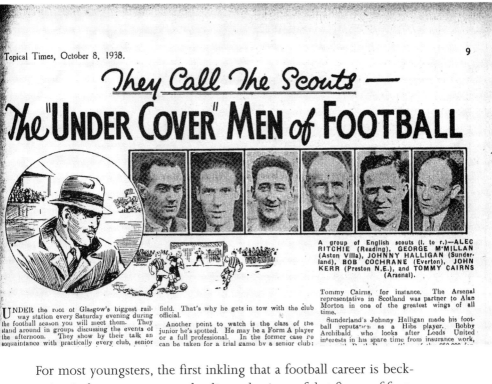

Topical Times, October 8, 1938.   9

They Call The Scouts —
The "UNDER COVER" MEN of FOOTBALL

A group of English scouts (l. to r.)—ALEC RITCHIE (Reading), GEORGE M'MILLAN (Aston Villa), JOHNNY HALLIGAN (Sunderland), BOB COCHRANE (Everton), JOHN KERR (Preston N.E.), and TOMMY CAIRNS (Arsenal).

UNDER the rule of Glasgow's biggest railway station every Saturday evening during the football season you will meet them. They stand around in groups discussing the events of the afternoon. They show by their talk an acquaintance with practically every club, senior field. That's why he gets in tow with the club official.

Another point to watch is the class of the junior he's spotted. He may be a Form A player or a full professional. In the former case he can be taken for a trial game by a senior club:

Tommy Cairns, for instance. The Arsenal representative in Scotland was partner to Alan Morton in one of the greatest wings of all time.

Sunderland's Johnny Halligan made his football reputation as a Hibs player. Bobby Archibald who looks after Leeds United interests in his spare time from insurance work,

For most youngsters, the first inkling that a football career is beckoning is the appearance on the distant horizon of that figure of football legend, the football scout.

In an industry that places so little store in paperwork and identifiable assessment criteria, the scout plays a key role. Perhaps an ex-player or manager, but often neither, he is able to apply that crucial but indefinable ingredient: experience. The good scout not only has to have an 'eye' for a good player, but also a knowledge of the peculiarities of the profession, and a sixth sense about those who will do well in it. Scouts are both talent-spotters and salesmen. They are often, incongruously, ladies' men, as mothers are frequently the key to success in the business – after all, the targets are young schoolboys.

Perhaps one of the attractions of this poorly paid and peculiar calling is the definite thrill involved in the undercover aspect of it: the secrecy and the subterfuge. Scouts tell tall tales, breathless accounts of mad car chases, of secret assignations on lonely railway stations following anonymous tip-offs. There is a calculated mystique about the business, contributing to the 'hidden world' aspect of pro soccer. Scouts are fishers of men: photographed with arms stretched wide, indicating the size of the one that got away.

Terry Venables recalled that the man who had been such an influence on his signing for Chelsea in the late 1950s was obsessed with secrecy: 'Jimmy Thompson, the Chelsea chief scout, who had taken Jimmy Greaves and several other good young players to Chelsea, was a hell of a man, a tremendous character, who loved nothing better than to make a melodrama out of his job. He often called round at our house to chat and offer advice, but he never wanted any of the other club scouts to know what he was doing. On one occasion, he was sitting in our kitchen when one of the other scouts came to the door, and Jimmy went and hid in the bathroom for an hour, until the other man had gone, rather than be spotted by his rival.

'My Dad saw him one day, watching a game in which I was playing, lying on his stomach in the long grass behind the goalposts. When Jimmy saw him, he whispered, "Fred, get down here quick. Don't let anyone know I'm here." Only when my Dad was safely down in the long grass alongside him, did Jimmy relax enough to indulge in some polite conversation. He also arranged to meet me at Waterloo Station once, under the four-sided clock. I stood there for twenty minutes and could not see him anywhere, and I was about to give up and go home when I heard someone going, "Psst, psst". I finally spotted him hiding behind a pillar and beckoning to me. When I asked him what was going on, he just said, "You can't be too careful. You can't be too careful."'

Scouts are 'private eyes' and, like novelist Raymond Chandler's Marlowe, they often appear to be hard up. In fact, in economic terms, scouts represent a form of 'producer subsidy', in that the vast majority of their efforts yield little or no wage. Scouts are usually reimbursed for travel expenses and paid a bonus (of, typically, a few hundred pounds) only if someone they recommend is subsequently 'signed on'. A few are awarded a small retainer.

emphasised ability, discipline, loyalty and clean living, along with an enthusiastic enjoyment of the game. Players with these attributes would be the lifeblood of the kind of club he was trying to build and he believed such qualities could only be found at schoolboy level, his 'good apples'.

Jack Hixon, by contrast, was seeking something simpler: 'Perhaps the most important thing for the modern game is pace. I don't think you can ever give a man immediate acceleration, you cannot make him "lift" to leave an opponent. Physical make-up, balance, execution – all these things can be worked on. But running power is different. You must also always study the youngster carefully to find out his margin for improvement over the years.'

Tim Ward was a scout for a number of years in the 1960s, following a distinguished career as a player for England and Derby and later as a manager. According to Ward, the key thing about scouting, the 'burning issue', was evaluating the standard of the game, its pace and skill level. Only then, he felt, could one judge one of its participants. 'The vital question was: what would happen if we took X out and put him in another team in another league? It was about comparing and contrasting.'

The first thing he looked for in the individual, however, was whether a player had good balance; then he looked for speed off the mark, the skills, the courage, the determination and so on. A player might have enough of one asset to make it worth taking a chance on the rest, but there was more to scouting than just watching the players: 'I like to find out about a player's character, too. That involves chatting to people, finding out about his reputation. It's nicer to find out from someone you know. I always try, if I can, to get near a player to judge his height. It's very deceptive with footballers.' Like Hixon, Ward was looking for pace:

'If a player hasn't got pace today, he's got to be very skilled, especially up front. He needs pace these days and he must turn quick. He must be quick enough to get away or he's in trouble. I was watching a player at Crewe once when there were several managers there. I was sitting next to Joe Mercer. I'd gone to watch a big, tall, raw left half and just before the end the right winger left him dead in a race for the ball. Joe turned to me and said, "Christ, he can't run, either".'

It often went deeper than simply identifying qualities and then offering the boy a contract. Young players with possibilities might find themselves being regularly monitored by a scout who would feed them tips and criticisms or who would play cat-and-mouse games with them to keep them on their toes. Alf Walton was keen to spot and cure idleness and bad habits in young players. 'I saw a really good goalkeeper one night, a big young fellow, but he was idle. You couldn't fault his keeping, his actual keeping: he could do everything he could kick a ball, he was agile, he had tons of agility, a capable pair of hands, but he wouldn't run to pick a ball up, he wouldn't run out to kick a ball. You can't cure that. But you can't find out until you talk to him, tell him, you've got to tell him, point blank, you've got to rub it [the fault] out completely. Well, you go again and you don't let him see you if you possibly can, and you watch him again, because if he thinks he's being watched, he'll cut it out. But if you were there and he doesn't see you, he won't. Teachers are useful to a certain extent. But I find out from the other lads as well whether the pupil and the teacher dislike each other. And if they do, that can be [the reason for] a diverse report, just because of his dislike. And then you take it with a pinch of salt. I speak to them on the quiet. As long as I've got permission to approach that lad, well, then I can talk to the other lads and talk about the teachers as well.'

Walton, like many other scouts, would form a relationship with a potential recruit. He would often assume a quasi-parental role: 'A boy under fourteen can't make his mind up. You'll see a school footballer go down [in his schoolwork]. Some of them are affected that way, and I can stop it with a few words. I'll threaten him, if he doesn't get back to his own standard, that we shall finish with him...and I say to the boy, if we finish with you, we'll tell anybody else not to sign you, we'll tell them. I tell them all, I threaten them, if you don't want to work hard in this game – and you'll lose a lot of sweat and you'll get a lot of knocks – it won't matter what you say, it's what they [the club] think. I've frightened quite a few off.'

The spotting of youngsters with the potential to become professional players was and remains an inexact science. The list of 'stars' discovered by any one scout might be long, but the list of failures will be immeasurably longer. Unfortunately for the boys concerned, they will often never know why they have been chosen, and thus will rarely understand why they have been rejected. Not that it matters when the club comes calling.

4. Signing on the dotted line

'Off the three of us went to my home in Main Street, Cambuslang, Scotland. Remember that I was then only sixteen years old and was not quite comfortable in the presence of the manager of a big English club. But I was not in the least scared. I knew exactly what I wanted. "And what terms are you prepared to offer me?" said I.'

Andy Wilson, Topical Times, May 1922

The moment when the forms are placed on the table and the prospective star is asked to sign has often been presented in players' autobiographies in almost mystical terms. After all, it's the dream come true, the moment a young boy's life is changed forever. It's also been a moment characterised by sordid wrangling and bartering, with young men being literally 'sold' by their parents like prize heifers.

Arthur Hopcraft, in The Football Man, recounts how Stan Cullis was taken by his father to see the Wolves manager, the legendary martinet Major Buckley, at his home. Buckley, Cullis said, 'looked like a retired well-to-do farmer, because he always wore plus fours. He looked like a man of the soil. No one ever thought of calling him anything else but "major". It was his rank in the First World War.'

The interview was short and staccato. Cullis said, 'He looked me up and down as I imagine a bloodstock owner would look at a race horse. He said, "Stand up". I didn't know what he meant. I thought he must mean something about my clothes. He said, "Are you frightened?" I said, "What of?" He said, "Of getting hurt". I said, "No". That was all he said to me. He had some words with my father which I couldn't hear, and I was a professional footballer.'

In many instances, the teenager concerned is faced with men who've spent their lives in the game and who understand the power they are wielding. Jimmy Seed wrote of the magic moment in April 1914 when he was asked to sign:

'Entering, I took in at a glance the manager, several directors and signing forms which were lying on the table. Nervously, I opened my mouth to announce myself to the nonchalant group, but since they were paying little attention, I closed it again. "Now, sonny," Bob Kyle's voice sang out, when eventually I was noticed, "how would you like to be a Sunderland player?" How would I indeed, thought I, but tried to assume an indifference consistent with the atmosphere. All the advice I had ever received took its departure from my whirling mind at that moment. I would have signed a death warrant just then. To sign for Sunderland. Why, it was like the climax of a fairy story. I stammered an affirmative, listened while I was offered 30s a week and £5 for myself. "There's five pounds to start with," said Mr Kyle, "let's hope it will soon be £500." I had never been in possession of such wealth. With a shaking hand and a heart that was rejoicing, I took up the pen and signed the necessary forms, picking the five golden sovereigns as a newsboy would a hidden treasure chest.

'Once on the other side of the door I collected my thoughts but before I could put these into words I ran into my three brothers, who were anxiously awaiting the verdict. They could see by my beaming countenance that all was well. I showed them the five jimmy-o-goblins while they gaped their amazement. Joyfully, we walked the two miles to Whitburn, singing as we went.'

Dixie Dean's great moment was far less auspicious. It was November 1923: 'I was just getting stripped after the match and a chap comes in to me and he said, "How would you like to have a trial with Tranmere?" I thought, "Well, this is a bit of a stepping stone." So I told him, I said, "Yes, I wouldn't mind." He said, "And if you do come off, they'll sign you professional." It was a chap named "Dump" Lee who used to be the main scout of Tranmere. I went and signed with them but I didn't get any summer wages. They played me the very next week. I signed for £4 5s a week. You got £1 if you won and 10 shillings if you drew, which, of course, in those days was pretty decent. But Tranmere should have been paying me £6 when I was playing with the first team. I made one or two enquiries but I didn't go any further with it and stayed on £4 5s.'

Dean's lack of guile continued when he moved to Everton a year and a half later, in March 1925. His parents had made all the financial arrangements but Tom McIntosh, Everton's secretary, had deceived Dean's parents: 'He promised my mother and dad that I'd receive £300 out of the £3,000 that Everton had paid for me; he said he'd kick me off with a bank book and I'd have 300 quid in it. Then I received a telegram, I went along to the ground, about a fortnight later, and he handed me a cheque for £30. So I turned round to him and I said, "You've made a mistake here. You've left an 0 off." He said, "I'm sorry, Dean, but that's all the League would allow you."'

Ted Harper, another free-scoring England centre-forward of the inter-war years, greeted his big moment with similarly youthful carelessness. A dockyard apprentice on 3s 8d a week, he was getting 10s a match playing for Sheppey United. In May 1923, 'Jack Carr, then manager of Blackburn Rovers, came down unknown to us and watched our game. I got five goals to celebrate the last game of the season. Whilst I was having my tea afterwards, a youngster came to the door and said to go to a nearby hotel where a Blackburn gentleman wanted to see me. When I got there I was introduced to Jack Carr. I was asked if I would care to sign for Blackburn Rovers. I didn't think long. They had started firing men at the dockyard and, as far as I could see, I was finishing my apprenticeship and then getting the sack. So I gave myself the sack and signed for Blackburn Rovers. I was given the usual £10 signing-on fee. I went home and gave the folks a fiver and told them what I'd done. I then collected my pals, went up to the soda fountain and filled them up with ice-cream sodas and ginger-pop. What a binge!'

Cliff 'Boy' Bastin was certainly not overawed nor particularly excited when he was offered professional terms. The future Arsenal and England winger was playing as an amateur for Exeter City in the

Third Division in 1928. Having just turned 17, Mr Syd Thomas, the club secretary, called him into his office and suggested he sign the professional forms on the table. Bastin had different ideas.

'I read the contract through, and saw that I was to be paid £4 for first team appearances, and a pound less for matches in the reserves. "That's no good to me!" I said. Mr Thomas' astonishment was almost painful to behold. "What do you mean?" he snapped. I pointed out to him that, as a first-year professional, I was entitled to a maximum wage of £5 a week, all year round, and that unless I received it I had no intention of signing for Exeter.'

Mr Thomas suggested that Bastin was suffering from a swollen head and that he wouldn't get such terms even in the First Division, but Bastin held firm. 'I gently informed him that it was all the same to me whether I signed for his club or not, and that if the City thought I was worth signing on as a professional, I was worth a decent wage as well.' Bastin got his extra pound.

There must have been something about the men that Arsenal targeted during the 1920s because Eddie Hapgood, another player who ended up at Highbury, was equally off-hand at attempts to lure him into the professional game. He was working in a dairy when his opportunity came. 'A Blackburn Rovers director came out to the dairy with a professional offer of £8 a week, and a place in the first team. I asked what I would do during the summer. "I have a coal business," replied the director, "and I can fix you up driving a coal cart." Gently, but firmly, I ushered him out of the house. I figured there was a social distinction between driving a milk float and a coal cart.'

Sometimes, what was offered had to be gratefully accepted, despite its paucity. Many fledgling players were from extremely poor backgrounds and were already earning pittance wages. Frank Swift signed for Manchester City in October 1932, at the 'magnificent sum of 10s a week. This was a little less than I had imagined, and I asked manager Wilf Wild, "Do I get anything if I get into the first team?" Mr Wild laughingly added a clause to the contract that my wages would be increased to 20s if I played for the senior side. Such are the riches which pave the path to fame!' Swift continued working as a coke-keeper but within two years he was on the top wage and making his debut on Christmas Day, 1933. 'As midnight chimed, the family, God bless 'em, wished me a happy birthday. I was nineteen.'

Raich Carter was another young man facing an uncertain future. His father had died and he wanted to be able to support his mother and sisters: 'Sunderland had not escaped the national slump of that period, and at the Forge and Electrical Company where I was serving my apprenticeship, practically all hands were on short time.' Sunderland FC then offered him professional forms: 'And so on that red-letter day in my calendar – 12 November, 1931 – I went with my uncle to Roker Park and in the Boardroom of the Sunderland FC met the manager, Johnny Cochrane. When he offered me £3 a week with £4 when I played in the reserve team, I was frankly disappointed.'

His uncle persuaded him to sign, however. 'We shook hands and Johnny Cochrane counted out ten £1 notes – my signing-on bonus. I had never known so much money. I walked through the streets with the notes clutched tightly in my hand, and to celebrate the momentous occasion went into a cinema for the afternoon matinee. Still holding on to the money like grim death – I dare not put it in my pocket and let go of it – I sat through the performance and then went home in triumph to my mother.'

And the experience would hardly alter from one generation to the next. Some twenty years later, Raich Carter was instrumental in bringing Jack Charlton into the professional game. Charlton recalled, 'When I walked into [club secretary] Arthur Crowther's office, I couldn't guess what lay ahead. He got straight to the point. "Jack," he said, "Raich has instructed me to offer you a contract. You'll get ten pounds signing-on fee, eighteen pounds a week in season and fourteen pounds off." The first thought that entered my mind was, "That's senior team money!" I left that office feeling ten feet tall. I realized that I might have a real future in the game. Within hours I was on a train back to Ashington, to give the good news to my mother and father.'

Four years later, in November 1958, a future England international team-mate of Charlton's was approaching his signing-on moment in a rather less deferential fashion. Alan Mullery was an apprentice at Fulham. Some months before he was about to turn 17, he learned that Fulham would be making him an offer. 'A great old pro in those days, Roy Bentley, who was an England international centre-forward, gave me some advice. He said, "Ask for £1,000 under-the-counter payment," but I said, "I can't do that." He said, "No, no, they'll give it to you, don't worry about it, they won't want to lose you." So I walked into the boardroom and there was Tommy Trinder, the chairman, the comedian, and [manager] Frank Osborne, who had a cigarette in the side of his mouth and drank a bottle of scotch a day and he tossed the contract down the big boardroom table which I used to polish every Friday, and the contract slid down and I looked at it – the usual £10 signing-on fee and £12 a week. I slid the contract back up the table.

'Osborne said, "What's the problem?" I said, "I want £1,000 to sign on," and he jumped up out of his chair and he got his hat and he threw it on the table and he went, "Get out, get out," and I got up and I walked out of the boardroom. Roy Bentley said, "Did you get your money?" I said, "No, he threw me out." He said, "Don't worry, you'll get it."

'The following day I came in and Frank said to me, "Are you gonna sign that contract?" I said, "No." "Well, I'm gonna report you," he said, "to the Football Association for asking for illegal payments," and I was absolutely worried. I went home and the weekend went by. I came in on the Monday and he called me into his office and said, "Look, I'll tell you what I'll do, you sign that contract and if you're not in the first team inside three months of your birthday, I'll give you the £1,000 out of my own pocket." I thought, "Well, that's not bad," so I signed it, and two weeks before the three months were up I was in the first team, so he didn't have to give me the £1,000.'

Because there was relatively little on offer before the 1960s by way of pay and contract flexibility, such lack of guile and help probably caused little pain. With the abolition of the maximum wage and as players' contracts began to evolve towards total freedom, 'signing-on' for top players started to get complicated. As a consequence, the player's agent, for long a dormant species, re-emerged in the 1970s. At first, such agents represented only individual prominent players. They were often friends or lawyers hired for the purpose and until the mid-1980s only a handful operated in England. Since the introduction of the Premiership, however, agents have proliferated and their remit in terms of services to players has expanded too. Agents now offer players a weekly service, helping with everything from finding sponsorship to shaping their image to meeting the demands of potential advertisers. They offer career advice, arrange car and house purchases, negotiate book deals, and even (it's controversially claimed) suggest when a player might think about leaving his present club.

They act, in fact, more like professional management companies and some agents now have hundreds of players on their books. However, they are now perceived by many football administrators as being something of a menace, some going as far as to describe them as a 'cancer' in the game. Loosely regulated and with an increasingly sinister influence on club managements, they can destabilise a player simply to earn money for themselves or can be used by a club to 'tap' a player illegally. In some ways, they have resurrected their original turn-of-the-century role as providers of players to clubs willing to cut corners in pursuit of the best men. Possible conflicts of influence are obvious.

They can also be as manipulative as clubs once were, taking advantage of the ignorance of young, impressionable players, persuading them to sign complex contracts the player later regrets. Many agents seek to sign promising players as early as 14 years of age (Jermaine Defoe of West Ham is one such player). In order to ameliorate some of the problems being caused, the Professional Footballers' Association, which offers all prospective professionals help with financial, educational and medical help, recently went so far as to establish a Platinum Group of young, gifted players. The group was selected from boys attending the FA National Soccer School at Lilleshall. Sponsored by adidas, which provides kit and lays on medical and 'lifestyle' advice at its Wellness Centre, the pilot scheme was devised to help young players with contract negotiations, media training, formal education, etc.

The PFA stressed that it was not attempting to create an 'elite' of any kind. It simply wanted to establish itself as an honest broker providing sound advice and objective guidance to young men (and their parents) who might otherwise be bedazzled by offers from unscrupulous agents. With hundreds of new agents entering the business each year, however, and with the complexities of sponsorship deals, 'Bosman' style contracts, 'image rights', etc., the influence of agents seems likely to expand ever further. Liverpool's Emil Heskey was signed on by agents SFX when he was 17 and he's been extremely happy with them. 'They have organised my commercial and financial affairs and my playing contracts, leaving me to concentrate on my game.'

5. On the groundstaff

'The following morning I was handed my equipment, and it didn't include football boots, shirt or shorts. I was given a pair of overalls and told to follow the motor mower all over the pitch, clipping any long grass stalks missed by the mower. A rake was provided too, but never a sign of a football.'

Len Shackleton, Clown Prince of Soccer, 1956

Len Shackleton went to Arsenal from Bradford in 1938 to be a groundstaff boy: 'I thought August would never come, but eventually I packed my bags, caught the train to London, and was met at King's Cross by Jack Lambert, centre-forward hero of so many Arsenal triumphs. Having been installed in Highbury Hill lodgings, I went with Lambert for my first peep at the magnificent Arsenal stadium. It was a real eye-opener. The mighty stands, the spotlessly clean terracing, reaching, to my eyes, into the clouds, the emerald green turf: these would have been sufficient to impress the bumpkin from Bradford, but to cap the lot, I saw – and recognised immediately – several of the favoured, fabulous, footballers, who had helped to make Arsenal great, helped, in fact, to make Arsenal "The" Arsenal. There they were, within hailing distance, Ted Drake, Wilf Copping, Cliff Bastin and George Male, yet I did not dare hail them, even with a "good afternoon".

'Enviously, I watched the "real" players doing their training stint – while I pretended to rake the gravel or cut the turf, without having the heart for either task. Each day a fresh face would join the stalk-shortening squad.'

Albert Scanlon, who joined Manchester United in 1953, remembered, 'My first job was painting the ground. They gave us a five-gallon drum of red oxide, a paint brush, and they said go out and paint everything red. Then when we'd painted everything red they'd come back with a drum of white and a different bucket and give you that and you'd go out and paint everything white that was white. You never got involved in anything else but just Old Trafford as it was then. We did all the odd jobs. There were dressing rooms but outside there was a gymnasium and the only thing in the

Evening Standard,

2 December 1932.

BERT GELDARD

—EVERTON'S NEW RIGHT WINGER— visiting CHELSEA

WAS TRAINING WITH PROFESSIONALS AT THE AGE OF **12**

AND PLAYING FOR BRADFORD RESERVES AT **14**

HE WAS A FIRST TEAM PLAYER AT **15**

GELDARD IS A FORMER SCHOOLBOY INTERNATIONAL AND WAS A PHENOMENAL MARKSMAN AS A BOY— .... JUST BEFORE JOINING BRADFORD, HE SCORED **125** GOALS IN A SEASON, INCLUDING **22** IN ONE MATCH !!

gymnasium was mats, big square mats and two medicine balls and a few weights. And Ted Dalton, the physiotherapist, he had his treatment room in there, and every day Monday to Friday we swept and locked and that was the job I finished with. And you were covered in dirt, dust, the water was rotten.'

Stan Cullis, in his book, *All For The Wolves*, talked about cleanliness of dressing rooms at Wolverhampton Wanderers' Molineux ground compared to elsewhere. There was a reason for it: 'The youngster who comes to Molineux is expected to work hard at his task and, if he is one of the half dozen lads whom we have on the groundstaff, he does not have a great deal of spare time on his hands. He will report to the ground shortly before the senior professionals arrive at 9.45 a.m. and will not leave until tea-time. His main duties will range from cleaning the baths and dressing rooms to clearing litter from the terraces and helping the groundsmen to weed and tidy the pitch. Between his other duties, he will train and practice with a football either on the field or in the gymnasium.'

Cullis was at least honest about the reality of the groundstaff boys' duties. Too often, boys were used as only manual labour, while their opportunity to train and be coached was severely limited. Cullis, however, added, 'I tell every lad who comes to Molineux that the club will arrange for him to take up an apprenticeship or to attend a technical college or night school if he feels he would like a second string to his bow.'

This was purely voluntary until the introduction of the Youth Training Schemes in the 1980s, and the idea of going back to school after having apparently escaped such drudgery and boredom was never going to prove attractive to a teenage boy. The experience of Alan Mullery in December 1958 was more the norm: 'The general manager of Fulham, Frank Osborne, who was a lovely man, said to me, "Do you wanna join the groundstaff or do you want to go to the city and work for two years and study something and then come back and be a professional footballer if you're good enough?" I didn't have a clue what you did as a groundstaff boy. I looked at my dad and I said "I want to be around the players and learn the game, so I wanna be a groundstaff boy". He [Frank Osborne] said, "Fine. Great. Go outside, see the groundsman and he'll give you some kit."

'It was a Thursday. I walked out onto the pitch and the players were playing a five-a-side over the far side from Fulham, over by the river, and the groundsman was cutting the grass for the Saturday match. I walked over and I said, 'I'm a new groundstaff boy, what do I do?' I got some kit, got some old rags on, a torn track suit, whatever, and he said, "Find yourself a cardboard box and pick up all this paper that I haven't picked up so that I can cut the grass." All the other part of the ground, other than one quarter, had paper blowing off the Thames and off the terraces onto the pitch, so I went picking up crisp paper and putting it in the box.

'The second day was even more exciting. I was given another job. I worked with a little guy. I remember his name – Jack Gordon. I can see him now, he was about 5ft 2in, had a cigarette in the side of his mouth, peak cap. I said, "I've been assigned to you". He said, "Fine. Let's get underneath the stand." So we went underneath the stand with a wheelbarrow and two shovels and a tin. I didn't know what was in the tin. He said, "Right, if you see any buns, pick up these buns," so I said, "Okay." I picked up these buns, and he got an old knife and he spread something like mustard on this bun, you see, and he put it down by the little kiosk there and said, "Right, we're gonna have a cup of tea now," so we went into the shed, had a cup of tea and I said, "Excuse me, what are we doing?" "Oh," he said, "you'll see before long." We went out and there was all these rats waddling around as if they were drunk. He picked up a spade and he smashed this spade on this rat and squashed it. He shovelled it up, put it in the wheelbarrow. He said, "Right, it's your turn now," and that was my second day at Fulham, the start of a great time.'

However, little changed with the introduction of the apprenticeship schemes of the 1960s. Steve Claridge was offered apprenticeship terms by Portsmouth when he left school in 1981: '£20 a week, going up to £25 in my second year. It was a great feeling; it felt like I had really made it, though I have to be honest and say that I thought I deserved it. In those days, because it really meant something to be chosen from all those kids, you really felt you were on the verge of a glittering career. That said, we were still cheap labour.

'I had to clean thirty-four pairs of boots every day. Each apprentice also had six sets of players' kit for which he was responsible, making sure it was all laid out properly each day. And we had to keep the boot room and all its contents clean. We would train with the first team and reserves at Eastney Common, a bleak and

windswept place, from 10.30 to midday, just making up the numbers, really. It was a bad system, I thought, because in that first
season there was no full-time coach to look after us or teach us
anything and we were left to our own devices too often, just kicking a ball around. The club manager was Bobby Campbell, who
went on to manage Chelsea. He was a fearsome sort of bloke,
though we didn't have much contact with him, thankfully. You never
mucked around in his eyeline.

'After lunch it was back to Fratton Park [Portsmouth's ground]
where we did fitness work, like running around the pitch, or swept
the terraces till home time. Pompey used to employ four old blokes
to sweep the terraces but one by one they died and the club never
replaced them. We apprentices did our best to keep them alive so we
wouldn't have to do it ourselves, feeding them vitamins and such
like, but we just couldn't halt the march of time. Then, after night
matches, we could be replacing divots until 11 p.m. In the summer
we would also have to paint the ground before we were allowed our
three weeks' holiday a year.'

The traditional 'apprenticeship' would appear to have been a
rough and ready method of 'socialising' young men into the strange
world of the professional player. Learning to accept the existing
hierarchy without question, developing a passive rather than active
approach to one's destiny at the club, closing out all distracting elements such as curiosity about non-footballing subjects and accepting the dressing room 'pecking order': these were the principal
items on the unofficial curriculum.

When YT replaced Youth Training Schemes in 1990, however, the
educational aspects of the apprentice schemes increased in importance. But the Professional Footballers' Association, overseer of the
education of young footballers, has always wanted to develop a
more holistic approach to the issue and in 1998 an ambitious
Football Scholarship scheme was launched in conjunction with the
FA, the Premier League, the Football League and adidas, the sports
equipment manufacturer. This, those involved hope, will significantly change the occupational culture of professional football. The
new scheme, to which most Premiership clubs have now signed up,
places much more emphasis than hitherto on academic study and
gaining qualifications, things that would seem to have little connection with the immediate business of becoming a player.

A young apprentice professional (henceforth described as a Scholar rather than a Trainee) is now educationally assessed prior to taking his GCSEs at school and asked to suggest areas of study that interest him. Once his GCSE results are known, he proceeds to a college near his club to take his chosen course, be it A-levels, AS-levels, GNVQ or BTec national diplomas. At some clubs, the educational elements are provided daily. At Derby County, for instance, scholarship players come in at 9 a.m. and are normally involved in education for an hour and a half prior to football training at 11 a.m. In addition, there is a half-day block period once a week when the scholarship players go to Loughborough College to continue their education. Most of the education, however, is provided on site at the Derby Academy (where some 125 youngsters aged between 10 and 15 attend for football skills training). Teachers from local schools and technical colleges come to the academy to provide a variety of courses.

There are also some twenty-one core skill elements involved in the three-year package that will take the prospective player from 16 years of age to 19, including media skills, dealing with the public, nutrition and diet, avoiding alcohol abuse, financial planning, lifelong learning and many more. The first cohort of scholars 'graduating' in 2001 showed significant successes at A-level – a third of those involved achieving grades that could take them on to university degree courses if they so wished.

Topical Times, 1930. Harry Johnson, ex-Sheffield United, with sons Tom (left) and Harry, also Sheffield United.

Dropping out of college will mean cancellation of the apprenticeship. In fact, Gordon Taylor, PFA Chief Executive, has said, 'We hope that, with a little bit of luck, the Scholarship will be the only way into professional football in the future.'

Not all clubs have embraced the concept wholeheartedly. Many of the 'old school' in football remain unconvinced about the programme's worth in terms of the development of young players as people as a whole and not just as footballers. It did, after all, represent, according to Micky Burns, Chief Executive of FFE and VTS, the body charged with implementing

The STARS THEN AND NOW

Old-Time Photos sent by Readers

JAMES McCORMICK
Tottenham Hotspur
outside-right

At the age of 13

JACK COULTER
Everton outside-left

ALEC HALL
Sunderland
right-back

TOMMY WALKER
Heart of Midlothian
inside-right

Captain of his school team 1924-25

Alec as a member of
his school team

Wearing one of his Scottish
schoolboy international caps

the programme, 'a radical change in the culture of the game and the way clubs treat their young people.' He continued, 'We are always going to be faced with the problem of trying to mature young men very quickly and that is becoming increasingly difficult now football is almost equivalent to the pop industry. I suppose what we are trying to create is a university within football to help with that maturing process.'

What it has done is banish, so it is claimed, the old-fashioned 'dogsbody' role for young men entering professional clubs. Dave Rushbury, ex-player and now physiotherapist at Chesterfield FC, where one of his sons is a scholar, has observed: 'Certain jobs, such as cleaning the pros' boots, can still be part of the young player's routine, if the pros are happy to pay the scholars to do it and so long as it doesn't interfere with their scholarship routine. But some of the other more menial tasks have disappeared. For example, they no longer sweep the corridors, weed the ground, clean the stadium seats or wash out the toilets – that's all gone now.'

The new scholarship system suggests that young men entering the game will be far better prepared for life if football fails to offer them the opportunities they so desperately desire. Sadly, however, many clubs instinctively turn to the transfer market when sudden team vacancies occur – managers with little time to make mistakes will opt for the finished article rather than gamble on an untried youngster. Being an apprentice or a scholar can, therefore, be a potentially heartbreaking business. At the same time, diligently getting an education can often seem like an unnecessary distraction from achieving that tantalising dream.

6. Rejection

'I cried for two weeks when the gaffer told me. I was gutted. I hadn't progressed as quickly as he'd expected. He put his arm round me, offered to help me find another club, gave me his home telephone number and said he'd always give me help or advice. I remember he said, "I'll always be your boss." That helped.'

*George Switzer on being 'released' from
Manchester United*

Professional football has always been extremely cruel on those seeking to enter its ranks. Certainly it has always had an extremely high wastage rate. In the 1890s, only 42.5 per cent registered to play in 1893–4 were still in League football after a year, and only thirteen per cent after three years. In the 1990s, fifty per cent of trainees taken on by League clubs at 16 years of age were released at the end of the two-year stint and only twenty-five per cent remained after three years.

For managers, the business of ending a young man's career must be difficult, particularly as most managers have been players once, and understand the pain. When Lee Glover was taken on as an apprentice at Nottingham Forest, he found he was one of a very small group. 'There were only three or four of us where other clubs might have twelve or fifteen. I think the reason was that Cloughie didn't like telling people they were being let go. So we only had a few every year at Forest, but most of them did get kept on.' It wasn't, he felt, that Clough was 'soft'. 'I would say he didn't want to dash people's hopes.'

For young men, being told that they have no future in the game can be a crushing blow, particularly as few talented youngsters give much thought to the alternatives. Very often, the alternatives do not bear thinking about. Len Shackleton, who would later find fame with Sunderland, recalled: 'A week or two before the end of the season, Harry Ward and I were approached by groundsman Rudd and told, "The boss wants to see you in his office." We imagined the summons was in connection with some neglect of our groundstaff duties: we both hoped it would not be a reprimand relating to the playing side of the job.

'In the magnificent managerial mausoleum I stood awkwardly facing Mr Allison, wishing, I don't know why, that the pile on the ankle-deep carpet might grow and keep on growing until it attained a height of 5 feet 2 inches to hide me from the eyes of my manager.

'Then followed an interview I shall never forget. With each pronouncement the facts became clearer. I was washed up, was not good enough for the Arsenal – or any other club for that matter; I would have to return to Bradford and become, perhaps, a miner, an engineer, perhaps a commercial traveller – but never a footballer.

'Mr Allison could not have been kinder: he handled that interview with diplomacy, repeatedly assuring me that he was advising me in my own interests, and told me not to take the news too badly. One day I would be grateful. He said, "Go back to Bradford and get a job. You will never make the grade as a professional footballer." I should have been thankful to have discovered such shortcomings so early in my career, but my only thoughts that day were the shame of returning home a failure, the epitome of "local boy doesn't make good", and I was not far from tears as Allison's verdict was pronounced.'

Kerry Dixon, who would ultimately succeed with Chelsea, was physically affected: 'One by one the lads were called to one side and assured they would be signed by the club now that their schooldays were coming to a close. All of us were looking for a job of work to do. I'd considered nothing but professional football. Only two players failed to attract the prized apprentice forms: Kerry Dixon and a close pal called Johnny Mawhinney. I was devastated. The usual defensive barriers were erected in my mind. I tried to make out I was a big shot who couldn't have cared less. What a joke. The feeling of nausea just wouldn't go away…'

Steve Claridge, similarly rejected, but later to sign for Bournemouth, was confident enough not to feel as bad as Dixon, and he understood what had gone wrong: 'Looking back, I was too cocky, too sure I was going to make it. I had this dream and I didn't think anything was going to disturb me. Being nice to myself, I suppose it was single-mindedness, but with that has to go hard work as well. Ability alone is never enough.'

Today, with many Premiership clubs creating their own 'Centres of Excellence' to produce players, and with elite squads of young men being selected and cocooned at Lilleshall to play for England youth teams, promising boys can be involved in professional game from the age of 9 in one way or another. In previous decades, as we have seen, apprenticeship schemes were often little more than a means to providing cheap labour for clubs and the young men involved were rarely encouraged to feel that they were part of the first or even second team 'pool'. Whether they liked it or not, many young men had been forced to serve industrial or commercial apprenticeships and thus had some contact with the outside world of work. The modern 'hot-house' system simply didn't exist. For those rejected from the contemporary game, life beyond the football pitch must feel unimaginable, the psychological and financial stakes being so much higher.

Paul Wheatcroft, an exciting young England youth team striker was signed by Manchester United from Lillehsall in 1999. He thought that his natural ability would take him into the first team but admitted that he hadn't appreciated how much hard work was necessary. One afternoon, he was selected to play in a 'so-called friendly' at Halifax.

'When we ran out there were hundreds of scouts surrounding the pitch and upstairs in the canteen looking out, and I was wondering, what's going on? And they'd set up a game for the lads who were, sort of, being put on the market and we weren't even told about it. There was a team sheet going round with our names on and different things – like a cattle market – and I thought it was disgraceful, treating players like that. I mean, I'm a talented footballer. I don't need to be treated like that. It just felt like, pieces of meat, really. A lot of the lads were very upset about it, just couldn't take it in. I've still got the team sheet. It was just an unbelievable way of going about things.'

Wheatcroft had been cast into the trauma of an 'exit trial', a kind of boot-sale for abandoned youngsters, which serves a grim economic function. Regular sales of such teenagers pay most of the bills at the new academies, where standards are now so high that the youth directors can congratulate themselves if they supply one new first-team player a year. Even clubs as rich as Manchester United have to re-coup costs. The economic necessities that drove Stan Cullis back in the 1950s, though dressed up in finer clothes, still apply.

Wheatcroft was picked up by Bolton Wanderers, who offered him a contract, but the bitterness and hurt ran deep. 'It doesn't pay to be a deep thinker, it's a roller-coaster ride.'

Kevin Nicolson was another England 'graduate' from Lilleshall in the same year as Wheatcroft. Captain of England Youth, he knew that the pressures of professional football would only reveal themselves when he was out in the real world, in his case, Sheffield Wednesday. A regular in the reserves, he found living up to expectations difficult. With a year to run on his contract, he went to speak to the manager.

'To be honest, as far as those kinds of meetings go, it was really quite negative. He told me that he thought that I was a long way off, and didn't really give me a lot to go on. It was quite disappointing, because I went in there hoping for some kind of constructive criticism and a bit of hope and when I came out of it I'd been knocked down a bit.'

Nicolson was later told by one of the coaches that he might not have a future in football, that he wasn't 'fit to wear the shirt', and that he was a 'moral coward, whatever one of those is'. Determined to prove them all wrong, he seized the chance of a first-team debut to put on a show, but despite performing well, he was never again selected for the first team. The manager ignored him from then on and, resentful and bitter, he faced an uncertain future with no explanations or constructive help.

'Realistically, I wouldn't have any idea what I would do if things didn't pan out for me in football. I've never thought about it. I've never wanted to think about it. And if it does happen I'll be very under-prepared. To be released at the end of the season is a nightmare because you go into a pool of players, there's so many of them, a position where you've got no power at all, you're just hoping really that somebody is going to pick up on you.'

After a few months with Northampton Town, playing in the first team on a non-contract basis where he felt people appreciated him, Notts County of the Second Division offered him a three-year contract plus a pay rise. He then had to make what he called a 'horrible decision', upsetting and hard, to take up the offer and leave Northampton. Needless to say, he was called a 'Judas' by some supporters.

The falls from grace can be dizzying. George Switzer was part of the Manchester United FA Youth Cup winning team of 1992 that contained Ryan Giggs, Paul Scholes, Nicky Butt and David Beckham. His was a dream-like existence: free tickets to Manchester United matches, £240 a week wages and training with Ferguson, Brian Kidd and Nobby Stiles. After his year as a pro, though, he was 'let go' by Ferguson. A move to Darlington FC proved disastrous. After three months, the manager who'd signed him was sacked and Switzer was dumped in the reserves. He eventually ended up playing semi-pro for Hyde United. Age 25 he was making lenses for Dolland and Aitcheson glasses, but supremely philosophical:

'I had ten years with Manchester United, played with some of the world's best players and was paid for my trouble. If you ask any guy in the pub, he would love to have done what I've done.'

Rejection would appear to be based on criteria difficult to pin down, a set of intangibles that are rarely defined and often hard to explain. Silence or ambiguous phrases such as 'moral cowardice' are resorted to by managers often only days away from being sacked themselves. As Steve Claridge said, 'Ability alone is never enough.'

Chapter **4**

Tools of the Trade – Coaching

1. It'll be alright on the night

'...You must catch your player young. Footballers aren't born – they are made! The start must be made at school and if football is to become more and more of a science, greater attention must be paid to the coaching of the young idea.

W Freeman, The Red Letter, 1909

For the majority of the last century, it would seem, the football profession made a point of leaving young men to their own devices before suddenly plunging them into a playing world, almost totally unprepared for what lay ahead. Apart from a few enigmatic words of advice, it often seemed to be a matter of 'sink or swim'.

Charles Buchan, making his debut for Sunderland in March 1911, sat in the dressing room, 'and with shaking hands, I began to put on my kit. Sitting next to me was my partner Jimmie Durrant, who spoke a few kind words to put me at ease. Then at the twilight

Topical Times, November 19, 1938.

9

Ever Wondered How A Newcomer To A League Side Feels? The Players Themselves Tell

— MY FIRST GAME —

By JOE JAMES
(Brentford centre-half).

MY feelings were a bit mixed when I played my first game for Brentford. I was 20, in my second season with the club, and the snag was that I was taking Jimmy Bain's place. You see, Jimmy, who is now assistant-manager at Brentford, had been a great pal to me, and given me many tips on the game.

I wanted to do well, but I didn't fancy the idea of keeping Jimmy out of a "shop." Jimmy solved my problem for me, though. "It's a great chance for you, boy—make the most of it."

Once the match started I had no time to think about Jimmy Bain. We were in the Southern Section, and played Southend at Griffin Park.

long as usual to get to sleep the night before the match.

Mind you, it wasn't just nerves which caused me to be such a flop in that Liverpool match. No, I just couldn't last the pace—my tongue was hanging out most of the game — and my positioning was almost too bad to be true.

On top of this, the Bolton players generally had a poor day. Liverpool licked us 7-2. Dick Pym had the bad luck to score two goals against himself.

Each time Dick kicked clear, and each

after that. Each game confirmed my first experience of him.

Barson certainly knew the value of the hefty shoulder charge. But I never once saw him foul a player intentionally. His wholehearted play, together with his natural brilliance, made him the perfect centre-half.

By JACK WEDDLE
(Blackburn Rovers and ex-Portsmouth centre-forward).

MY first game in league soccer was against Burnley at Portsmouth. I shall never forget that day, for it was the first time I had ever played at centre-forward.

I went to Pompey as an inside-left, and had played all my soccer in that position

---

of his career, Jimmie was an experienced hand at outside-right, almost of international class.

'As we stood waiting to go out, Jimmie said to me:

"Charlie, can you do a lot of running? And will you do exactly what I want?"

"Yes," I replied, "I'll run as much as you like. What do you want me to do?"

"When I get the ball, run to within about ten yards of me every time. Then I can give you the ball."

"What happens when I've got the ball?"

"If I shout, push it forward along the wing so I can run on to it. If I don't shout, do whatever you like."

I carried out these instructions to the letter.

Almost forty years later, and Jack Charlton was equally in the dark as to what he should be doing when he made his debut: 'Incredibly, [manager] Raich Carter never came near me that day, never told me why he had put me in his team, nothing. And when I climbed aboard the first-team bus taking us to Doncaster the next day, I was left completely alone, without as much as a word from my new team-mates. I mean, nobody told me what I was expected to do, no tactical talk, nothing. I was left to my own devices until Eric Kerfoot, perhaps sensing my predicament, came across and said, "Son, they've picked you because they think you're good enough. Now, go out and prove them right."'

In most professions, there is a body of knowledge that has to be mastered before one can claim to be a member. Pro footballers sit no examinations, no case law and, until recently, there were no academies. The only qualification was and remains 'doing it'. As Jesse Carver, a great coach from the inter-war years, summed it up: 'Young British footballers learn from example rather than tuition, both in terms of individual skills and team tactics.'

Walter Winterbottom, who would become the Football Association's first national director of coaching and England team manager in 1946, wrote: 'The use of the ball for training during the week, apart from the game itself, was very limited. There was no tactical awareness, you just played football, and people didn't have much knowledge of how to help each other, how to build a system.' One of the game's main problems, he felt, was the secrecy regarding the transmission of information, a reluctance to discuss football issues with other people in the game, even one's own team-mates. He cited the example of one player who, having passed on some technical advice, urged him to 'Keep it to yourself'. A former England international, George Hardwick, agreed that football knowledge was disseminated orally during the 1940s and the written word was frowned on and was not generally accepted within the game. When coaching manuals finally appeared, such as the one Winterbottom produced in 1952, Hardwick claimed that many people did not like it because such knowledge 'had never been put in a book of words'.

No wonder, therefore, that the young players were often bewildered when the moment came for them to take the big step on to the pitch. Malcolm Allison, who would prove to be one of the most influential coaches in the British game, recalled his first game as a professional for Charlton Athletic during Christmas 1949, and his lack of preparation, both physical and mental.

'In my ignorance I had burned myself out on the training pitch. My strength should have been growing a little with each of those games, but instead I was shattered after the first. Mentally I was in a fog. There was no communication between the bench and the field.'

The trainer at Charlton Athletic at that time was Jimmy Trotter, who doubled as the England coach. Trotter was one of the key figures in the English game and his career stretched back some forty years. Yet Allison felt that going to work at that club, '..was like getting into a time machine and finding yourself travelling in the wrong direction'.

Trotter, he felt, was a fine physiotherapist and a good man, but, 'It seemed to me that he could never have given a moment's thought to the need for developing new ideas about the preparation of the professional footballer. We were asked to jog aimlessly around the training ground. You could see boredom on every face. Training gear was ragged. It reflected the lack of thought behind our work.'

So what was taught early on? Very little, it seems, because trainers were more concerned with physical fitness than with technique. That side of the game was left to the individual, although even before the First World War there was concern that players, especially young players, were not being encouraged to develop necessary ball-skills and techniques.

In 1913, in *The Football Players' Magazine* under the headline, 'Do Players Need More Ball Practice?' Charlie Roberts, ex-Manchester United and England centre-half, wrote: 'At present the players stand about six yards away from the goalkeeper and shoot, which any navvy could do. There is no running about or dribbling, feinting, passing with the inside or outside of the foot, trapping or heading the ball, placing it with the head like you do with your feet, judging distances, etc., indulged in at all. Players, in my opinion, should try and do the things with the ball they have to do on a Saturday...'

Peter O'Rourke, manager of Bradford City, agreed: 'I am certain that the day will come when ball practice during the week will form a fundamental part of the training of the professional footballer. When that day does dawn there will be far less hustle and more cleverness and combination.'

An un-named trainer interviewed for the magazine disagreed, however: 'There has been a lot of talk about this ball practice, but in the end people have had the sense to see that a trainer knows his own business best. Take my word for it, we know what's what without any interference from the public. For my own part, I am about tired of this talk from people who have never done a day's training in their lives. I know what to do with my lads without being told to do first this and then the other. What are we trainers for? To take orders from every Dick, Tom and Harry?'

The inter-war period would see little change in the training routines of professional players. They would continue 'lapping' and skipping while shunning ball-work almost entirely although isolated outposts of enlightenment were occasionally to be found. In 1933, in an article in *Topical Times* on trainers and their methods, Charlie Bates at Burnley was lauded for his 'scientific' attitude to the game.

Bates, 'built devices for everything. He has a shooting board at Turf Moor. It is the size of the ordinary goals. Three players can use it at a time. There are boards attached to it. They are at various angles. The ball rebounds from all angles. The players are supposed to catch it on the bounce. Teaches them to use either foot. And to be ready for anything.' Bates appeared to be a good teacher, grasping the simple truth that players needed to enjoy what they were doing: 'Bates spends hours working out ways of doing what seems obvious. Corners, kick-offs, throws-in. He tries stunts for doing these in a manner not stereotyped. If the players can work the idea, all well and good. If not, he drops it and tries again. The youngest boy whose heart is in football has a friend in Charlie Bates…'

The game, however, continued to be played at a faster and faster pace, obviating the need for players to train as runners first and foremost. As Brian Glanville concluded in his book, *Soccer Nemesis*, the relative decline of English football in terms of skill and technique came about because:

'British managers and trainers have for years broken hearts, built up the resistance and pared away the initiative of their players, by setting them monotonously to lap the track, since this is the safest means of preparation. A team trained in this unimaginative manner will be at least a team with stamina, capable of pursuit and endurance.'

In fact, the formal, systematic coaching of young players began outside the professional game. In 1928, FNS Creek, an amateur, ex-Corinthians player and schoolmaster was asked by one of Her Majesty's Inspectors of Physical Training to devise a soccer skills course for schoolmasters under the auspices of the Board of Education. 'To the best of my knowledge, no one had even analysed our game before, and for the life of me I could not imagine how I could fill in the time allotted to soccer – two lectures each morning for three days, with practical work in the afternoons.'

Creek devised a course that included the teaching of various 'abilities': how to run fast, quickness off the mark, how to swerve, dodge and feint, how to kick the ball with either foot, to head it, to trap it and then dribble with it and, finally, the ability to combine into a team with his ten colleagues.

His work impressed the then master in charge of Physical Training at Watford Grammar School, Stanley Rous. Six years later, Rous was appointed Secretary of the Football Association, and he encouraged Creek to continue with his courses. He led the first soccer 'Summer School' at Loughborough in 1934, 'teaching coaching to dozens of schoolmasters. With a few new ideas each year, I went there every August, and the gospel began to spread.' He was joined in his endeavours by one or two ex-professionals. Len Graham, who had had a distinguished amateur career before signing forms with Millwall in 1923, recalled: 'In 1934, the FA scheme for coaching in the schools began. Along with "Bert" White (an ex-Arsenal player), I was chosen to impart what football knowledge I had. I did this to the best of my ability for two seasons, but was then reluctantly forced to resign as the scheme was not then on a sound financial basis.'

In fact, the involvement of professional players in the coaching revolution would prove to be one of the major problems for Stanley Rous and the Football Association. When Walter Winterbottom began offering official FA coaching badges to those who could complete a specific three-day course at Lilleshall, the FA's training centre, the reaction from among the professionals was mixed. There were serious doubts expressed on two counts: first, whether you should even try and teach a young player how to play, and second, whether anyone, other than a talented professional, was worth listening to in the first place.

Len Shackleton was a sceptic. In 1956 he wrote: 'I sometimes wonder if we are putting too much emphasis on coaching – a dangerous practice when, as sometimes happens, it changes natural style, curbs individual ability or tends to make the pupil think through the mind of his coach rather than go ahead with his own ideas.'

Almost twenty years later, Derek Dougan, ex-Wolverhampton Wanderers player, wrote: 'I have an ingrained suspicion about coaching. It isn't the be-all and end-all of the game. In the final analysis, it is only for those who need it – and a natural player doesn't need much of it. I have never had a coaching lesson and I have known many players who, like me, liken it to painting by numbers.'

It was almost as if the professional footballer feared that his secret world, established in opposition to the demands of formal education, was suddenly being colonised by middle-class teachers who would turn it into something 'boring', something for which one might even have to 'qualify'. Most professional players had escaped education as fast as they could; most would try and avoid the educational obligations placed on them by apprenticeship schemes and Youth Training Schemes.

Winterbottom understood the antipathy professional players might feel towards an 'academic' approach to the teaching of the game's skills and he was reliant, to some extent, on persuading respected professionals like Joe Mercer to turn up at the Lilleshall sessions and convert the sceptics. But the endemic suspicion of those who hadn't actually 'done it' on the pitch was hard to shift. As Shackleton claimed, 'the FA system allows many great players to be rejected as unacceptable, while poor players are given Lancaster Gate blessing to pass on their doubtful knowledge.'

Quite simply, the unofficial 'degree' in football is tangible success. If you have won a cup, or earned an international cap, you have qualified as a 'master'. Even a long career at the top will do. Once that has been achieved, other professionals will listen to you. Otherwise, you face a crippling credibility gap.

Lee Chapman outlined the problems this attitude created for managers like Lennie Lawrence: 'Lennie was an obvious enthusiast who had to endure many snipes behind his back because of his lack of League experience. This is often the stock criticism made by players about coaches or managers who have not had a substantial League playing career.'

2. Teaching the teachers

'When I used to finish training with the youth team, I would go over and watch the first team for an hour. I was in digs at the time so I never ever had anything to rush home for. So I would watch Marcel Desailly and Frank Leboeuf, and then go and try the things they were doing.

That improved my game. The first couple of times I trained with the first team, I asked Marcel Desailly and Frank Leboeuf loads of questions. They were looking at me and thinking, "Little kid, give it a rest". But it paid off. They would spend ten minutes with me, advising me on how to position myself when the attacker came in. They told me to always stay on my feet as long as possible, to always watch the ball rather than the attacker's legs. To learn off two World Cup winners is brilliant.'

John Terry, Chelsea, 2001

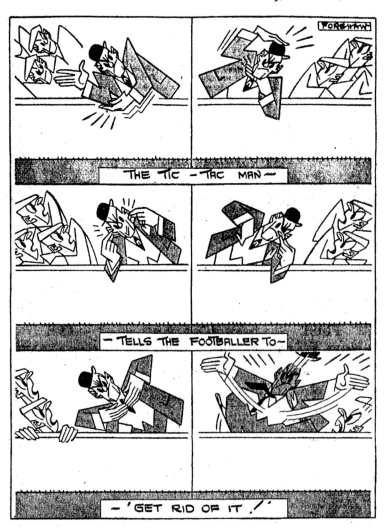

The Manchester Football News, 31 October 1931.

In many ways, the argument between the sceptical professionals and the 'amateurs' at the FA was a false one. Winterbottom's principal concern in those early days was not so much what one taught but how one taught: how a coach stood up in front of a group of players and demonstrated something so that they understood it and were able to put it into practice. He cited Alex James in this respect: 'A talkative chap, but get him in front and try to organise anything and he couldn't do it. And, as for demonstrating and talking at the same time, and then getting other people to do it – that sort of thing – those skills were without him.'

It was an aspect of the task that Malcolm Allison was intrigued by: 'Some people talk about communication as though it is a very simple thing, a matter perhaps only of clear language, and they are the worst communicators because they take too much for granted. In fact communicating is the most difficult thing in the world – certainly in football. You can tell somebody something, he can nod his head, and you can assume, quite wrongly, that the message has been absorbed. But it is not like a schoolmaster writing something down on the blackboard and his student copying it.

'You have to get inside both the mind and the instincts of a footballer. You have to hammer information into his subconscious, set up instinctive patterns of thought and reaction. And you have to keep on doing it until the thought process is removed. You have to get things so that they flow naturally out of a player. And technique and skills are only one aspect. The central challenge is to motivate the languid, the over-confident, and the insecure. It has always been for me the most fascinating work.

'At Charlton I had done a little basic coaching with younger players like Eddie Firmani and Stuart Leary, simple techniques in kicking and heading the ball. It was all very basic, pathetic really when you consider that this was supposed to be a professional business and that there were people about who were being paid to do a job that they had never understood.'

Allison realised that he needed help to progress: 'There were great gaps in my knowledge. And certainly when I first arrived at Lilleshall and met Walter Winterbottom I felt I was coming face to face with the messiah. Here was the man who would teach me how to teach,' and although he struggled at first, 'it was enough to be in an atmosphere where people were talking intelligently about the game, where new ideas were being tried, and the old, tired training chores were being tossed contemptuously on one side. And the great breakthrough came when I was allowed to take a class of my own.'

Lee Chapman, a player under Allison some years later, attested to his skills: 'Far from being the extrovert character I had read about in the newspapers, I found him (Allison) to be an introverted, almost shy person. His fedora hat was never seen, and only the occasional Havana cigar was ever smoked. Malcolm's training sessions were always enjoyable and never repetitive. He was constantly innovative and always searching for something new.'

That coaching was a skill in its own right, one that could be learned like any other, would take professionals in Britain many years to accept, despite the occasional emergence of such charismatic characters as Allison. The teaching of young professionals at clubs up and down the country would continue in haphazard fashion, with little system and continuity between clubs. There were, however, a few natural teachers and, though nothing was written down, coaching skills and techniques of a highly sophisticated kind were being implemented in the post-war years.

Manchester United's manager, Matt Busby, produced some of the finest young professional sides and players since the Second World War. It's been said that Busby was not a coach in the formal or technical sense of the word, but rather a preacher of a simple gospel. Football was a simple game, made complex or difficult by bad players and poor coaches. While he believed that good coaching was important, he felt, 'The great danger of coaching is that it might take the fun out of football'.

In fact, Busby was in agreement with those who felt the club shouldn't have to teach a player how to play. If the scouts had done their jobs properly, the players involved would have the basic ability when they arrived and would not need a great deal of technical coaching. All that was required was for 'schoolboy bad habits' to be broken. And while keen to encourage self-expression and attractive play, he was conscious of the fact that beautiful, flowing football would not of itself produce results. To be successful in professional football management, a balance had to be found between artistry and other qualities such as fitness, determination and courage.

Bill Foulkes, a long-time Manchester United player, offers the following insight into the coaching at the club in 1950 when he first arrived as an amateur player. 'As soon as I came here it was all ball work, we just played with a ball, worked with a ball all the time. With Assistant Manager Jimmy Murphy and his assistant Bert Whalley it was passing practices, movement, shadow play, which was really imagination. We didn't do anything in theory at all, we just enjoyed it. Jimmy and Bert would be giving instructions, giving advice. Not planned, not particularly planned, just using the ball, playing the ball. And then, after a while, we'd do certain technique practices for heading, control, passing – particularly passing. Jim was a stickler for passing. Accuracy of passing, weight of passing, he was always stating this, you know. But then, after that, it would be a short-sided game, and then we'd have a full-scale pitch match. And that was basically what we did for the two training days, Tuesday and Thursday.'

Wilf McGuinness, who joined the club three years after Foulkes in 1953, describes similar training sessions: 'The idea that you just went out and played and did what you wanted – that didn't happen. Bobby Charlton was coached, I was coached, Duncan Edwards, who was the greatest, was coached. You were taught the areas to play and how to play, but it was coached in an understanding way. We did shadow play, playing against nobody, sometimes playing without a ball.

'Jimmy would be down there, during the game, before the game, telling us something of what he wanted individually and collectively as a group. Then, once the game started, he would stop the game and point out certain things and stand on the side. He didn't stop it all the time, you know, he let it flow. But if there was something very important he would emphasise [it]. So that's how the form of the coaching went.'

The shadow play mentioned by McGuinness is a complex coaching technique designed to help a player acquire a higher level of team work and game understanding. It involves practising soccer movements with the ball but with restricted or even no opposition. Thus, players are required to use their imagination in order to rehearse specific movement patterns in the game. The use of shadow play by Jimmy Murphy and Bert Whalley should dispel the myth that Manchester United's young players did everything by instinct or intuition, while Henry

Frank Powell,
Clapham Orient's
trainer, repairing
boots and footballs,
Sports Pictures,
August 1924.

Cockburn, another former international-class player recalled: 'Matt always used to say, "Keep the ball flowing". When I finished playing and went on coaching courses, they had invented one-touch and two-touch games as part of the coaching system, and it was only then I realised that Matt had had us playing like that unknowingly.'

Busby had a vision of football that guided the way he and his assistants coached his players. He once said, 'There are two aspects of the game that have always impressed me, I love its drama, its smooth playing skill. On the great football occasions, I feel a sense of romance, wonder, and mystery, a sense of poetry.' The problem for young British players in the second half of the century was that too few managers saw the game as 'poetry'. The relentless drive for results and success has seen systems of play developed that have severely curtailed the acquisition of ball-playing skills. The British game has preferred to produce artisans rather than artists.

3. Route One

'This slam, bang, wallop stuff will be the death of foot-ball. Football in which players are controlled by off-pitch Svengalis, backed up by batteries of statisticians and ana-lysts will never hold the magical appeal of what Pele called "the beautiful game".'

Allan Wade, Ex-FA Head of Coaching, speaking in 1989

The effect that team tactics and the coaching that accompanies them can have on the development of young players' individual skills was demonstrated in the 1980s with the development of what has become known as 'Route One' football, in which attack-ing play was dominated by counter-attacks, passing the ball to the space beyond the opponent's last line of defence. It was highly successful and popular because it brought results and, while Terry Venables felt that to dismiss the style as 'kick-and-rush' was too harsh, he went on, 'The Route One approach has not done our game any good and it was not the right way to go. It is not a ques-tion of believing in short passing as opposed to long passing, it is a question of combining the best of both.'

It was a style that seemed to run counter to the lessons that had been learned in the 1950s, when English footballers at the very top had been exposed for their lack of technical skills and tactical nous. The Hungarian defeat of England at Wembley in 1953 had highlighted the need for coaching that emphasised keeping possession, and building attacks via a succession of accurate passes. Allan Wade, Walter Winterbottom's successor as the FA's Head Coach, had produced an influential book called The Principle of Play, in which 'possession' was seen as the all-encompassing attacking principle. Young players were to be encouraged to control the ball, to feel comfortable with it and to be able to pass it accurately to a team-mate.

During the 1970s, players like Alan Hudson of Stoke City were trying to play the game in such a fashion. Hudson was of the opin-ion that all football 'starts from the back', and that 'the high ball down the middle for me is not the game. It's alright for the lower teams and the teams that get relegated would do that. We want the players at the back not to panic and use every ball. The more they use the ball, then the more chances we've got. If they belt it up the middle and we have to challenge in midfield for it, then we've just a 50-50 chance of getting it.'

But there would always be an impatience in the English game with such a careful, intelligent approach, particularly if it didn't reap immediate results. With the crowd baying, 'Get rid of it!' the temptation was to lower the head and whack the ball forward. As Hudson observed, 'The average supporter doesn't know anything about football. The majority don't know what they're looking at. I would say the majority of pressmen don't know what they're looking at. If people don't see you rushing around about 100 miles an hour and tackling everyone and kicking everyone they think you're not trying.'

But for those who favoured the more robust, less complicated, 'English' style, dismissed by Hudson, the theories of Wing Commander Reep, a mathematician and a keen fan of Herbert Chapman's Arsenal sides of the 1930s, were music to their ears. Reep argued that, while the aim of attacking is certainly to score goals, possession is also one of the aims of defensive play. The defence was not there simply to prevent the opposition from scoring but also to win back possession. Thus, instead of possession being perceived as the overall purpose of attack, Reep felt that penetration should be regarded as the main attacking principle. What's more, in his analysis, the position of the ball came to be more important than who was in possession.

Reep's mathematical theories had highlighted the role of chance in football. As he put it, 'Anything can happen at any time in any match' and while admitting that, 'the factors of skill and merit are (of course) enormously important in affecting the result,' Reep insisted that, 'goals come at random just the same.'

Reep persuaded Stan Cullis, manager of Wolverhampton Wanderers in the 1950s, that this direct approach to the game, of getting the ball into the opponent's half as quickly as possible so as to maximise the number of scoring opportunities, was the one most liable to reap results, and he was right. Cullis' Wolves carried all before them for a period, winning League titles and FA Cups, though not succeeding in Europe where a more sophisticated approach was necessary.

Reep went on to advise many other League clubs in the 1960s and 1970s, but it wasn't until Charles Hughes took over as Head of Coaching at the FA that the major problems began. In 1990, Hughes 'borrowed' many of Reep's theories, and re-presented them in a book entitled *The Winning Formula*, thus establishing himself as the father of 'match performance analysis'. The Football Association were to play a key role in spreading the gospel of 'Route One' football, an idea that would have saddened Walter Winterbottom.

Many within the coaching fraternity were appalled by the Hughes 'doctrine'. In 1994, Terry Venables wrote: 'We have many good qualities in our game, but our technical abilities have grown worse, if for no other reason than the mere fact that the long ball cut out a lot of work in the middle. It became just a matter of "Let's

'Soccer', February 1948.

get it up there as quick as we can, and catch them out," but when we played against the best teams, it did not work.'

He also felt that the co-operation between the Football Association and those in the professional game, so carefully nurtured by Winterbottom, Stanley Rous and their successors, had been undermined: 'An FA man called Allan Wade used to do a particularly good job in bridging the gap between the two sides, [but] something went wrong, somewhere, after that, however. Charlie Hughes, the new FA director of coaching, tried to get on with the pros, and show them what was wrong, but came up against a bit of a wall with the players. He felt he was right about many things, but instead of pursuing it, and convincing the doubters, he decided to walk away from the confrontation, and the split grew wider.'

John Cartwright, ex-technical director at the old National Football School at Lilleshall, disagreed so violently with Hughes that he resigned after two years in the job. Today, Cartwright blames Hughes for the continued failure of the FA's coaching system to produce English players who, in his opinion, are as skilful as young Frenchmen such as Thierry Henry, Patrick Viera and Nicolas Anelka.

'Some of the academy system – the facilities and the criteria, for example – is right. But the Achilles heel of academy football is coach education. The coaches running the academies have come through the Charlie Hughes era and they really are grey in many ways. Winning football matches is at the bottom of everything, and I feel we aren't producing a different type of player as a result.'

Cartwright's credo is that the development of individual skill should be a compulsory starting point in the coaching of young players. 'For me, football at the beginning of the coaching structure has to be about the individual, about making that player comfortable in possession of the ball. You encourage him or her to be clever on the ball, to stay on it, not give it away, and then make sure there is an end product. I seem to be the only person worried about the skill deficiency that we have.'

The Hughes controversy and the obvious damage it caused in the development of young English players had one beneficial fall-out: the professionals, once the sceptics, have now become the apostles of enlightened thinking where the art of coaching is concerned. In the mid-1990s, the Professional Footballers' Association produced a report on coaching in England called 'A Kick In The Right

Direction'. Comments from within the profession on what coaches were producing were universally negative; there was little creativity and interchange of positions in the English game and a need to improve players' ability to pass and run with the ball diagonally. There was a lack of creative midfield passers and forwards who were capable of dribbling past defenders and unlocking organised defences. Coaching in general 'lacked charisma' and there was now an awareness among professionals that if the quality of the teacher was limited then the content of what was being taught would be equally limited.

As England struggled to make headway in the opening stages of the 2002 World Cup, commentators noticed how the England manager, a Swede who had found success in Europe during the years when the Long Ball theory was all the rage, was suddenly emphasising the need for the England team to 'play the ball forward quickly, with not too many passes in defence'. Paul Hayward, writing in the *Daily Telegraph*, felt that, though Eriksson was right to spot that surrendering possession was still an English disease, he was wrong to assume that he could get round it by reverting to the long ball, a 'retrograde' approach.

But Eriksson was a realist. The English game has been producing a certain type of player for years. His direct tactics were a reflection of those careless English traits. As the PFA report concluded: 'Unless we establish player development programmes and high-level training for our coaches, we run the risk of drifting into fatal stagnation, which will result in mediocrity in comparison with progressively thinking countries.'

STEPPING OUT
with
JACK SMITH
SHEFFIELD UNITED GOALKEEPER

At shooting practice.

Polishing up the car.

Making the cinders fly.

Attention from Trainer Livingstone.

A word with Fred Ashton (left).

Corinthian bagatelle with his fiancee, Miss Nan Williamson.

Chapter 5

Football and the Body

1. Treatment for injury

'The athlete is already a being who has hypertrophized one organ, who turns his body into the seat and exclusive source of a continuous play. The athlete is a monster, he is the Man Who Laughs, the geisha with the compressed and atrophied foot, dedicated to total instrumentalisation.'

Umberto Eco, Reports From The Global Village, 1969

The professional soccer player has one major resource, his body. It is a finite resource, subject to sudden breakdown and inevitable decline. In a sense, a player goes through a complete life-cycle before he reaches early adulthood. By 35 years of age or so, his body will no longer carry him through a season. At this point his athletic 'death' and the eclipse of his professional identity can be traumatic. Some players suffer such a 'death' well before their mid-thirties. Thus, for a professional footballer, getting injured can be more than just an occupational hazard. Such injuries also confronted the fledgling professional game with major economic and physical problems.

When professional league football began in the 1880s, the frequency of injuries to players necessitated a rapid expansion in the number of men retained. Wealthier clubs employed as many as twenty-five players by the turn of the century. When the Football League expanded to a two-division, forty-team format in 1905, member clubs were employing well over a thousand footballers.

The increase in the number of opportunities available was more than offset by the risk of injury, which shortened many a playing career. During the 1913–14 season, *Cricket and Football Field* computed the starting line-ups for teams in both football league divisions, for the Southern League, and for the Scottish League. By New Year's Eve, 1914, only 169 of the 1,701 players had survived the risk of accident or illness and were able to start each match. By mid-April the number had fallen to 61.

By as early as the late 1880s, the exceptionally high rate of player injuries led insurance companies, such as the Boiler Insurance and Steam Power Company Ltd of Manchester, to issue policies for injuries and surgeons who were keen to treat players advertised their services. Writing in *The Weekly News* on Saturday 9 March 1901, the 'Secretary' wrote: 'For a premium of £10 some clubs secure for their players a certain weekly sum in case of accidents. The companies provide the most stringent rules and regulations as to how an injured player might "lay up" and in most cases had a tabulated form of injuries which occasionally makes very gruesome reading.

'Injuries to wrists, ribs, thighs, etc. are detailed and allowed for accordingly. Twenty-one days is the limit allowed for the healing of a broken nose. Then for "total loss by complete separation of one or more fingers" a football insurance company will allow for compensation for thirty-five days while sick pay for perhaps ninety days is granted to a footballer who suffers "total and irrevocable loss of one or both eyes". £50 if killed on the field or as a result of accidents thereon is a fair average allowance.'

Football was hardly a lethal occupation, however, although the occasional death cast a long shadow. Di Jones of Manchester City died of blood poisoning contracted through a cut on his knee sustained during a pre-season friendly match in 1902. The club

resisted claims of liability and sought to blame Jones's insistence on walking from the field to the ambulance as having 'caused more trouble than anything else'.

However, at the inquest, the jury, 'wanted to impress upon football clubs that they should not allow a man to walk off the field in a case like that'. The Coroner, however, demurred, stating: 'Are football clubs to supply a medical staff on their field? I don't think there is any obligation on them to do that...' In fact, there would be no obligation for many years to come.

Operations before the First World War on knee ligaments and cartilages were not very efficient. Billy Meredith opined: 'There is no

---

MATLOCK HOUSE,

HYDE ROAD, MANCHESTER,

IS NOW

UNIVERSALLY RECOGNISED

AS THE

FOOTBALLERS' HOSPITAL

THE Proprietor has for 24 years made a special study of injuries to the Knee-Joints and Limbs to which Football Players are especially liable, and the most obstinate and apparently hopeless cases have yielded to his combined system of Massage, Swedish Exercises, Vibration, and Radiant Heat Baths.

During the past season more than 90 per cent. of the Players who have been injured in LEAGUE MATCHES and ENGLISH CUP-TIES have been successfully treated at the FOOTBALLERS' HOSPITAL.

For particulars apply to

THE PROPRIETOR,

MATLOCK HOUSE,

c. 1900.

getting away from the fact that very few men are ever the same again after they have had knee trouble and the inevitable operation. Any player who has a knee trouble I also strongly advise to go to the best surgeon in town.'

There is also more to a fracture than just the breaking of a bone. For a professional footballer there is often a formidable mental struggle to overcome. There are long weeks of idleness, seeing his team-mates going out to train and play while he has to carry out irksome and monotonous remedial exercises. There is the lurking fear that he might not recover in full. When one's body is one's living, the strain can be intense. From the earliest days of professionalism, particularly where valuable players were concerned, these fears could be dealt with at Matlock House, in Manchester, the first centre for the treatment of soccer injuries in the game's history.

John Allison, a local businessman and Director of Manchester City FC, had studied massage in the late 1870s, travelling to America and Sweden in search of new ideas. When called upon to treat a Bolton millionaire and MP, the latter was so impressed that, on his death, he left Allison enough money to establish a centre where he could extend his system of massage.

Matlock House was initially intended as a hydro for ordinary patients, and in the early years his clients were mainly hunting men who'd had accidents while riding. JJ Bentley, a famous football journalist and manager, noticed Allison's work and soon a stream of footballers were being referred there.

A visiting journalist in 1898 noted some of the greats of the game who'd spent time there recovering from various strains and muscle tears. These included Jimmy Crabtree, John Devey, Howard Spencer and Willie Foulke, among many others. Crabtree, it was revealed, spent almost a month at Matlock prior to the 1897 Cup Final between Aston Villa and Everton. Allison was treating him right up to the kick-off and was even in the dressing room at half time to treat his damaged knee.

Matlock House was used mainly for rehabilitation. The aforementioned journalist outlined the routine for a footballer with a damaged knee: 'On his arrival at the footballer's hospital he will be carefully examined by Mr Allison or one of the attendants. If the injury is of a nature requiring surgical treatment, he will immediately be put in the hands of the visiting surgeon. If no surgical aid is required, Mr Allison will at once proceed to mete out his own special treatment.

'The first step in this treatment is to fit a machine to the patient's leg which will keep the knee in constant movement. This machine of Mr Allison's, by the way, is rather a wily contrivance: it serves the double purpose of helping to heal the knee and effectively curbing the wearer's propensity to roam. Footballers aren't fond of captivity and most of them after being a day or two in the hospital show a strong inclination to get outside and explore the beauties of Manchester, especially as Mr Allison regulates his household on strictly teetotal principles.

'When he is freed from the trammels of this machine the damaged footballer is next subjected to a course of what is called radiant heat treatment. It isn't easy to describe on paper all the details of this treatment but, to put it briefly, a tremendous heat is applied by means of electricity, and localised upon the injured part of the limb'.

'Radiant Heat' had been invented in the 1880s by an electrical engineer called HR Dowsing and was considered the most up-to-date form of treatment available at the time for hastening recovery. Dowsing incidentally had a football connection in that he was good friends with the wife of a Southampton director, R Sarjantson, whose wife was one of the few people in the country trained to use such equipment.

Matlock House continued in business for over thirty years. In 1911 a *Weekly News* journalist took a trip to see for himself. Inside the clinic he found 'a variety of apparatus at Matlock House to assist in the curative treatment, including a specially constructed stationary bicycle, a rowing machine, shoulder developer, and spinal exerciser, not to mention the electrical vibrators and electrical heating bath. When there is any doubt as to the location of an injury, or displaced bone, the X-rays are brought into operation. Indeed Matlock House presents a little history book of the national pastime and has certainly extended the careers of many famous players who might otherwise have been lost to the game.'

Matlock House closed down after the First World War and wasn't replaced. Football league clubs went their own ways and for the pro player at the top or the bottom of the game, treatment of injury could differ dramatically according to who employed him. Gradually clubs acquired machinery to treat injury, though it was often a haphazard process and the men employed to operate the machinery were invariably untrained.

In 1938, 'Peeping Tom', a journalist on *Sports Budget*, took a trip around the football clubs to investigate the dramatic increase in electrical gadgets used to hasten players back into fitness. 'Tom' claimed that such machinery was now installed 'in nearly every first-class ground I have visited,' and the article drew on visits to West Ham, Bolton, Leeds and Bradford.

At West Ham he received some treatment for himself on an electric massage machine: 'My leg was bared and two small steel pads were strapped on, one above the ankle, the other just above the knee. Each of these pads was connected with a wire which passed into a large apparatus standing against the wall and resembling a radiogram. As I was strapped up, I asked how many stations they could get on it. "You'll soon see," assistant trainer Billy Moore replied laughingly. All was now ready. The current was switched on and I felt a slight tingling in my leg as a buzzing sound came from the "radio-set" behind me. The tingling increased. Then I was handed a small switchboard and told to control the current myself…'

Charlie Paynter, West Ham's trainer-manager, claimed that such a machine replaced the old hand massage method. It cost £1,000 but repaid the cost in speed of recovery. 'Serious injury a few years ago meant a long lay-off from active service, followed by weary weeks of hand massage.'

At Bolton Wanderers, Bob Young the trainer showed 'Tom' a 'gleaming chromium radiant heat lamp'. 'In the old days it took a trainer the best part of a week to massage every one of his players. Now, with the help of this apparatus, the job takes only a few hours.'

The descendants of Dowsing's Radiant heat lamps were in use at Charlton Athletic, too, where Jimmy Trotter demonstrated how a deep bruise could be dealt with in a couple of hours. At Leeds United, Arthur Campey, who claimed to be the first qualified expert to apply such treatment to football players, showed off a treatment room he'd installed himself, while at Brentford, trainer Bob Kane, a white-haired, ex-naval man, gave 'Peeping Tom' a sun-ray session.

'Tom' left Brentford with, 'a face like a boiled lobster and my skin was all aglow. I wasn't used to it, you see, but according to Bob Kane, ten minutes a week of sunray treatment is almost as good as a week at the seaside.'

But Peeping Tom's optimistic belief that technology and expert skill were revolutionising player treatment was misplaced. After the war, the equipment he'd seen at various grounds was ever more expensive to install and many clubs took decades to refurbish and replace equipment which had fallen into disrepair or been taken for military use. It took a number of football touring parties across the Atlantic to North and South America in the late 1940s for English footballers to discover just how far behind the 'home' of football had fallen. Don Featherstone, Southampton FC's physiotherapist, whose team toured Brazil in 1947, explained: 'Their treatment rooms and staff are able to X-ray a fracture, put the injured man under an anaesthetic and put his limb in plaster, thus enabling the man to return home with his team, having suffered no delay by being detained in the local hospital. Some clubs even possess a dietician to supervise the player's food, one particular club reporting that they had not had a single case of "tummy" trouble during the season, whereas prior to the engagement of the dietician they had had thirty-eight cases in a single season."'

There was thus dawning a gradual awareness that medical welfare meant more than the use of electronic gadgets. Treating injury should also coincide with prevention, which was probably even more important. Suspicions, however, as to why players injured themselves so frequently had been raised many years before.

In 1911 Billy Meredith, writing in Thomson's Weekly News, said: 'Every day I am more and more convinced that the clubs have fallen into a great error in the system of training and to a certain extent I blame this for all the knee injuries we hear of in the present day.'

His analysis of the problems regarding injuries was simple: 'Now, what is the great idea of the modern day trainer? It is to get another half-yard out of the men, to make them all sprinters. The result is that constant sprinting exercises develop certain muscles and ligaments to a fine degree and, in my opinion, to a degree that makes them give way easily when the leg is twisted and turned suddenly. The footballer's muscles and limbs require to be trained for the particular work they have to do.'

Unfortunately, it was a lesson only slowly learned. In 1954 Don Featherstone, revealing that twenty per cent of Southampton's injuries were to the knee joints, wrote: 'I am firmly convinced that the frequency of torn cartilages in English football is solely due to incorrect methods of training, in that the type of training carried out has little or no relationship to the stresses, strains and general movements of football.'

2. Trainers: the men with the magic sponges

'Fred Tilson, the reserve team trainer...sat all day in his little room picking horses and sleeping. Fred was a legend at Manchester City. He had scored two goals in the 1934 Cup Final and that seemed to ensure him a job for life. I received one single piece of advice from Fred in all my time at the club. "You should have your bleedin' tonsils out," he informed me in his thick Barnsley accent, as I complained one day of a sore throat.'

Fred Eyre, Kicked Into Touch, 1981

The job of trainer to most pro football teams in the early part of the century usually went to ex-professional runners or boxers. Such men simply implemented regimes that they knew best. 'Secretary', in the *Weekly News* of 1901, outlined a typical routine: 'To get a player into condition, he is generally put through a course of running exercises, half a mile or so to begin with. Then this is increased as the player progresses. To this is added fifty or sixty yards of sprinting in spiked shoes... After this there is a moderate amount of dumbbell work and Indian club-swinging (the clubs generally being about two pounds weight each) winding up with a few rounds with the gloves at times. Boxing is a most useful exercise in training players. It is excellent as a developer of urbanity of temper and so on...After the gloves we follow with a few exercises on the rings, ropes and bars in the gymnasium (I refer to where such are found – and one is desirable in every club), the whole ending with cold sprays, hot baths and a rub-down – not a heavy scrub, but a gentle rub.'

Many of the early professionals were sceptical about training. W Freeman, giving readers practical hints in the same paper in 1909 on 'How To Become A Star Footballer', felt that football, 'does not consist in training. A good man can be thrown away in the process of training just as a mediocre man can be made. I am not an exponent of vigorous training, believing as I do that it is far better to be under-trained than over-trained. What I favour are light exercises and fresh air.'

Billy Bassett, writing in *The Book of Football* in 1906, was of the opinion that having a job outside football was the best way of keeping fit. He felt walking was the best way to get men in trim; it provided fresh air and enough exercise although, 'there was a time when walking was overdone. There was an individual connected with Wolverhampton Wanderers in the old days who used to walk the men off their feet. He would take them 10–12 miles at a fast pace, day after day...' As a consequence, their muscles hardened and they became prone to injury.

In 1905, at Woolwich Arsenal's training quarters, Indian clubs and dumbbells were much in evidence, as was a skipping platform. The resident trainer, Bob Dunmore, was, like Bassett, a great believer in walks, though rarely in the morning. A *Fry's Magazine* journalist explained, 'It will interest advocates of the "early to rise" dictum that one of the tenets of Dunmore's creed is that a man is never himself in the morning. Men, he says, do not get into form until about twelve and as for playing a football match in the morning, if such a thing were ever dreamt of outside India, it would be an absolute impossibility! On walk mornings Dunmore assembles his men for a start at 10.30 or 11.00 and they return about 12.00 or 12.30, the pace being, as it is with an army on the march, that of the slowest.'

Tottenham Hotspur's trainer Sam Mountford worked on similar lines. Mountford was a 50-year-old ex-professional Powderhall sprinter who became a trainer in the 1890s, working at Walsall, Bristol City and then Tottenham. Mountford's routine included a half an hour's sprinting, followed by ball practice with turns at skipping, followed by a bath and maybe a stroll. In strict training, however, (usually followed when the team was playing away), 'the men are up at eight sharp and they go for a walk before breakfast. After breakfast, it's sprinting followed by a conducted walk of three to four miles, followed by tea, then another walk.'

As the years passed, the ex-boxers and sprinters were replaced by ex-professional players. There was, however, little academic theory to refer to and the knowledge-base hardly deepened at all. Men simply repeated the fads and foibles they had gleaned from the ancient elders. Dave Willis was trainer to Raith Rovers, Nottingham Forest and Derby County after a playing career that began with Sunderland in 1899, followed by Newcastle United, and ending with Jarrow Town after the First World War. The father-in-law of Alex James, his career spanned well over sixty years. In the 1930s he outlined his methods, which he claimed to have learned under such great trainers as JQ McPherson of Newcastle United and B Williams of Sunderland, two men whose careers started in the 1870s!

His methods have a familiar ring to them: 'Walking will keep anybody fit — for anything. I also like my players to do a little "lapping" on the ground, but there's nothing I'm more opposed to than trying out players as "marathon" runners and having them lapping for more than a few minutes. Sprinting and skipping are the more violent forms of training that I prescribe, the sort of training to bring men "down to fighting weight".'

He differed, he claimed, in one crucial respect from many other trainers: 'I only allow ball practice on one day of the week. Some people advocate ball practice as often as possible but I claim that this exercise hardens men's legs and in some cases gets them "fed up with

The first professionals?

FA Cup winners with Blackburn Rovers in 1884, four years before professionalism was legalised. (*Above left*: Fergus Suter; *above right*: Hugh McIntyre).

Arthur Turner, the subject of Madame Tussauds' first soccer waxwork (*below left*).

Jimmy Crabtree – not the first, nor the last top player to succumb to alcohol (*below right*).

N.L. Jackson, the famous English amateur international who opposed the payment of players.

John Goodall (*above*): English International and Preston North End legend who defended the paid player.

A pre-First World War hopeful (*left*).

Sunderland's Raich Carter as a young boy (*right*).

Hope springs eternal in a young man's breast

Len Shackleton, the future 'Clown Prince' of football, tending to Arsenal's pitch in August 1938 (*above left*).

The big time: The England Youth Team in 1963 (*above*): back row: Willie Evans, Sammels, Cowan, Chatterley, Harris, Whittaker, Smith, French, Sissons; front row: Jones, Badger, Shaw.

Future Manchester City and Brighton forward Mike Robinson with doting parents (*above*).

1978: Coventry scout Alf Walton congratulates young discovery Danny Thomas (*right*).

Football's men and motors

Billy Walker, soon after signing for Aston Villa in 1920, with his brand new car.

Notts County players hitching a ride in 1925.

Liverpool's Steve Heighway shows off his Volkswagen Beetle in 1971 (*top*).

Rio Ferdinand arrives at Leeds United in style (*above*).

Treating injury: The first sixty years

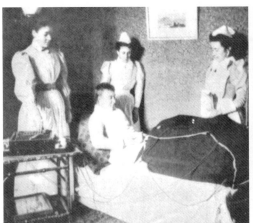

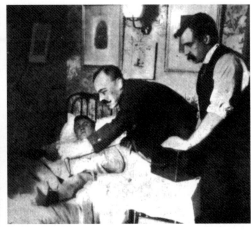

Inside John Allison's Footballer's Hospital in 1895 (*both above*).

West Bromwich Albion's club doctor examines a damaged knee with the trainer looking on (*left*, 1906).

Aston Villa's medical room in the 1950s (*below*).

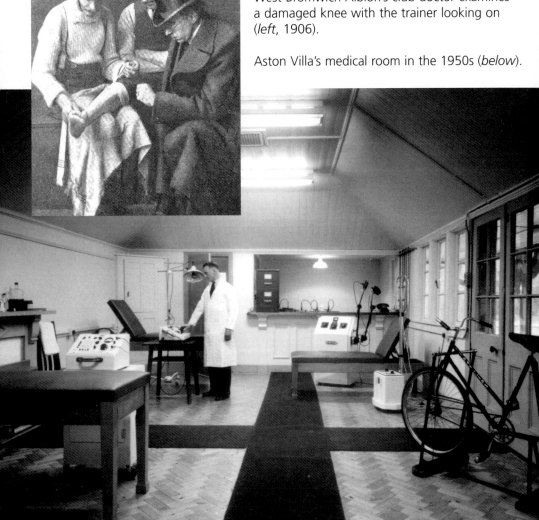

Post-war coaching

Stan Matthews, George Hardwick and Stan Mortenson perform for an instructional film at Hendon FC in the early 50s.

Alex James shows Arsenal's youngsters how it's done at Highbury (1949).

Boots and glory

Danny Blanchflower, Aston Villa and Northern Ireland, modifies the studs on his boots (1953).

Building that elusive 'team spirit'

Manchester United Players relieve the monotony (1911).

Brentford players bonding in the bath (January 1950). Future England manager Ron Greenwood is second from the left at the back.

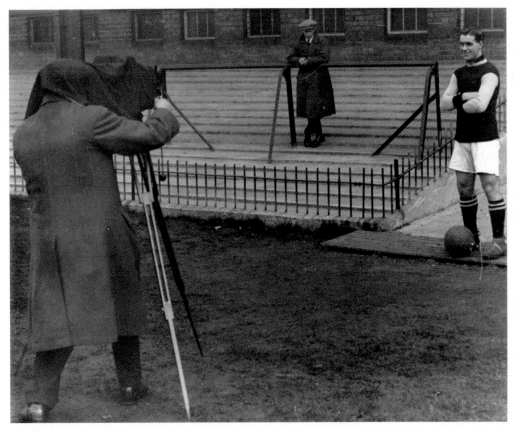

Albert Wilkes* photographing Aston Villa's Billy Kirton, c. 1924.

Albert Wilkes* with Billy Meredith in 1924.

* Albert Wilkes was signed by Aston Villa in 1898 and retired in 1909, having earned five England caps. Always a keen photographer, he snapped players as they relaxed and had fun (see opposite). He subsequently built up a prestigious press-photo agency. As a respected ex-player, Wilkes was able to gain exclusive access to training grounds and social clubs.

Birmingham City players help the trainer to roll the pitch (1923).

West Bromwich Albion players gamble away their win bonus (1925).

Footballers' real wives

West Brom's captain Reed plus bride and club mascot (*top left,* 1925).

Everton's Ted Sagar and his wife enjoy an evening at home in 1932 playing, appropriately, 'Housey, Housey' (*top right*).

(*Above*) Billy Wright's new wife Joy (*centre*) with her singing Beverley sisters at Wolves in 1958.

Pop star Louise and Liverpool's Jamie Rednapp at a film première (*right*).

Soccer's style warriors

Derby County and England star Steve Bloomer poses awkwardly in 1906 (*left*).

Arsenal's Denis Compton obliges the ladies (*above*, 1949).

Kevin Keegan, Gerry Francis and Mick Channon play it cool (*below left*, May 1976).

Arsenal's Ian Wright struts his stuff on the catwalk. (*below right*).

After the cheering stops

West Brom's Tommy Glidden and wife outside their tobacconist's shop in 1932.

Ex-Bradford City and Spurs forward Harold Walden took to the stage in the 1920s with his singing and mimicry act (*far left*).

Ex-Bradford City and Everton's Albert Geldard had aspirations to be a conjurer in the 1930s (*right*).

Ex-Doncaster Rovers' fullback Charlie Williams (*left*) hit the big time in the 1970s with the Comedians.

England and Southampton's Mike Channon made his millions training horses in the 1990s (*below, left*).

Ex-Wimbledon and Sheffield United 'hard man' Vinnie Jones, seen here with Angelina Jolie (*right*), is soccer's one and only international film star.

Modern-day icons

Dixie Dean in the distinguished Tussauds' company of cricketer Jack Hobbs and explorer Commander Shackleton (*left*, January 1929)…

… and as he appears today outside Goodison Park (*right*).

William Ralph 'Dixie' Dean
1907 – 1980
377 goals in 431 games, including a record 60 league goals in season 1927 – 2
FOOTBALLER · GENTLEMAN · EVERTON

David Beckham's Tussaud figure on the Trafalgar Square plinth during World Cup 2002 (*left*).

Today, statues and images of Britain's famous pro-players appear inside and outside football grounds the length and breadth of the country – evidence of their enduring and increasing significance as figures in popular social history.

Cull and Archibald decide to have some ball practice in spite of trainer Vallance's edict of 'sprints first'. *Topical Times*, 28 September 1929.

the sight of the ball". In my playing days we never saw the ball from one week's end to another and we were always keen to get to it.'

How this strange notion became so much a part of soccer training lore is a mystery, particularly as men like Billy Meredith recalled that when they had started in the 1890s, 'we used to train very largely with a football. We were out on the ground every day dribbling and shooting and kicking…nowadays, the players of most clubs see little of the ball in midweek…'

However, fitness, stamina and speed, regardless of the consequences to the men concerned, were forever the order of the day at most professional clubs, largely due to the relentless Football League programme which, by the 1920s and 1930s, had become almost industrial in its rhythms and demands, placing heavy emphasis on results. Army-style methods and mentality were the closest the game came to developing any 'theory' of training before the war, Major Frank Buckley at Wolves being the prime mover in this respect.

His post-war successor and pupil, Stan Cullis, would take things a step further. In his autobiography Cullis wrote: 'Training for football today is far removed from the old days when three or four laps, half a dozen sprints each morning and a bit of kicking comprised the programme. Today, the training section at Wolves and some other clubs is a highly organised scientific department dealing with the fitness of both body and mind.' Intricate ball-play and passing combinations were not part of the Wolverhampton team's style of play. Running for ninety minutes was. Thus, his players were 'scientifically' trained to play a peculiarly English game via a military-style assault course, led by ex-service men. Stamina was the key. 'By the time the season opens, the players are as hard as nails, able to play at a cracking pace not only for ninety minutes but for one hundred and twenty minutes if necessary.'

During the season, the Wolves players followed a weekly training routine as follows:

Monday:	*Light ball-work for 100 minutes in the morning.*
Tuesday:	*A three-mile run, sprinting, hurdling, and agility training for 100 minutes in the morning. Weight-training and ball-work for a similar spell in the afternoon.*
Wednesday:	*A morning practice match or training in football boots for two hours in the morning.*
Thursday:	*Sprinting and running, ball-work in the morning. Positional and individual coaching in the afternoon.*
Friday:	*Sprinting, exercises and light ball-work for an hour.*

Such a regime was designed to produce a team with a very particular 'Route One' job in mind, and the success of Wolves during the 1950s and 1960s cannot be argued with. What's more, the emphasis on endurance, power and agility was ahead of its time. Today, the sciences of physiology, nutrition and even psychology have raised the levels of fitness way beyond those obtained by Cullis' Wolves as British football has continued to strive for ever more speed and power. However, the intensely physical approach to the game adopted by Wolves exploited an attitude towards injury current in the game that at times has proved disastrous.

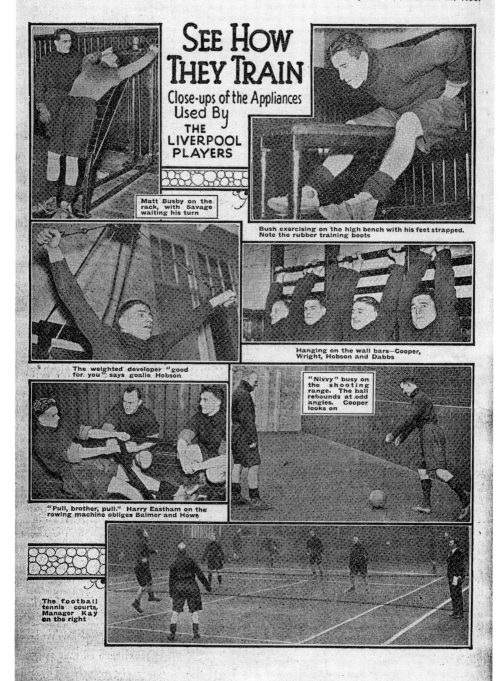

Topical Times, December 26, 1936.

14

SEE HOW THEY TRAIN

Close-ups of the Appliances Used By THE LIVERPOOL PLAYERS

Matt Busby on the rack, with Savage waiting his turn

Bush exercising on the high bench with his feet strapped. Note the rubber training boots

The weighted developer "good for you", says goalie Hobson

Hanging on the wall bars—Cooper, Wright, Hobson and Dabbs

"Nivvy" busy on the shooting range. The ball rebounds at odd angles. Cooper looks on

"Pull, brother, pull." Harry Eastham on the rowing machine obliges Balmer and Howe

The football tennis courts, Manager Kay on the right

3. The pain game

'Get up, Barratt, you're not hurt! Like a big tart, I'm not kidding. Somebody ruffles his hair, he wants his pants changing...'

Al Reid, comedian

After the war there were calls for more expertise where treating injuries was concerned and the importance of properly trained physiotherapists was underlined. According to Don Featherstone at Southampton, not only were trainers getting a much better grounding in the medical problems of the game by means of annual courses held at the Carnegie College of Physical Education but, 'more clubs are appointing full-time physiotherapists to treat their injured stars. It is a sound economic move which relieves the trainer of the anxiety of having to carry out involved medical treatments for which he is often not properly trained, and of having to use complicated electrical equipment. It enables him to concentrate on the job at which he excels – that of keeping his players at their peak of physical fitness after they have been progressively trained to that degree. He is also able to give more time to coaching the younger players and in general doing a first-class job.'

All of which sounded good, but the actual number of trained physiotherapists remained scandalously low at football clubs up and down the country and would remain so for decades. In 1953, a survey for Charles Buchan's *Football Monthly* could identify only a handful. The two most prominent men in the business, Jimmy Trotter and Tom Whittaker, didn't actually possess medical degrees, but the reporter wrote complacently, 'both are capable of results with sports injuries far exceeding those obtained in any hospital – a fact which proves that they possess innate skills and a sense of vocation beyond any number of certificates or parchment rolls.' Of the three who were qualified, one had been sacked [by Queens Park Rangers] a couple of years previously in a cost-cutting exercise.

Thus, the reality where treatment was concerned at some clubs could be grim. Charlie Williams had been a professional with Doncaster Rovers for some twelve years without suffering any serious injury until he went in for a tackle and ripped the tendons behind the knee, top and bottom. 'They strapped me up at the ground and had me walking to and from home every day. I don't think this did any good at all – I should have been in plaster. Then I had to start training and the tendons broke down and I was as bad as ever. I was out of football for three months until the injury healed. When I went back I was put into the reserves and on to the transfer list.'

Young, fit and enthusiastic men can endure pain and often will rather than come off the pitch. Williams considered himself a 'quick healer': 'I had a couple of ankles done in through men coming in with both feet, chopping, but in a month to six weeks I was back in action. At Lincoln City I got a dislocated collar bone, but it was a straightforward job – spring in, spring out – and I was back on the field in a couple of weeks.'

Such an approach to physical pain and discomfort was encouraged and even expected in a profession that placed great store in its macho image. Continental innovations were often scoffed at as 'namby pamby'. Here's top journalist Bob Gray writing about Jesse Carver, one of the world's finest coaches, in the *Weekly News* of 1955:

Come Off It Mr Carver!

This is the end. It must be. I mean those wooden shoes with which Coventry City players are being issued. Man behind this innovation is Jesse Carver, new manager-coach. Idea is that they will prevent the players' feet getting cold when they step out of the bath on the concrete floor. Well, well. What comes next? Fur-lined shirts? No training on wet days? I'm wondering just where this mollycoddling in football will stop...'

It's not surprising that Carver made little impression in England, the land of his birth.

More appreciated were characters like Jimmy Hagan, whose approach to the athlete's body was straightforward and uncompromising. Jeff Astle recalled that Hagan, when managing West Bromwich Albion, had once, during the winter of 1963, been horrified when players ran out on to the pitch wearing tracksuit bottoms: 'He ordered them to take them off. The players refused and went on "strike". For several days the dispute raged. It made the national headlines and most people sided with the players. Medical experts confirmed that the risk of strains and other leg injuries was far greater when the limbs were cold. A sensible compromise would have been for the players to warm up wearing the track suit trousers and then discard them. But not Hagan. He was adamant. His players weren't going to be mollycoddled. They should be able to withstand the cold weather. And to prove his point, Hagan continued training with a few of the youngsters who hadn't joined the senior players' strike. His dress: socks rolled round his ankles, brief shorts and a thin training vest, the sleeves rolled up to the elbows.'

'A halt for repairs':
Stoke v Notts County
(c.1906).

In part, such attitudes stemmed from a residual suspicion on behalf of both management and fans concerning the very nature of professional footballers; that they were 'shirkers' and prone to 'playing the old soldier'. As far back as the early 1900s, John Lewis, a director of Blackburn Rovers, felt that players pampered themselves: 'I do not wish to appear callous or brutal, but there have been constant complaints this season of the frequency and length of stoppages, and something seems necessary to be done to remind players that football is a game in which knocks must be expected and taken as a matter of course.'

Even John Allison at Matlock House felt it necessary to invent a special plaster which he called his 'sham detector'. 'The exact composition of this plaster is a secret, but its chief virtue is that it is diabolically painful as well as lasting in its effects.'

It's ironic, however, in the light of such suspicions, that an immunity to pain has long been a hallmark of the professional player. In 1909, Billy Meredith wrote concerning the 'astonishing powers of endurance shown by footballers. [Do you] fancy going

Potts of Leeds United on the rowing machine watched by team-mates Edwards, Hart and Cochrane.
Topical Times,
3 October 1931.

through three-quarters of a stiff League game with a broken collar-bone? TT Fitchie, the popular Woolwich Arsenal player, did so at the beginning of the present season. Another, Robert Hardy, had a particularly gruelling time of it. Hurt in the first half of a match played at Sunderland, he retired to have his broken wrist temporarily bandaged but returned and played to the finish. His injury was, however, continually getting in the way and the look of agony that came into his face every time a forward and he collided plainly showed the intense pain the plucky Rover was suffering.'

Worse still was the experience of goalkeepers in the early years, who could be charged and buffeted by opposing players while clearing the ball. Meredith recalled: 'Herbert Broomfield, goalkeeper for Bolton Wanderers, while playing against Sunderland played for twenty minutes with his shoulder out and one arm swinging behind him – useless, like a piece of rag, as he puts it. Twice while he was like that the big Sunderland forwards "put" him in the net…'

This 'Iron Man' approach, though a quality highly lauded, was expected of players. To take the knocks was 'manly'. To complain wasn't to show the right spirit, an attitude encouraged by the tough school of management exemplified by men like Jimmy Hagan, but traceable back to the amateur origins of the game. All too often, however, it has been rewarded with poor medical treatment and exploitation on behalf of managers and club directorates.

Tom Finney has admitted: 'I've got to confess that I fell for it on several occasions, had injections, and probably didn't do myself any good by playing when I wasn't 100 per cent fit. The trainer would watch you run round and say, "Well, you're going fairly well, it doesn't look as though there's anything wrong." I said, "Yeah, but I can feel that if I want to go that extra yard it's gonna go." I got through a game but I wasn't doing the injury any good and consequently it put you back another two to three weeks.'

In some cases, the lack of knowledge on display can only be laughed at. Fred Eyre recalled his trainer at non-league New Brighton: 'His favourite remedy to injuries was: "It's in the mind – run it off." Many an ankle looked black and blue to me but according to him we were only imagining it was bruised.'

For others, there was very little to laugh about. Derek Dougan, when playing for Blackburn Rovers, twisted an ankle in a reserve match but X-rays were inconclusive: 'For ten weeks I tried to get myself fit, but my ankle didn't seem to improve at all. The management and the trainers thought I was trying to pull the wool over their eyes by not responding to training and by maintaining that my ankle was sore. It was very painful and I just couldn't run on it properly. They told me that it was impossible that there was anything wrong, because a sprained ankle should have been better after six or seven weeks. I was disillusioned and upset by all of them not believing that my ankle wasn't getting better.'

After the ankle broke down again in a 'comeback' third-team game he was taken to hospital again, where an X-ray now showed a broken ankle: 'When you have been nearly ten weeks trying to persuade people that there is something wrong with you and no one believes you, you do not feel too good. The manager and the trainer just stood with their heads near enough between their legs. If only they had said to me, "We're sorry about this. We didn't realise your ankle was broken all the time."' Instead, they ignored him and he was unable to play for some months. 'The whole episode filled me with despair.'

However, few players have committed to print the intimate details of injury and pain the way Jeff Farmer managed in his book, *The HeartAche Game*. Farmer was a bright young Wolves star in the late 1950s under Stan Cullis. Cullis, according to Farmer, had an 'abrupt and often vehement style,' which Farmer felt could often destroy the confidence of more timid characters.

Playing for Wolves in January 1961, Farmer received a bad head injury. 'Joe Gardner was quickly at my side with the magic sponge and was draping a towel over the top of my head. As he took the towel away [team-mate] Norman Deeley who had come across to give assistance remarked, "Take him off, Joe," and I knew my skull was cut open…'

George Palmer, the Wolves physiotherapist, told him that he had several smallish cuts at the back of his head and that each one would require stitching. The club doctor gave him three or four injections and started to sew the wounds. Just as he was pulling through the first stitch the door opened and in rushed Stan Cullis who shouted: 'Get him out, we are one up!' and, as if in a nervous trance, rushed around the room and disappeared as quickly as he came in. I received twelve stitches in three gashes at the top of my head and after the doctor had performed this task George Palmer looked into my eyes for pupil dilation and said, "Take no notice of Cullis. You only go back when I am satisfied."'

Farmer then spent five minutes sitting in a chair, had a bandage wrapped round his head, then returned to the fray with a throbbing headache and a certain nervousness at heading the rain-soaked ball.

A couple of months later, in April 1961, Wolves were playing Manchester City. Farmer recalled: 'Man marking and heavy tackles were the order of the day and in the fourth minute of the match Dave Ewing's elbow found its way into the pit of my stomach. I was very sick and severely winded, taking several minutes to compose myself and get on with the match. I couldn't shake off this sick feeling and with challenges coming in from all corners the match developed into a farce.

'[At half time] Cullis was in a complete rage and I was very unbalanced and quite ill. I went to the toilet to try and get myself together but was horrified to see thick brownish blood gushing through my penis when attempting to urinate. Norman Deeley was in the toilet at the same time and when he saw my condition he advised me to see the club doctor. I was now very concerned and with our dressing room hushed through Cullis's ravings, I beckoned George Palmer and the club doctor to examine me. Just as I had finished explaining my symptoms, Cullis pushed his way through and asked what was wrong. "He is passing blood through his urine," the doctor explained. "Wait till it comes through his backside before you take him off," was the manager's enraged reply.'

Amazingly, Farmer was allowed to continue playing, though he wondered why the doctor allowed it. He had to be treated on the touchline many times, and at the end of the match, dressed and went home. 'I was in a very distressed state, still passing blood but now continuously and on the verge of collapse, when my parents finally called in our family practitioner.' He was rushed to Dudley Guest Hospital where a specialist diagnosed damage to the wall of his bladder. He remained in hospital for a week during which time no one from the club came to visit him.

Some time later, he was playing at Everton in a reserve match when, 'I was unceremoniously tackled to the ground by Parnell, the Everton right full-back. On the second occasion I retaliated and, gripping the front of his shirt, bellowed, "The next time you attempt that I will break your ****** neck." Early in the second half, the next time came all too quick. His tackle sent me off the pitch and into the wall that surrounded it. My right leg was doubled up under my fallen body and as I hit the wall I heard a sickening crack followed by extreme pain in my lower right leg.'

Stretchered off, he feared a broken leg but the Everton physiotherapist thought there was no serious damage. He returned to Molineux where Cullis, for a change, insisted on taking him to the local hospital. X-rays revealed a slight fracture and a chipped ankle bone. After four weeks, he resumed training but felt pain at the top of his right leg. Everyone was baffled. He was injected with cortisone by the club doctor and continued playing, but the pain also continued. He demanded a meeting with Cullis and George Palmer during which Cullis now declared that Farmer was a hypochondriac: 'A headache would be a tumour on the brain, a pain in my side would be appendicitis...' They insisted he played on.

Eventually, he went to his own doctor and arranged a consultation with an orthopaedic surgeon who diagnosed a broken fibula just below the knee. According to Farmer, physiotherapist George Palmer was not surprised and 'rather smugly asked: "What does Cullis think now?" Cullis made no comment but the local newspapers reported: "Farmer discovers a broken leg five weeks late".'

Cullis would be sacked a year or two after Farmer's agonies. But Wolves were one of the most successful teams in the land, where treatment of players was considered scientific and advanced. By the standards of the day, they were wealthy and well-equipped in terms of medical facilities. But the relentless drive to get results led to the club pushing young players like Farmer beyond the limits of their physical endurance. Doses of cortisone plus accusations of hypochondria, combined with an indifference as to the long-term consequences of such a philosophy, have long been a hallmark of the English game in general.

4. Dog eat dog

'Sport provokes a desire to do violence to others and likewise [to] be attacked and suffer.'

Theodore W. Adorno

Players get injured because the body cannot stand the stresses and strains inflicted upon it by the physical demands of the game. However, a further complication has been the tendency for professionals to injure one another deliberately. Though not freely admitted in some quarters of the professional game, deliberate foul play is directly responsible for many sporting injuries. Curiously, and for reasons connected with long-established sporting mores and customs, linked to the 'macho' image of robust play, any notion of cheating by inflicting physical injury has been underplayed, if not ignored.

In the early days of the game, physical contact was acceptable to a degree that would be unthinkable today. It was a game of very hard knocks but as the game grew in popularity, some commentators felt that roughness and 'dirty' play were increasing. In an article in the Football Players' Magazine of 1913 entitled 'Is Football Getting Rougher?', George Robinson of Bradford City suggested that nothing had changed, except that, because more people were watching, offences that had once been overlooked were being given greater prominence.

Robinson was of the 'old school' who felt that tripping an opponent was much worse than the old-fashioned shoulder charge. He was also of the opinion that those watching the game didn't really understand it. 'There are very few really "dirty" players, probably not so many as would be found in most other competitions of less importance than the three big leagues. After all, players have a rough and ready way of dealing with really "dirty" players at times and that style of football does not always pay as much as some people think.'

Dixie Dean certainly had a way of dealing with such people. Aged 17, in 1924 he was playing for Tranmere Rovers against Rochdale in a league match, 'and Rochdale had this centre-half, a chap named Davy Parkes, one of these big six foot two fellas and a big strong man. I went down the middle a couple of times and got two early goals. And Davy Parkes, as I passed him going down the field, he said, "Tha'll get no more bloody goals today, you've finished." So right away I said to him, "By the looks of you, you've finished, you've had it."

'I'm afraid that he was a great tipster because when I did come sailing down the third time, he kicked me where I didn't want kicking and I'm afraid that if the ground had opened that day I only wish it would have swallowed me. But any rate, I had to go into the hospital and have a testicle out. So they strap you down there to this here flat-bed affair and you've got to wait until this thing stops swelling. Then they gave you a little touch of the old gas lark and away you go. But while this thing was swelling, I turned round to the specialist and told him. I said, "You'd better hurry up – if this thing blows up it'll blow this bloody hospital up." At any rate, it didn't affect me in any way afterwards, in after life.'

He was playing again within five weeks: 'I've never wished anybody any harm but I always said to myself that I'd come across that man somewhere or somehow and I'd get a bit of revenge for it. And I did. I met him in Chester about seventeen years later. He sent me a pint across the bar. When I asked the barman who sent it he pointed to him and I couldn't quite place the face for a time. But I did. And then I done his face up and they took him to the hospital, so we're evens! That's about the only time that I've ever, it was the only time as a matter of fact, and ever since, that I ever retaliated. The only thing I used to do was turn round to the man. I had fifteen operations throughout my football career. To the bloke that broke a bone or gave me a broken rib or a broken shoulder blade, or whatever it was, I used to just turn round and say to them, while I was laying there, "Has this done you any good?" and that was it.'

Such physical damage can have a devastating effect on a player's career, but taking legal action against an opponent who oversteps the mark is rare in professional football. In 1898, action was taken as a result of death in a soccer match, but it would be another seventy years before one player took another to court over an alleged physical assault on the pitch. Suddenly, in the late 1980s and early 1990s, the game seemed rife with such cases. An on-field incident in January 1988 led to Chris Kamara of Swindon Town becoming the first player in the history of the British game to be fined in a court of law for an assault on another professional. Kamara was fined £1,200 for causing grievous bodily harm to Shrewsbury Town's Jim Melrose, who suffered a broken cheekbone due to Kamara's use of the elbow. In the same year, Danny Thomas received £30,000 for a tackle by Paul McGuire that ended his career. There were further cases involving Peter Beardsley and Neil Ruddock, and Paul Elliott and Dean Saunders.

In a court case in 1993, a Torquay United player, John Uzzell, took Brentford's Gary Blissett to court for an elbowing offence. Blissett, who was defended by FA Chief Executive Graham Kelly, was found not guilty. Blissett had been sent off, but Kelly claimed the challenge with the elbow was 'routine' in the game. As *Daily Telegraph* journalist Paul Hayward noted during the 2001/2002 season, 'Like most vices, elbowing remains alive and well as a means of getting a point across with one of the body's sharpest implements, especially in games where two clubs have developed a tradition of mutual belligerence.' Not long afterwards came the Gary Mabbutt case, where another such assault by Wimbledon's John Fashanu almost led to Mabbutt's career being prematurely ended.

The spate of legal cases during this period and the subsequent bad publicity they generated for the professional game have been attributed, however, less to changing masculine codes of conduct on the field or an upsurge in player-on-player violence but rather to the increasing involvement of lawyers at all levels of the game. Gordon Taylor, Chief Executive of the PFA, has commented that it is 'sad' that players are sometimes encouraged by lawyers to go to court. Particularly sad when the case cannot be proved. Quite recently, Crystal Palace's Darren Pitcher lost his case in the High Court in London for more than £1 million damages against Huddersfield Town. Pitcher had claimed his career had been ended by a 'negligent' tackle by Paul Reid while playing against Huddersfield on 31 August 1996.

Such actions are fraught with difficulty because it has to be proved that there was either malicious intent involved or a considerable element of negligence. In a physical game like soccer, bodily collisions are inevitable, expected and encouraged from both the terrace and the coach's bench. Whether it's called 'getting stuck in' or 'putting oneself about', the lexicon of the game is littered with such euphemisms for actually hurting an opponent.

In an article in the professional players' house magazine, *Players' Journal*, Gordon Taylor sought to categorise the various scenarios: if it's an 'off-the-ball' incident and a clear assault then the player has no defence. If the incident is 'on-the-ball' and a legitimate tackle, then the player has nothing to worry about. If, however, it's on the ball and deemed negligent, then there's a problem.

As an example of the complexities involved, in 2001 Bradford City striker Gordon Watson received nearly £1 million in damages from Huddersfield's Kevin Gray for a tackle that ended Watson's career. During the case, the following evidence was taken into consideration: Gray's FA disciplinary record; the referee's immediate booking and match report; the report of the referee's assessor; the video evidence of the incident and events leading up to the tackle; the height of the tackle; the evidence of eye-witnesses; statements made by manager Brian Horton to the press; as well as both players' versions of the incident. Various football 'experts' such as Jimmy Hill were also called in to add their comments, as well as evidence to suggest that Gray was exacting revenge for Gordon Watson's alleged elbow on another Huddersfield player. However, Gray was not being accused of intending to break Watson's leg. What had to be decided was whether it could be proved, on the balance of probabilities, that a reasonable professional player would have known that there was a significant risk in what Gray did and that it might have resulted in a serious injury to Watson.

As Taylor commented in the aftermath of the case: 'We have told our members that the football pitch is no oasis from law and order and they do owe a legal duty of care to colleagues and, particularly, opponents.'

The apparent admission by Roy Keane, in an autobiography published in the summer of 2002, that he had deliberately set out to cause damage to an opponent via an 'over-the-top' tackle shocked the football world. It also brought a prompt response from the player on the sharp end of Keane's assault. Alf Inge Haarland, a year or so after the incident, is still unable to resume his career. He and his club, Manchester City, launched a £5 million claim for damages against both Keane and Manchester United, while the FA, who had already punished Keane for the offence, indicated that they would look again at the incident and at what Keane had written about it in his autobiography.

"What do you mean, cut out the rough stuff —that's what I've been picked for!"

'What do you mean, cut out the rough stuff – that's what I've been picked for!' Charles Buchan's *Football Monthly*, c. 1966.

Keane's admission, if that is what it turns out to be, is shocking only if one holds a sentimental view of human nature in general and of professional soccer players in particular. Michael Parkinson, a respected commentator on the game and a harsh critic of the contemporary player, has made much in his various newspaper columns of the fabled 'Skinner' Normanton, who played for the Barnsley team of Parkinson's youth. Normanton's physical excesses, his rugged tackling and rough treatment of opponents (especially wingers, who were regularly deposited by 'Skinner' on to the gravel track surrounding the Oakwell pitch) are regarded by Parkinson as simple manly fun and not to be equated with the 'thuggery' of today's players.

But to assert that Keane and Normanton's actions are somehow different in kind is to let nostalgia replace common-sense. Players have always settled old scores one way or another, either in the fashion of Dixie Dean, but more often in the style of Roy Keane, biding their time until the opportunity arises to make their point on the field of play. (And it's interesting that the retribution is usually made in full view of the rest of the world, rather than down a dark alleyway.) It's unpleasant, but has always been a part of the game, though increasingly, with so much money at stake, something that receives much more attention than once it did.

It can generate bitter memories, however. In the mid-1990s, Zilwood March, who played for Brighton Hove Albion and Portsmouth in the early 1920s, recalled his worst memory as a player: 'Well, getting knocked out and going completely blank. I woke up in the dressing room, dressed and ready to go home. We were playing Plymouth Argyle in the League and we were two up, you see. And either one or the other had to win the League. Moses Russell, I don't care if he's alive and hears me, he butted me in the mouth, that's the whole rubber. Next thing I was in the dressing room, dressed up to my waistcoat. I thought to myself, "I can earn my living better than this".'

'Zack', who turned 100 years old in 1993, reverted to amateur status and took over the family building trade.

5. Football's a drug

'There are some who advocate artificial restoration by means of tonics, but I would shun these as I would the plague. There are many admirable pick-me-ups, no doubt, but they can only serve their purpose for a time and leave the player in a worse condition than he ever was before.'

W Freeman, The Red Letter, 1909

The pressure for success has led management and players down many a strange 'scientific' alleyway. Pain-killing injections were once given without a second thought. Before that, the galvanising of weary men was attempted in other ways.

The 'Football Secretary' wrote in 1901: 'Before a big match some of the players are attended to in the way of tonics, etc. but on such we won't dwell – the players' faces show that the subject is not the pleasantest. Sometimes the tonic given previous to the match includes a little spirits but its use is strictly from a medicinal standpoint. Lemon and barley water is frequently used...'

Whatever was available before the First World War would appear to have been fairly innocuous. In the immediate post-war world, stranger substances were becoming available. Leslie Knighton was manager of Arsenal in 1925 and under pressure to get a result in an up-coming FA Cup match: 'I was sitting in my office in Highbury with my head in my hands, wondering how on earth we could make sure of putting West Ham out of the Cup, when a card was handed to me. It bore the name of a distinguished West End doctor.' The mystery man told Knighton that, 'What the boys require is something in the nature of a courage-pill. Occasionally, we administer such things to patients requiring abnormal stamina or resistance for a particular purpose. They do no harm, but simply tone up the nerve reflexes to produce the maximum effort, and they leave no serious after effects.'

Knighton considered the idea. 'It's big hearts that win cup ties,' he reasoned, 'and against the Hammers we should need hearts as big as bullocks.' Assured that there would be no harmful after-effects, Knighton agreed to administer the pills. He continued: 'We went to Upton Park. I had talked the matter over, and, as a sign of good faith to the boys, I had offered to take my pill when they took theirs. And I needed it! One hour before play began we sat solemnly round, each swallowing his silver pill. No one made a fuss about them, but I can tell you mine felt as big as a marble. In the middle of the gulps and sighs, Alf Baker suddenly guffawed. Then we all saw the comic side of it – heads tilted back, glasses in hands, eyes and faces very strained. There was a sudden yell of laughter, half of us choked, the water spilled and spluttered; but I saw to it that every man did his duty and swallowed his pill. Then we sat around nervously awaiting the results.'

Just before kick-off, Knighton noticed that his players were getting restless. 'So was I. I felt I needed to run, jump, shout. There was something in those pills. I felt I could push down a wall with my fist.'

Unfortunately for Knighton and his pepped-up team, the game was called off because of fog! He was then left with the task of getting them back to Highbury. It was, he said, 'like trying to drive a flock of lively young lions. Those pills not only left us "roaring to go" but steadily developed the most awful bitter taste, and the most red-hot, soul-destroying thirst I have ever known. And, mind you, I have known some thirsts! We drank water till I thought the Thames would dry up. It became painful. Nothing quenched that thirst – whatever we poured down made it worse and worse, and the bitterness in our throats was like gall.' Not for the first time in the club's history, Arsenal players found it hard to quench a thirst.

When at last they took to the field some days later, Knighton felt he could see the pills working. 'Just before half-time I noticed a change. The Arsenal boys seemed like giants suddenly supercharged. They tore away with the ball, and put in shots that looked like leather thunderbolts. They monopolised the play… There was no defence against the pluck-pills…'

There the experiment ended, however. They drew 0–0, the players refused to take the pills for the replay, which they drew again and they finally lost the second replay. The doctor never told Knighton what the pills contained, though he thought it might have been strychnine, 'the stimulant drug used sometimes by students to nerve them for a hard examination'.

Knighton was sacked the following summer and had died before the next drug sensation hit the English game in the late 1930s. On this occasion it was Major Frank Buckley, the Wolves manager, who decided that intravenous injections of animal secretions might benefit his players. A number of doctors had been interested in what was then termed 'rejuvenation' and had been experimenting with the transplanting of testicles from monkeys to humans to overcome the effects of syphilis and gonorrhoea. It was an early form of sex therapy. How the idea came about to use monkey secretions (sperm?) to increase a player's physique and bodily strength is unclear, but Buckley felt it was worthwhile, even if only for the publicity. In the *Weekly News* of May 1958, Stan Cullis, who was a member of the Wolves team at the time, admitted:

'We received these injections once a week for twelve weeks. No fuss. No bother. Most of us thought the whole business was a bit of a joke. We were so fit we had stacks of stamina. We needed no artificial aids. Actually the injections made no apparent difference.'

In 1938, the FA held an enquiry into the affair and announced that players were at liberty to decide for themselves whether or not they received such injections. When Wolverhampton Wanderers met Portsmouth in the 1939 FA Cup Final, Portsmouth manager Jack Tinn, ever the publicist, had his players pictured drinking extracts from 'monkey' glands. The Minister of Health was asked in the House of Commons, 'whether his attention has been directed to statements that gland extracts from animals are being administered to professional football players…and whether he will order an investigation into these allegations and whether he regards this practice as desirable in the interests of national health'. No enquiry followed.

Remarkably, despite a recent series of cases in Europe involving performance-enhancing drugs such as Nandrolene, scandals concerning drug-taking have hardly touched the British game since then.

For many commentators, however, the fact that no player has tested positive in Britain is not down to innocence, rather, it's due to the football authorities' desire to hide and conceal the truth. Unlike other sports, professional football in the United Kingdom tests its players infrequently and across a wide area. The FA claims to test around 1,200 players a year but this includes players from the Premiership, the three Football Leagues, the Football Conference and even youth and women's football. In total, the tests cover less than one per cent of games played.

What's more, the Football Association does not allow home testing, the selected matches are agreed beforehand and players are tested on Mondays. Four names are asked for and two players from each side are chosen at random. This ponderous procedure provides massive windows of opportunity for evasion, perhaps the reason why Lazio player Jaap Stam's Nandrolene traces were not picked up in England when he was with Manchester United. No surprise, perhaps that since the commencement of the testing programme three years ago there have been only two positive tests of youth team players taking recreational drugs.

It's often been claimed that soccer players do not need performance-enhancing drugs and it has always seemed unlikely that there is a drug that could combine a clear head with the reactions and stamina needed for a 90-minute soccer game. However, many players, including those in the Premiership, have been given creatine, a supposedly steroid-free body-building supplement.

It's true that the prevailing culture among British players has always looked askance at drugs. The late Trevor Ford, a player in the 1940s and 1950s wrote: 'There should be no need for some clubs to revitalise their players with pep drugs. They've tried oxygen, phenobarbitone and Dexedrine but I'll tell you – if players have to be doped to get them on to the field of play they ought not to be in the game. They ought to be painlessly put away. And if a hypodermic has to be used, I know what I'd do. I'd give them one prod in the right place and I wager they'd move faster than with any pep drugs.'

However, it could be that British footballers have been too busy imbibing rather more traditional dangerous substances down the years to be bothered with more modern products.

6. Who ate all the pies?

'Every Saturday night after a game, we'd come in, get changed, have a shower, straight round to the Black Lion. The lady there would make a load of sausages and God knows what on the counter, and we'd all get stuck into that. I don't think there was any diet in those days.'

Harry Rednapp, ex-West Ham United, speaking in 2002

Doncaster Rovers players, Walker, Tindill and Goodall, have a good tuck-in the night before a Cup Tie, 1953.

Perhaps the last redoubt defended by British players against the sweeping tide of continental reform has been that of the dinner table. Food has rarely figured in players' lives except to fill stomachs, hopefully with traditional wholesome fare.

When the 'Football Secretary' quizzed top players for the *Weekly News* in 1901, there was a clear consensus: Johnny Holt, centre-half of Everton, liked 'plenty of good wholesome food, avoiding spirits and beer'. The latter were apt to 'make a fellow short-winded and bloated'. Billy Bassett liked his food 'the plainer the better', while John Southworth, Blackburn Rover's centre-forward, admitted that he 'didn't go in for any special diet: good, plain, wholesome food is best, with very little pastry'.

Preston North End's John Goodall's guidelines were similarly simple: 'I always have what I fancy, never restricting myself to any particular food. I seldom take coffee and my favourite drink with my dinner is "lemon and dash". Always take meals at least two hours before playing.'

The author of an article, 'Footballers and their Worries', in *The Red Letter* of November 1908, felt that, though smoking was frowned on, 'the question of diet curiously enough plays a very small part in the training of the footballer, except on the day of the match. For breakfast, fish, ham and eggs and tea or coffee may be taken, but only a light luncheon is allowed and on no account must potatoes or pudding form part of the menu. Stimulants of any kind prior to the match are absolutely forbidden. When the contest is over the seals of bondage are broken and the player is at liberty to follow his own inclinations for the remainder of the week-end.'

For most of the first half of the twentieth century, there would have been nothing but simple common-sense advice for footballers to follow, as dietary fads and the science of nutrition were subjects far removed from working-class experience. What's more, the majority of ordinary people ate poorly, as horrified war recruitment officers discovered both in 1914 and 1939. Footballers by contrast were able to afford

'good, wholesome food' and they were inclined to indulge in it and most men followed a simple routine usually determined for them by their mothers and later their wives.

Dixie Dean of Everton explained: 'On the Saturday morning [before a match] my mother, before she brought me a cup of tea, would always bring me in a spoonful of Phosferine and this happened every Saturday that she was alive. Then I'd have an egg or something like that. About 12 o'clock, I'd have a bit of boiled fish round and a bit of toast.'

In 1938, in a *Topical Times* series entitled 'The Human Side of the Players', Jack Dodds of Sheffield United, who also lived at home with his mother, was said to be, 'pretty strict in the matter of diet. He goes in for fruit and fish and seldom tackles a real hefty meal of the steak and chips and apple pie and cheese to follow variety'.

When it wasn't mothers, it was wives who supplied the nutritional discipline. A *Topical Times* reporter profiling Huddersfield Town's Ken Willingham in 1938 revealed: 'Mrs Willingham has complete control over Ken's diet. It is small and compact, for Ken easily puts on weight. She diets him on fish, salads and tomatoes. Especially tomatoes. They're Ken's favourite dish. He can eat them raw by the half pound any day in the week. Ken has an unusual appetite – after a match he can never eat anything until about nine o'clock at night. But his wife has such an expert and varied way of preparing his food that Ken has no food trouble.'

These were carefully tailored pieces, of course, reflecting a conservative mind-set unburdened by theory and one that would survive even the culture-shock of foreign travel. Stoke City's Neil Franklin went to Bogota in Colombia in the 1950s as part of the abortive 'break-out' of top British players in search of better pay and conditions. He had more money offered to him than he'd ever experienced in Britain, but his principal memory was food-related: 'Maybe it is hard to believe, but it took us a couple of weeks to teach them how to cook bacon and eggs, and can you imagine an Englishman without his bacon and eggs?'

Even a successful British 'export', Eddie Firmani, who went to Italy in 1953, confessed that, 'my biggest disappointment is not to be able to have a real English breakfast of fried eggs and bacon.' Firmani soon learned, however, that diet was an important aspect of Italian training and preparation.

On the morning of his first match for Sampdoria, Eddie was up at 10 a.m: 'After a cup of coffee I had to report to the Restaurant Bolognaise where I was told the team would have lunch at 12.30 – four hours before we were due to kick off against Trieste. I'll admit I had been warned that I was in for a shock when I saw the large quantities of food my colleagues would enjoy, so I went to the Restaurant Bolognaise with an open mind and prepared to see footballers enjoying something much more substantial than the boiled fish and toast, which is the accepted pre-match snack in England. Despite that I was shocked – and I mean shocked – when I saw the magnificent "feast" prepared for us as only Italians can serve up a meal. We had boiled rice – yes, RICE! – grilled steak, a raw egg, wine if we wished, and espresso coffee!

'Another shock for me was to see several of my colleagues wading into rolls. It wasn't until later that I discovered that they took out the centre of the rolls and ate only the crust! Although I was given to understand – and my friends stressed this point – that a dietician had produced this "balanced meal", I was still worried at the prospect of playing on a tummy full of rice. But my fears were unfounded.'

British players, meanwhile, did have vague suspicions that diet might lead to improved performance. Tommy Docherty used to have two raw eggs before a game when he played for Preston North End in the 1950s, though without Firmani's sumptuous Italian meal to supplement it. '11 o'clock in the morning! No breakfast, just two raw eggs. I felt it did me good. Horrible to take, two raw eggs and a drop of sweet sherry in it as well. Swish it all up and take it. Vile! Vile to take!'

Terry Venables also had more than an inkling as to what a player should or shouldn't eat. When he was a Chelsea player in the early 1960s, he recalled being given a lift to a game by team-mate Jimmy Greaves. They stopped off at Greaves' favourite pre-match lunch spot in Gant's Hill, where Venables ordered a healthy grilled chicken breast. Greaves, in stark contrast, ordered roast beef, Yorkshire pudding, carrots, peas, cauliflower and potatoes, roasted and boiled. That was followed by steam pudding and custard. 'I gazed at him in disbelief,' said Venables. 'Was this any way for a professional sportsman to carry on? Evidently it was. We won 6–1 that afternoon and Jim scored five of the goals.'

For the most part, players simply pleased themselves about what they ate and drank. Not surprisingly, most of their ideas concerning what was best for an athlete turned out to be wrong. Lee Chapman, a player in the 1980s, wrote: 'Our ignorance about preparation also extended to diet. Large steaks were believed to be the essential food for top athletes. It was also thought that any carbohydrates such as potatoes and bread should be severely rationed. Many players would consume steaks at every opportunity. Some would even eat fillet steak as a pre-match meal, two and a half hours before a game. They would consume negligible amounts of bread and potatoes, and pasta was not even contemplated. It is amazing how these players managed to perform at all.'

Today, it is understood that soccer players are endurance athletes and making the right food and fluid choices can help enhance their individual performance. Nutrition is now seen as the key to providing energy which can optimise performance and minimise injuries that are often caused by an early onset of fatigue. Maintaining adequate carbohydrate reserves, plus a daily energy intake, all appear to be well understood by players, principally because of the influence of foreign coaches.

Sean Davis at Fulham admits to having changed his habits under French manager Jean Tigana: 'I eat more healthily and at the right times. Before I would eat an hour before training and would be all heavy. Now we get told: "Eat three hours before training, chew your food, sip your water and you will get more energy and will be fresher and livelier." It's working. Last season, the boys were a lot fitter than before. It's carbohydrates and protein: the normal chicken, pasta, bread rolls, toast and fruit. We get fat-tested and weighed all the time. We can't really go out and eat too much junk food. I used to do that. In the past I would have a chicken sandwich without thinking about the way it was cooked.'

Some, however, remain unreformed. Lee Bowyer's eating habits, according to Leeds United's coach Eddie Gray, are not what one would expect from a highly tuned athlete: 'He loves fast food, especially McDonald's hamburgers and fries. It has become a standing joke among the players. On European trips you immediately know that the town or city has a McDonald's outlet by the cheer that emanates from the back of our coach when it passes one.'

In many ways, however, players can hardly be blamed for remaining ignorant about the influence that food could have on their performances. As a senior lecturer at the University of Aberdeen put it during a conference on nutrition in the mid-1990s: 'Diet is a big problem. Most clubs leave it all to the physiotherapist, but you don't go to a dietician with a broken leg.' Another contributor stated, 'The present degree of nutritional naïveté, ignorance and confusion displayed by coaches and players alike only serves to further misunderstandings, and ultimately to impair the development of individual players.'

7. Old footballers never die

'When Jack finished at Luton he injured his foot and couldn't play properly any more and they didn't give a damn. When they had a post-mortem on his body (because he dropped dead), every part of his body was worn out through football. It just shows what a toll it takes on people, doesn't it?'

Norah Ball on JT Ball of Luton Town, speaking in 1995

The physical damage the game does to a professional player has only recently been taken seriously. Professional football takes a heavy toll on young bodies. Paul McGrath, who played for Manchester United and Aston Villa in the 1980s and 1990s was eventually forced to retire because of chronic damage to both knees. 'I pushed things so far with so many injections that it all became too much. The doctors laid it on the line: it was either stop playing or carry on and risk being in a wheelchair for the rest of my life.'

Only now, with the realisation as to the sheer economic cost of such injuries, is there a concerted attempt to reform this crucial area of the game. An audit of football injuries, the first of its kind in the long history of the game, was carried out in 1999 involving all the clubs in the Premiership and the Nationwide Leagues. It calculated that, based on an annual wage bill for the 1998–9 season of approximately £400m, and with, on average, ten per cent of any squad being unavailable to train each week, injuries were costing the game some £40m a year in lost revenue. Add in the cost of treatment and insurance premiums plus diminished prize money as a result of lower final league positions for individual clubs, and the amount of cash being lost by clubs in dire need is clearly enormous.

And yet, health care at the majority of League clubs in England still falls far short of good medical practice and fails to measure up to Continental standards. A 1999 report cited individual examples of players being forced back into competitive matches with inadequately healed injuries, of 'unacceptable pressure' from managers to allow injured players to resume and that half of all physiotherapists working in English League clubs are not chartered and therefore not qualified to work in the NHS. Peter Evans, of the Association of Physiotherapists in Sports Medicine, stated: 'Many clubs continue to employ unchartered physiotherapists who might have had as little as a few days training. This is a false economy.' What's more, a majority of club doctors are appointed through the 'old boys network' and have no specialist qualifications.

As the England team headed out to Japan for the World Cup, they were accompanied by a good coaching team, physiotherapists, a cook, a nutritionist and two doctors. However, neither of the latter had any specialist or formal training in the diagnosis or treatment of sports injuries. Most other national teams have qualified sports doctors who have spent a large part of their careers treating the ailments of elite competitors.

In many senses, English football suffers from a wider problem concerning the training of doctors. In the United Kingdom there are only two consultants in sports medicine. In reality, sports medicine does not exist in the National Health system. There is no longer any scope in medical training for a young doctor to specialise in this field and next to no recognition within the NHS of the importance of caring properly for an exercising population. In Australia, to become a qualified sports physician takes a further four years on top of the basic training. In Europe, countries like Italy, Holland and Ireland have rigorous training programmes and high standards of care for their sporting communities.

Thus, Gerard Houllier, the Liverpool manager, can hardly be blamed for seeking Belgian medical advice for Steven Gerrard's persistent groin injury, or Jimmy Floyd Hasselbaink flying in a Dutch sports doctor in his chase for fitness before the 2002 Cup Final, nor Juan Sebastian Veron in returning to Lazio to get treatment on his injured heel. Jamie Rednapp of Liverpool and now Tottenham Hotspur, who suffered a bad knee injury a year and a half ago, made regular visits to a German doctor in Munich, before being forced to turn to Dr Richard Steadman, an American knee specialist who had operated on Patrik Berger and Alan Shearer. He had to fly to America on four occasions after the operation, and finally returned to playing late in the 2002 season. And there is nothing new here. Kevin Keegan fled the English team in the 1982 World Cup and went back to Germany to seek treatment on a stubborn back problem

The day-to-day medical skills are possibly available in this country but not formally trained and certainly not within a cohesive structure. As one prominent doctor put it: 'When an athlete is in trouble in this country it is a Yellow Pages job. In other countries everybody knows who the key people are. In this country it is a case of hunt the thimble.'

However, league clubs have always been slow to catch on to whatever medical advances were being made in the treatment of injury. The sudden plethora of hamstring injuries to top players in the Premiership towards the end of the 2002 season led to suggestions that many of the players were simply not fit enough. A top consultant physiotherapist, Kevin Lidlow, however, suggested that the problem was probably due to a certain part of a player's

FORSHAW.

TO-DAY'S BEAUTIFUL THOUGHT
FOOTBALLERS PAD THEIR FEET WITH COTTON WOOL~

IN ORDER TO CAUSE AS LITTLE SUFFERING AS POSSIBLE,
SHOULD ONE INADVERTENTLY KICK ANOTHER.

Manchester Football News, Saturday 14 March, 1931.

vertebra being placed under too much pressure. 'Stress and fatigue combine through this part of the lumbar spine, which is a little bit exposed and that in turn puts pressure on the hamstring. The fault isn't necessarily with the musculature of the hamstring itself.' Football clubs, however, did not seem to be aware of this, according to Lidlow, a perfect example of their parochial attitude. That and the ever increasing workload they thrust upon their star men.

The sudden occurrence of three metatarsal injuries to key England players within the space of a week or two was considered by some to be sheer bad luck. Dr Jumbo Jenner, director of the sports injury clinic at Cambridge's Addenbrookes Hospital, simply felt that players played too much: 'All these metatarsal fractures are not bad luck but more an indication that England's top-class footballers are just spending too much time on the pitch. The amount they play makes them more susceptible to stress fractures and it is no surprise that there have now been three of them.' As evidence, he compared the numbers of games played by the three men concerned: Liverpool's Danny Murphy (55) and Stephan Gerrard (46) plus Manchester United's Gary Neville (50), with those played by Juventus' Zinedine Zidane (40) and Roma's Francesco Totti (35).

The longer term consequences for individual players of such over-use of their bodies was revealed by a number of high-profile court cases in the late 1990s. Tommy Smith, the ex-Liverpool 'hardman' of the 1960s, was the most prominent. Smith had lost his disability allowance after being seen taking a penalty kick in a charity match. He claimed he had to take constant painkillers and had even needed help to dress for the match where he made a brief guest appearance. Though just 53 years old, since his retirement he had had two new knees, a hip replacement and an artificial elbow. He also suffered from osteoarthritis and rheumatoid arthritis.

Allen McGraw, 58, who began as a professional for Morton aged 19, was forced through injury to stop playing some ten years later. He had been unable to walk without the aid of a stick since the age of 33: 'Just about every bone in my body has been broken – the sticks are with me always.' In his last year as a player he had twenty-five cortisone injections in an attempt to kill the pain. In the thirty years since he stopped playing he'd had three new joints in his left knee and two in his right. His third operation on his right knee was due shortly: 'People say it is bravery to keep playing but actually it is stupidity.'

There have been even more serious consequences for much older players, however. Raich Carter's father, 'Toddler' Carter, played for Burslem (later Port Vale), Fulham and Southampton before the First World War. Raich recalled, 'A kick in the head had put him out of the game, and he suffered the most appalling attacks of pain in the head. In fact, my main recollection of my father is his persistent headaches and my mother telling me not to worry him or make a noise. He died when I

was 14 from a tumour on the brain, which undoubtedly resulted from the kick on the head. Understandably, I suppose, the
injury killed my father's interest in football.'

In 1998, Billy McPhail, aged 70, made the news by attempting to
gain Industrial Injuries Disablement Benefits because of memory loss
'due to heading footballs'. The government agency concerned had
previously refused him. McPhail, who'd played for Queens Park, Celtic
and Clyde, revealed: 'I'm in a hopeless way because my brain has been
half-flattened. Sometimes the ball came to you like a bullet and, if it
was a wet day, it really soaked up the moisture. These days, the ball is
as light as a feather, but the old one gave you a real thud…'

McPhail had been examined and found to have wasting of the
brain tissue and reduction of the cerebral blood flow to the high
frontal regions. Doctors advised that the most likely factor to have
caused the damage was Mr McPhail's previous occupation as a pro
footballer. It was claimed during the hearing that there were up to
sixty ex-players suffering with pre-senile dementia symptoms similar to the punch-drunk syndrome many boxers have that leads to
Alzheimer's Disease.

Tommy Docherty commented: 'I played alongside Billy and we
always used to punt the high balls to him because he was so good.
There's got to be a link between heading these balls and problems
in later life. People were knocked out, especially if the ball hit the
crown of the head.'

The late Roy Paul of Cardiff and Wales also suffered from Alzheimer's and nephew Alan Curtis, a former Welsh international, says: 'I
believe Uncle Roy's condition could have been linked to heading a
hard leather ball. He was like a boxer who'd taken too many punches.'

Reports on the effect of the modern ball, however, show that
no damage is now caused. Nevertheless, according to Peter
Hamlyn, a specialist in brain injuries, measurable evidence of
chronic traumatic brain injury had been found in a study published in 1999. 'It's been clear for some time that football, like
most collision sports, has its risks and these include brain injury.
The first danger arises from acute major head injury, causing loss
of consciousness. These usually result from heading objects other
than the ball – each other or a goal-post.'

The death of Jeff Astle in late 2002 reignited the debate. Astle
retired in 1977 but was found to have suffered from degenerative

brain damage caused by heading balls. This, it was claimed, led to his premature death. Dr Leslie Murphy, a chartered clinical neuro-psychologist, immediately called upon the FA to introduce headgear for footballers. 'Anything that's going to reduce the incidence of head injury is a good thing. Footballers could well suffer from headaches, nausea, concessional injuries and more long-term effects such as dementia. The more frequent the blows are, the more likely it is that actual damage occurs.'

The football world, predictably perhaps, was sceptical of the idea of head-gear. Steve Avery, the assistant director of the Charlton Athletic Football Academy, said, 'The important thing is to be taught how to head the ball correctly. We've played football for long enough without protective headgear so I don't see why we should start now.'

The FA has, in fact, invested £116,000 in a ten-year study of thirty young players who play in a variety of positions and who head the ball on a regular basis. They are subject to regular MRI scans to examine the effects of heading on the structure of the brain. Peter Hamlyn feels that such data collection is essential. 'We don't even know if the new football is any safer than the older. They say it's lighter but does that mean the players take on more challenging balls, more often?'

Pro players' bodies down the years have clearly suffered from medical neglect and physical abuse and, as the game changes its nature, becoming faster and more athletically demanding, the strain on muscles, limbs and even brain tissue will inevitably increase. As a commodity, the footballer has increased in value in recent years, encouraging clubs and governing bodies to invest in modern medical facilities and know-how. One suspects, however, that there is still a long way to go before all pro players receive the protection they deserve.

Chapter 6

Playing Away
(With the Lads)

1. With the lads at home

'When we have had our baths we spend half an hour in our recreation room which, by the way, contains two billiards tables, wireless set, piano, dominoes, draughts, chocolate and mineral waters, the latter two which, of course, we pay for. The recreation room is open from 10 o'clock in the morning till ten o'clock at night, and all we pay is one penny each week for our electricity bill. It is our own club and no outsiders are allowed in unless permission is obtained from our officials.'

Topical Times, Footballer's Weekly Diary, 1937

For many professional players down the years, the principal problem when coming to a strange town to work with strangers was coping with loneliness and boredom. Until the 1960s or so, the majority of towns and cities in the United Kingdom provided little by way of diversion other than public houses and cinemas during the week, and church on Sunday. Without television or radio, life beyond the football pitch could be bleak.

No surprise then, that many of the first professionals insisted on being allowed to work during the week at a job or trade. It wasn't simply a matter of money. As Bob Holmes of Preston North End put it in 1910: 'Wherever possible I think every footballer should have some business interest outside of the game itself. It relieves the monotony and is the unceasing enemy of listlessness, the most insidious of football microbes.'

David Steele of Tottenham Hotspur put it thus in 1909 in *The Red Letter*: 'When you come to think of it, in the playing season, the life of a professional may be said to be lived on the pitch. Day after day he has to turn up at the training ground to put in practice, and when it is over he has no time to journey much further than the local music hall or the corner of the street.'

The temptations laid before players in the early years of the century may have been limited but they were potent, drink and betting being the principals. The earliest popular image of the pro player confirms this. 'Stiffy the Goalkeeper' made his bow in 1906 in a Fred Karno sketch called 'The Football Match'. Stiffy was a hapless character played by a great music-hall comic, Harry Weldon. Prone to drink (Stiffy kept a flagon of beer behind his net), he was the object of a bribery attempt to influence a match result for betting purposes.

Apart from Weldon's comic genius, the continued success of 'The Football Match' was attributed to its realism. The training quarters were set in a pub, much skulduggery took place in 'smoke rooms', while the appearance on stage of real live football greats made the illusion all the more compelling. One of the most popular would be Jimmy Crabtree, a star with Aston Villa and England during the 1890s and a great friend of Weldon's. In March 1908, Crabtree died from the effects of alcoholism. Weldon would succumb to the effects of drink some years later. 'The Football Match' was more real than the patrons knew.

Alcohol had caused the professional game problems from the very start. From the 1880s on, too many players over-indulged. As the anonymous 'Football Secretary' writing in *Thomson's Weekly News* in 1901 put it: 'Footballers have a weakness for celebrating victories in their own way. It is often a case of "deliver me from my friends" for "friends" (so-called) spoil many a player; they're ever ready to treat him to a drink and then he ofttimes knows not when to stop.'

Some top internationals were even suspected of taking to the field while still inebriated. The 'erratic' behaviour during the 1898 England–Scotland international of Jimmy Cowan, the best centre-half Scotland produced in the 1890s, caused a scandal. Steve Bloomer, England's greatest player before the First World War, was regularly fined for reporting to the ground still 'under the influence'. Inevitable, perhaps, as many football clubs were centred on public houses. From the 1890s, for instance, Manchester City's players' headquarters was the Hyde Road Hotel, which backed on to the club's Hyde Road ground itself. For almost twenty years after the founding of the club, players changed in the pub and walked along a pathway beneath a railway arch to reach the pitch.

In the first decade of the twentieth century, professionals tried to convince the public that times had changed. Harry Reason wrote in *The Red Letter* in 1908: 'Footballers can be and are as good citizens as any other class of men. Our life is not made up of drinking, squandering our hard-earned money and betting. We have something else to live for.'

Two years earlier, however, Guy Thorne, a prominent writer on sport, dealt with the subject in an under-cover documentary-style article called 'Sport and Drink' for *Fry's Magazine*, a popular and influential periodical aimed principally at the leisured middle-classes and owned and edited by CB Fry, a great amateur soccer player.

Thorne told of visiting a large northern hotel and spending a quiet evening in his room: 'Next morning after breakfast, I smoked my pipe in the bar parlour. At one side of the place was a counter which formed a barrier between it and the ordinary tap-room. Three young and powerful men came in – it was about 9.30 in the morning. They asked the barmaid for a drink I had never heard of – "three warm sodas, please". The girl opened three bottles of soda, poured some hot water into each glass, and gave it to the customers. When they had gone I asked her what was the meaning of this. "Oh," she said, "there was a football supper last night. These lads were all drunk. They often come for a warm soda in the morning; it sobers them."'

Thorne continued, 'Drunkenness, distinct drunkenness, was very common. The members of the two teams were often the core of a welter of riot. The players themselves were treated by their admirers until they became intoxicated. Quarrels of all sorts were of almost momentary occurrence. "I hate all big sporting days," she said. "You've no idea what we girls have to put up with. They all seem to go mad. But there, the takings are enormous, so I suppose sport's good for trade!"'

Thorne's article, though melodramatic, revealed a problem that many club directorates were aware of. Some tried to counter it by providing social spaces for players where they could gather away from the prying eyes of fans and where, hopefully, they would eschew drinking and gambling.

Tottenham Hotspur would take the lead in catering for their players' needs for entertainment in a controlled environment. In 1905, the writer CE Hughes visited the ground for *Fry's Magazine*. Spurs were then being managed by John Cameron, the enlightened, intelligent man who had begun the first Players' Union before the turn of the century, and who was well aware of the pitfalls awaiting vulnerable young men in the big city. The social club was situated in a small building close by White Hart Lane railway station: 'Once past a padlocked door you will find that this tin tabernacle affair is in reality a fine large room – a comfortable homely-looking room, with two fireplaces, two billiard tables, and, in the corner, a small bar. It is the "Spurs" social club.

'On your right as you enter is a smaller room for reading and writing, round the larger room are seats, and little tables for chess, draughts and cards – solo whist, for preference. On the walls are pictures – some of them portraits of the team. Of these, the one over the mantelpiece at the end is a large-sized portrait of the men who won the cup – an excellent specimen of photography. Near by there is a bookcase, well stocked with readable books, the gift of Mr G Cox, one of the directors. In a glass case on one of the side walls is a stuffed squirrel, captured at Chingford, while the team was there in training.

'Across the far corner from the door is a bar, presided over by the major. Troop-Sergeant-Major Sinton served for twenty-one years in the First Royal Dragoons, and he has been the club steward ever since the room was opened some five years ago. He rules over his small dominion with a combination of dignity and joviality, and a

Above: Inside the 'Spurs' Social Club. Not only do the members of the Tottenham Hotspur team meet on the field, but they enjoy one another's company at the Club's social headquarters adjacent to the ground. Here the comforts of a home are provided, and the men may read, write, play billiards or cards, as fancy takes them. Needless to say, the club is greatly appreciated.

Below: Shooting at a pocket often follows shooting at a goal.

CB Fry's Magazine, 1906.

pride in the things under his charge which would make any social gathering a success.'

However, it's clear such places were rare up and down the country although, in 1905, Woolwich Arsenal, busy re-building their Plumpstead ground, planned to include, 'rooms where the men of the Arsenal team may read, or write or talk or play billiards or cards. It will contain the substantial elements of a social club, which will give the "reds" a bond of union out of working hours which does not at present exist.'

In general, however, football-club economics usually meant that the establishment of players' social areas came a long way down the list of priorities. The ubiquitous billiards room could usually be found tucked away inside the ground somewhere, a shabby, desultory place. Most men, it was hoped, would marry and set up home, thus taking care of their own free time. For many players, both single and married, however, home during the playing season would often consist of a rented room, the footballers' 'digs'.

For married men, 'digs' were only contemplated when it proved too expensive or disruptive to uproot the whole family and move to a new town. Where single players were concerned, however, it was demanded that, unless they were able to live at home with their parents or family of some kind, and be able to get to the ground each day with little trouble, they must live in club-approved lodgings until they married. In 'digs', the young single man could be watched (by the club landlady) and, to some extent, controlled.

Living in digs, a sort of adolescent boarding school life, would start for many players at 15 or 16 years of age, and could be an experience often as difficult as the business of playing itself. Peter Doherty initially suffered from homesickness, having left his home in Ireland to come to Blackpool in 1933, but he eventually came to enjoy it. 'On the Friday before a home game, we would all report at a local hotel for tea. [Manager] Sandy MacFarlane would treat us to a show, and then order us to bed about ten o'clock, rather like a Victorian father. Often, if we were spending the Friday night in the digs, Jack Charles [second team trainer] would call round to make sure that we intended to have an early night. It all made me feel that at last an interest was being taken in me. Gradually, as I got used to the routine, I grew happier and began to settle down. With me in the digs were Sam and Tommy

Jones, and we quickly became firm pals. We neither drank nor smoked, and none of us had a girl: an occasional visit to the pictures suited us perfectly when we wanted an evening out. We were inseparable, and the rest of the lads at Bloomfield Road quickly got into the habit of calling us the 'Three Musketeers'. They would shout, "They don't drink, they don't smoke and they don't go with women. What do they live for?" We three knew the answer to that: it was football.'

Manager Stan Cullis described a similar regime for young players arriving at Wolves in the 1950s: 'As soon as he arrives at Wolverhampton, he will be met at the station by George Noakes, the club's chief scout, or by one of his assistants, and taken to his new home. His landlady will become a "second mother" for she will probably have been on the club's list for several years. We know that her house will provide exactly the right atmosphere for a young footballer, that she will insist that the young man keeps good hours and she will provide him with good food. The lad, in turn, will feel at home immediately, which is a most important factor to anyone starting a new career.

'I could quote several examples of youngsters who have grown up to like their new home so much that they have been reluctant ever to move away. The best-known, perhaps, is Billy Wright, the former England and Wolves captain, who stayed with his original landlady, Mrs Colley, from the time he first came to the club in 1939 until he married Miss Joy Beverley, the singer, nearly twenty years later. Another is provided by Joe Gardiner, the head trainer of the club, who arrived at Molyneux a few months before myself. So far, he hasn't deserted the ranks of the bachelors and he now lives with the son of his original landlady. Altogether the "foster mothers" are a grand bunch who play a valuable part in helping us to establish the condition we require for our players.'

The digs for Manchester United players in the 1950s was a boarding house near Old Trafford, which consisted of two large houses knocked into one, which meant the landlady concerned could cater for up to twenty lodgers. The house was also used by commercial travellers and lorry drivers from time to time. 'It was a relaxed, warm house,' according to Eamon Dunphy, where Bobby Charlton, Duncan Edwards, David Pegg and Tommy Taylor all resided at one point. The club made a point of vetting and approving all such houses where they knew the landladies were 'homely and motherly types'.

One such was Mrs Fullaway, probably the most famous club landlady in the history of British football due to the fact that George Best stayed with her for most of his Manchester United career, and even beyond it. Best's account of arriving in Manchester in early 1962 sums up what must have been the experience for countless thousands of young boys down the century, on the thresholds of their playing careers: 'On the first day after training, we were taken to our digs in Mrs Fullaway's council house in Chorlton, which was another shock. Our room was nice enough but it wasn't home and trying to deal with another change in circumstance was probably too much for us. In one day, we'd already travelled on a boat and an English train for the first time and met all these star footballers. Now we were sitting down to a meal with a strange woman in a city that was a mystery to us. After our tea, we went to our room and locked ourselves in. I don't know why we locked the door, we were hardly going to be attacked by anyone but it just made us feel a little more secure after our day of surprises. There was no TV to watch, no radio to listen to so we just sat on our beds, both feeling over-awed by everything...'

Best and his playing pal Eric McMordie eventually ran away back home to Belfast, not the first youngsters to abscond, according to the club's chief scout. Best returned, however, and settled down: 'Mrs Fullaway did her best to make me feel at home, too, but she did have one irritating habit which, if I hadn't been so shy, I would have told her about. She would come into my bedroom in the morning and, if I wasn't awake, she would tickle my nose to rouse me. It was a horrible way to be woken up and several times I jumped up in shock but she kept on doing it. Manchester United landladies were supposed to operate a strict curfew on their precious charges, which was probably about 10.00 p.m. to 10.30 p.m. in those days. But she didn't say too much if I came in late and, knowing that I would probably be home after the curfew, I got in the habit of leaving my bedroom window open. The man next door was a window cleaner and left his ladders in the little passageway, though he probably worked out why they were often propped up against the wall of our house in the morning.' Mrs Fullaway eventually gave him his own keys.

Due to their unusual working hours and prescribed living quarters, single footballers would tend to spend a lot of their free time together. Wilf McGuiness, an apprentice with Manchester United in the 1950s, remembered: 'We used to go for lunches together to a place called Snack Time. We went out together at night to the cinema and dance halls, to each other's houses and digs and we also went on holiday to Ashington. Eddie Coleman, myself and Bobby Charlton went up there for a week's holiday and then we all went over to Butlin's together…part of growing up.'

Fifty years later, young players continue to prefer one another's company. John Terry of Chelsea had this to say in 1999: 'Manchester United and Leeds have a brilliant team spirit, especially Leeds because of the young players they've got. After training the Leeds players go for something to eat together, which builds team spirit, and that helps on the pitch. They go paint-balling and go-karting and that's something we are trying to do here because it brings the lads together. The young lads like myself, Eidur Gudjohnsen, Jody Morris and Frank Lampard tend to stick together, have a laugh and play little games of one touch. If you are having fun with your teammates, you trust them more. A couple of times here, the lads have come in, trained and then gone their own ways. But sometimes we get everyone together and go for a meal. We went go-karting the other week and are trying to arrange paint-balling. It's good for the team spirit; we came into training the day after go-karting and everyone was buzzing.'

Professional clubs have always been keen to foster such camaraderie and, although unwilling to construct club rooms such as the one at Spurs, they had other ways of keeping the players together. That special 'bond' referred to by Hughes, McGuiness and Terry, that 'spirit of comradeship' so essential to establishing 'team spirit' can also be facilitated by the hours and hours spent cooped up together travelling to matches, preparing for matches, recuperating from matches. It was and still is a rudimentary form of social control.

From very early on in the game's history, pro clubs insisted on regular 'special training': team get-togethers organised in order to prepare for cup matches or away games at holiday times. The 'training' usually took place at comfortable hydros or good hotels and was often little more than a form of athletic purdah. Billy Meredith's tart comment on being inconveniently removed from his home at holiday time summed up the experienced pro's attitude to such excursions: 'Yes, they took us to Norbreck and Buxton but I always thought it a waste of time. Still do. Had to go for long walks to stop stiffening up in armchairs.'

However, 'being with the lads' and all that this entailed – the laughing, joking and playing of pranks – was (and remains) a significant aspect of such trips and often conjures up more nostalgia among ex-pros than memories of winning medals and scoring goals. Much of the humour and fun is fairly juvenile. Here's a moment recalled by Sheffield Wednesday's Frank Bradshaw in Thomson's Weekly News of February 1909: 'I don't know of any club that enters upon special training more light-heartedly, but nonetheless earnestly, than Sheffield Wednesday. As a rule we go round Middlewood every week but instead of coming straight back we generally have a 'boat' race, which is in very truth a great sporting event with us. We are at liberty to construct any kind of craft we choose. It may, in fact, be anything we like. It is usually constructed of elderberrywood, and selected no doubt from a knowledge of the fact that it is practically waterproof. Old John Davis, the assistant trainer, sets our "vessels" off, and the betting at times is very fierce, I can tell you. You have no idea of the fun our weekly contest creates. The shouting and yelling that goes on reminds you for all the world of a swarm of bookies on the racecourse.'

Half a century on and the juvenile fun and games remain remarkably similar. Charlie Williams, with Doncaster Rovers in the 1950s recalls: 'We had some great times skylarking among ourselves. If the lads had been out skylarking and got locked out – we were supposed to be in by twelve – they'd climb in through the back windows. And then they had to find their beds. Generally they'd been dismantled and hidden on tops of wardrobes. Then they'd open their wardrobe door and find somebody else's clothes in there. In a hotel in Plymouth there was a cot on the landing for anyone who arrived with kiddies. Alick Jeffrey was the baby in our team, and one night the lads locked him out. When he was pleading to be let in his room, they chucked him some blankets and said, "Gerrin t'cot".

'In the dressing rooms we used to have some fun. In the winter the lads used to run in with shovelfuls of snow and sling it into the hot bath. And summer or winter there'd always be someone who

Charlie Williams and
Alick Jeffrey entertain
Doncaster Rovers
supporters in 1958.

would run in with a hose and turn it full on to the lads in the hot
bath. Ee…that were cold.'

Thus has developed the specific footballer 'mentality', referred to
here by Arsenal's Alan Smith in 2001 when summing up his fellow
players: 'A loveable, decent breed in the main but sometimes susceptible to outbursts of immaturity. Cosseted from the real world
until they overstep the mark, nothing gets taken too seriously in a
dressing room full of jokes.'

It has been said that although footballers become very worldly at
a comparatively early age, their sense of responsibility and maturity
develops at a somewhat slower pace. The fact is that a player's existence is so highly structured by the club that many players become

dependent on the resulting way of life. This dependency was noted by the 'Football Secretary' as long ago as 1901. In 'Bossing a First Class Club' he wrote: 'Some players require as much looking after as little children, perhaps more so because children can be slapped when they're naughty and footballers can't.' The Secretary continued: 'The railway rides when on tour are often considerable items. Saloons must be booked and the men seen safely inside. I verily believe some of the men would stand and watch their train go out of the station if they were not told every detail. In travelling they get so used to being attended to in every little matter that they have no thought or sense to look for themselves. In one case I know, while the club "sec" was getting tickets two minutes before the train was due to start he found, on his return to the train, only half the number of players therein; the other half — where? He rushed to the refreshment room, bookstall, but "not there my child". In the meantime the train moved off, and the "sec" was left behind. A few minutes later he spotted the remaining four of the players chatting as unconcernedly as possible on the platform on the other side of the station. In such cases, however cross or worried an official may be, he mustn't show it too much, for some footballers are champions at sulking and their play suffers consequently. The only excuse of the wandering ones was that they'd met Tommy What's-his-name and he'd kept them talking!'

Club strategy encouraged, in so many ways, a prolonged adolescence, which is an unusual form of development to impose on competent adults. Indeed, the 'Football Secretary' revealed that, from the very start, players' pranks and behaviour were close to juvenile delinquency. Players often stole things from shops on the way to the ground 'for a laugh'. 'Footballers are ever fond of their little larks. I know it's a fact that some hotel keepers positively refuse to receive football teams. At times, especially after a victory, they're like a lot of madmen let loose, in some cases; on the other hand some are as quiet as lambs. But there's oft-times the "horse-play" of the rougher element to contend with: they're so fond of pouring the cold liquid contents of the water jug over certain of their comrades and such like trifles. A bit of fun is alright; the only difficulty is when players go too far...'

It was rare, however, that such behaviour featured in newspapers. Lurid headlines in *The Red Letter* of 1908 such as 'Why We Burgled The Hotel: Footballers' High Jinks in London' (by goalkeeper George

Whitburn, then of Leyton but with Sunderland on a trip to London) turned out to be no more than a midnight raid on the kitchens of the hotel where the Sunderland team had been staying. The episode ended with little more than a reprimand from the hotel manager.

In 1977 Rotherham United players staying at a hotel also went on the search for food and raided what they thought was a large fridge. It was, in fact, a large oven, roasting ducks on a spit. Two players grabbed at the ducks only to find them too hot. They dropped them on the floor, grease spilling every-where. Finally, they wrapped the ducks in a collection of phone directories and took them back to their rooms. Later, they threw the leftovers on to another guest's car outside. All were banned and fined.

As ex-Leeds and Nottingham Forest player Lee Chapman put it: 'Life was one long quest for laughs and good times. We never burdened ourselves with questions of morality, no matter how insensitive or immature our actions were.'

2. With the lads on tour

'Gazza's on a pre-season tour of Italy. The waiter asks him, "Do you like scampi?" and Gazza replies, "Yes, I like all the Disney movies." True story.'

Eric Hall, football agent, on Paul Gascoigne,
speaking in 2002

The sense of being cut off from normal society, of being enclosed in a special little world all their own, was emphasised when football teams travelled abroad, a regular feature in players' lives from the start of the twentieth century. Players on such tours were, in fact, the very first working-class package tourists. Walter Bull of Tottenham Hotspur, writing on board the *Araguara* heading for Argentina in 1909, felt players deserved the time to relax. 'Some people don't seem to realise the strenuous life the average footballer must nowa-days lead.' He felt the long boat trip would bind the Spurs players together, while many of them 'fully appreciate the opportunity to see a bit of the world'. Continental tours were also an eye-opener, especially the Channel crossing: 'It was a beautiful moonlit night when we crossed to the Hook of Holland and the Spurs spent the night on deck with not a thought of turning into bunks. The concert that was served up that night would have done justice to any house of entertainment...'

Dan Steele, on the same trip, felt that travel broadened the mind. 'If every club were to arrange a foreign tour for its players in the off season we would speedily have our ranks filled with a better class than at present. Mind you, I have nothing to say against the present player as a man. My whole contention is that there is none of us so good that a little rub up occasionally would not make a huge improvement.'

Sam Hardy, on an England international team tour of Austria and Hungary in 1909, apologised to his *Weekly News* readers for not talking about the football: 'For I am rather going to give you my impressions of the countries through which we passed and the people with whom we mingled during the tour.' The train journey was 'every minute an education'. On arrival at Budapest, every player was given a medal bearing the Budapest coat of arms and there was a horse and carriage put at their disposal. However, it was the condition of the people that caused him concern: 'My lot has been cast among the English labouring class and with them I have often brooded over their undoubted grievances...' But looking at the lot of the poor in Hungary: 'I was proud to think that I had been born an Englishman, if only an Englishman of the common kind. Watching the fine types of womanhood carrying produce into the market of Budapest like beasts of burden, no man worthy of the name could help feeling a great horror that this should be so. They live as we lived in primitive times. I know that the footballer is reckoned little more than a machine by the vast majority of Englishmen. But even a footballer, I submit, has some notion of the essentials that go to make up a decent, moral life...'

However, foreign club tours could also encounter various local difficulties. A couple of years later, Tottenham visited Germany and Italy. In Pfzorzheim, after a 3–0 win, the crowd turned on them. Tattersall, a Spurs player, was attacked by a German spectator aided by the Pfzorzheim goalkeeper; stones were thrown and the Spurs chairman was robbed of £15. On the other hand, Bradford City, touring Europe at the same time, encountered no such problems. According to the accompanying journalist, they enjoyed themselves enormously in Zurich. 'Each player received a memento in the form of a large view of Zurich to remind him in the years to come that even his professional football days were not exactly of the "slave order" which many fanatics would have people believe.'

In 1926, the England team toured Canada. Joe Smith of Bolton described how, during the voyage there, the players settled down to a regime of deck quiots, badminton, tennis and shuffleboard and evening dances. There was a small social embarrassment, however: 'Laurie Edwards, our trainer, was the first to be up doing a jazz. The lady asked Laurie what college he graduated at and all poor Laurie could reply was "Wigan".'

Even on the high seas, a certain uncomfortable social reality crept in: 'In the fore part of the ship the passengers are all foreigners, travelling third class. One night we had a trip along to break the monotony. We went into a room where all the men were playing cards while all the womenfolk seemed down and out. We waited a little while, having a joke in our own sweet way, when somebody shouted, "They are all knifers". "What do you mean?" we asked. The reply was, "When you see one put his hand in his back pocket he is going for his knife." The boys were all eyes and watched carefully until one of the dagos dived his hand in his pocket (to get some money out I think). That was enough to give the boys the knife cue and off they shot in the dark, two up and two down the steps till they arrived back at their own quarters.'

As the political mood on the continent began to alter for the worse, so English teams began to receive a less than happy welcome. In 1929, Newcastle United were in Italy, where their behaviour and demeanour were criticised by the local press. At home, the *Weekly News* reported on allegations that the Newcastle players were brutal and unsportsmanlike during games, that they weren't taking the tour seriously, that they behaved derisively towards the crowd, and even took to the field with several players 'in a deplorable condition'. The Newcastle players, for their part, were said to be disgusted with the reception they received and with the tour in general. Because the British National Anthem was booed, the players responded by walking off the pitch when the Italian anthem was played. The Italians tried to stop the players leaving and various scuffles took place. After the game, local Black Shirts (Fascisti) surrounded the team charabanc to prevent demonstrators getting at the players. 'One of our players set the fireworks going when he made a derisive gesture to the crowd. A Fascisti officer immediately pulled out a revolver and pointed it straight at the player's head...'

After the war, the tours and the culture shocks resumed. In 1948, Southampton made the last such boat trip abroad, travelling to Brazil. From then on, teams would travel by air. The Brazil tour was interesting because it demonstrated how far pro players still had to travel socially. The team were in First Class accommodation. However, they made such a commotion on the first morning as they made their way up from their First Class quarters on the Lower Deck to their training area up near the funnel, 'running up the stairs, bouncing their balls', that other passengers complained. They had to find a less obtrusive route.

They also opted out of eating in the First Class dining room. Ted Meech, their trainer, explained: 'They're only ordinary fellows, these footballers. The upper society, some very wealthy people, big meat barons, used to travel in those ships, had dinner at eight. [The play-ers] wanted to eat at five o'clock. They were hungry. They were just young lads kicking a ball about. They didn't want to wait. On top of that, people in the First Class all dressed up [in more formal attire than the] blazers and club tie. They felt a little bit out of place, a big mob of them, coming into the dining room. I think a lot of these upper-crust people looked down on them a bit, because they weren't exactly quiet when they moved about.'

They did otherwise endear themselves to those passengers whom they entertained with exhibitions of their coach's favourite form of training: head-tennis. The team suffered, however, from the effects of over-eating, which was blamed on the dietary leap from the strict war-time food rationing at home to the plentiful amounts of rich food available at sea. The ship's waiters (many of them Southampton fans) invited them to 'go through the menu card'. This was not what athletes required, especially as the facilities on board for training were rudimentary. Pampered and unfit, the Southampton players arrived in Brazil to be shocked by the poverty they saw. The writer observed that, 'notwithstanding the depriva-tions of his early teens, Ted Bates, then a Southampton player, had never previously come in contact with real poverty. It shook him up at the time – the contrast between people.'

When teams travelled to the USA, as Sunderland's 'Team of all the Talents' did in June 1955, yet another factor made itself clear: the contrast between their 'celebrity' status at home and their virtual anonymity in the wider world of entertainment. Sunderland player Ken Chisholm, after telling his readers breathlessly that the players were given an allowance each day and 'allowed to eat wherever we wished', wrote: 'Ted Purdon and I had a wonderful night out before leaving New York. We gate-crashed a big dance called the "Bal Fantastique". We met a policeman on the door who had Scottish grandparents. He told us how to get in through the kitchen of the hotel and even met us inside to guide us into the hall where the dance was being held. Tickets for the dance cost $25! Marilyn Monroe, Dane Clark and hosts of other film, radio, stage and TV personalities were there. The costumes – and lack of them – made the Chelsea Arts Ball look like a Sunday School outing. Luckily we were wearing our club blazers and nobody paid us the slightest attention…'

All in all, throughout the 1950s, one still has the impression that players travelling abroad were learning something about the world around them. Jackie Milburn of Newcastle United was in Germany in 1955 and was struck by the fact that, 'many of the thousands of people employed clearing the bomb rubble and repairing roads in Berlin are women. We were amazed at the way in which they can use a pick and shovel…' Wilf McGuinness described the value of overseas tours as an England schoolboy international thus: 'Going together as friends and going around cities and having new experiences – like seeing they had trams in Zurich, which we didn't have here in those days. They were driving on the right-hand side of the road. These were things that stuck in our minds. Seeing various things and trying to explain to taxi drivers or people where we wanted to go in a foreign language. I always tell the story of the hotel where they put lettuce on the side plate, and I didn't know if you should eat it before the meal, during or after, you know, things like that. And our first "crème caramel" – what was it like? These sorts of experiences – cultural, definitely cultural…and the duvets, we didn't have duvets at home. I always remember thinking, "What's this on the bed? Where's the blankets?"'

There was also still a sense that they were somewhat privileged to be given such opportunities, in stark contrast to their working-class peers. Nat Lofthouse of Bolton Wanderers remembered a trip from the 1950s: 'My team was going to South Africa free for nine weeks. I'd left my house at half past seven to be picked up by the coach at the bottom of the road. There's a works down there and the men were rolling in. Half past seven, that was, and I was there with my cases going to South Africa for nine weeks, all paid with £2 a day spending money.'

3. Over the top

'As part of a professional sports team, you can quickly lose your grip on reality. You're immersed in your own little world. You train together, travel together, totter from bars together. The talk is always of sport and sportsmen. Or sex. You don't watch news programmes or read anything except the back pages of tabloid newspapers. You don't go to movies, relying on your limited stock of favourite DVDs to play at home or on a laptop.'

Simon Hughes, Daily Telegraph, December 2001

Over the last couple of decades, the naïve fun and games of previous generations of players have been replaced by gratuitous acts of violence and drunken stupidity. Drinking and 'clubbing' would appear to have escalated out of control. Indeed, it's almost as though the 1980s and 1990s were a re-run of the 1880s and 1890s, that infamous period of unlicensed debauchery and bad behaviour that set professional football off on such a bad start.

Although it might appear unfair to condemn a whole profession for the behaviour of a few, as we shall see, a certain set of behavioural traits can be traced back to the unusual socialisation and control of players within football clubs. Lee Chapman attempted to rationalise the debauched behaviour of footballers on tour by suggesting that because players today had 'all the benefits of education, money and foreign travel', they simply enjoyed 'regressing'. Terry Butcher put it more simply: 'I'd get absolutely slaughtered. I was a young idiot, crazy, bananas. Under Bobby Robson at Ipswich, I'd be fined every year, without fail, on the pre-season tour in Holland.'

However, it is not just excessive alcohol that has characterised the most recent examples of player excesses. The treatment of others outside the game, women in particular, seems to have plumbed new depths. Lee Chapman described how, in the 1980s on a flight to Barbados, one particular fellow player, after trying unsuccessfully to 'chat up' two girls, slipped sleeping tablets into their drinks and then sexually assaulted them while they slept. Another incident, recounted almost deadpan, involved the public humiliation of a drunken girl by a large part of the team.

Chapman felt that single players, 'exercise what they believe is their right to do whatever they want with whoever they want. In the somewhat male chauvinistic world of football, single players especially treat women with scant regard. For many, they [women] are there to be used and abused at every opportunity. Although it is something that happens in most walks of life, it tends to be much more exaggerated in the world of football. Single footballers have a great attraction for the opposite sex, and opportunities are plentiful. Who could blame any hot-blooded single male for taking full advantage of this situation?'

But even Chapman's unsavoury tales from the 1980s rather pale in the face of contemporary antics. In the summer of 2000, Rio Ferdinand and Frank Lampard, at the time with West Ham United, plus Kieron Dyer of Newcastle United, made a pornographic video on a drunken holiday in Ayia Napa, Cyprus. The film showed young girl fans in degrading sex scenes, which were secretly filmed by the three players. One holidaymaker who became a part of the player's party claimed: 'They were drinking themselves into oblivion most days. They treated the women who flocked around them like pieces of meat.' Also on the video were Chelsea stars Jody Morris, 21, and Michael Duberry, 24, both of whom would feature in later high-profile scandals.

Whether at home or abroad, incidents involving drunken players at all levels of the game proliferated through the 1990s, coinciding with the sudden increase in levels of remuneration brought about by the formation of the Premier League and the vastly increased revenues paid to clubs by TV companies. Gary Speed, Dean Saunders, Jason Dozzell, Chris Kiwomya, Paul Ince, Mark Hughes, Lee Sharpe, Ray Parlour, Tony Adams, Terry Phelan, Mark Crossley and many, many others fought with one another or with patrons of night clubs and bars, smashed up hotel rooms, littered pizza parlours with glass and let off fire-extinguishers with tiresome regularity. The catalogue of woe reached its peak with the vicious assault on an Asian teenager in which several drunken Leeds players became embroiled in 2000, to be followed soon afterwards by the disgraceful behaviour of various young Chelsea players who drunkenly mocked and abused American travellers in an airport lounge following the World Trade Center attack.

The succession of such incidents prompted massive media coverage and various attempts were made to explain why young players were behaving in such a fashion. Paul Merson of Arsenal and Aston Villa, whose fight against alcoholism and an addiction to betting made him a frequently consulted expert on such matters, felt it was a matter of increased media exposure and public resentment of the wages players were now earning: 'The drinking is no worse than before but the focus is bigger. When we were winning trophies at Arsenal we used to go out every Tuesday without fail and get well tanked up and it was never in the papers. Nowadays you could play for the worst team in the world and still get the headlines if caught drinking. I wasn't a wine-bar merchant, drinking bottles of champagne or being jack-the-lad. Now footballers are earning £30,000 a week and most of the stories are about them going out drinking, burning £20 notes and showing off. That's why people get the hump.'

Alan Smith, a former team-mate of Merson's at Arsenal, agreed: 'Is it a new phenomenon? Not really. Unseemly incidents have always happened when footballers hit the town. The West Ham player who [recently] relieved himself on the bar of a London nightspot is not the first to unzip his fly in public. A former team-mate of mine, an absolute menace under the influence, always preferred filling up a pint glass to making the tiresome trip to the gents. Revolting, yes. But par for the course.'

A lead article in the *Sunday Telegraph* recently linked the poor behaviour to professional players' deprived social origins, poor education levels and a 'soccer world where any kind of intellectual curiosity is treated with suspicion'. Writer Kevin Myers suggested that the problem was peculiarly British: 'The footballers are themselves not to blame for this intellectual dysfunctionality. They are merely very visible representatives of their class and its limitations; and thereby, the society from which that class emerges.'

Tony Adams of Arsenal, another recovering alcoholic, pointed to an overly tolerant attitude within the game towards such behaviour: 'What's wrong with society? I used to go into a pub and smash the gaff up. Yet somehow there seems to be a feeling that that is not as strange as slipping into a church and getting a bit of peace. Where are we going?'

More compelling connections were made, however, with the violent behaviour of various American pro athletes. In 2000 alone, an American pro footballer was murdered by his wife while another was on trial for shooting his pregnant girlfriend while already on drugs charges. One basketball star was charged with reckless driving after crashing his Porsche and killing a team-mate (they were racing), while another was acquitted of 'driving while impaired' and injuring another team-mate. New York Jets footballer 'Jumbo' Elliott was awaiting trial for assault; one former team-mate had pleaded guilty to third-degree assault; and another had recently served ninety days in prison for a drink-driving accident that resulted in the death of a woman.

The reasons for such disasters appeared straightforward. Here were young men from disadvantaged backgrounds who made sums of money which they could only once have dreamed of. Accorded with an exaggerated sense of self-esteem and granted physical and monetary power to accomplish whatever they want, they have things their own way for their entire competitive lives. It is therefore not surprising that trouble erupts, often when they are out in public with a group of friends when drink or drugs have eroded their judgement even further.

The 'friends' syndrome has been particularly noticeable in many of the more extreme incidents. The last thing a sports star from a poor background wants to do is walk away from his old friends, even when the latter are leading him into trouble. The Leeds United and England star Rio Ferdinand, no stranger to trouble as we have seen, admitted in 2002: 'I'm very passionate about my roots [his native Peckham, south London, and the tough Friary Estate where he grew up]. When I was younger we always used to say you must never sell out, however successful you might become. That's why I'm still close to my friends.'

While all the above rationalisations have value, they ignore the way the profession itself leaves so many young players psychologically vulnerable. The writer Germaine Greer, seeking to explain the 'suicidally wild behaviour of players when off duty' has noted how professional players are considered 'pieces of property' owned by their club. The players are, 'afraid of managers and coaches, afraid of each other, aware that they can be knocked off the gravy train by something as trivial as a hamstring. They also suffer the phallic anxiety that afflicts men who, as athletes, become identified with the body and thus feminised. They are dominated and often humiliated in the workplace by managers and coaches, not to mention the psychological carnage fans do.'

Oddly enough, however, despite the existence of such social and psychological regimentation, few people with responsibility within football clubs stand up to athletes when they err. Following the porn video scandal, a Newcastle United spokesman announced simply that Keiron Dyer would meet manager Bobby Robson 'for talks': 'Kieron Dyer will have a word with the manager on his return for pre-season training. We're not happy with these headlines. I have to accept that something is going on. These headlines are not helpful to him or his career.' Which barely begins to approach the main issues at all.

Two years later, the Welsh international and Newcastle United forward Craig Bellamy was cautioned for being drunk and disorderly, and for an alleged incident of common assault on a 21-year-old women in the early hours of the morning. Bobby Robson, the club manager, seemed unsure as to what line to take on players who misbehaved: 'We've hammered them with fines. They're more than stupid if they don't learn. But most of the players are good guys. I respect them. I admire them. What happened last week was a shock to me. But they've got to go out. Monks don't play football. They're young, they're single, they're good-looking, they've got money. They need a night out. They are stuck to a ball and chain 72 hours before every kick-off. That's the way it is in this industry. Some of them – not all – they go out with their mates or their wives or their girlfriends, drink eight pints and get semi-drunk. We warn them. We say, why punish your body twice in a day? Playing football in this hectic game makes great demands. The power and the pace are sky high. They come in exhausted and go out three hours later. Why do that?'

Bobby Robson, considered something of a football sage these days, was born in the 1930s and started playing in the 1950s. Throughout his long career, the money available to players never approached the levels seen today, and though he may be a kind and sensible man in many ways, the world into which his young players disappear when the match is over is one he cannot possibly comprehend. Robson, and the generations of players who came after him and who now manage clubs, coach players, and 'spot' youngsters, grew up in a culture of almost total neglect where the education of young players was concerned. It is not surprising, then, that when players become involved in serious drink and drug problems, it often seems that they are left to seek salvation for themselves. The football club transforms and moulds them into something useful on the field but, all too often, the same institution remains on the periphery when things go badly wrong. Those in control of clubs are too unaware or unwilling to accept that they have helped create the problems. Apart from fining players, clubs usually overlook antisocial behaviour as being nothing to do with them and thus reinforce destructive patterns of behaviour.

The influx of foreign managers and coaches into England has put the issue into an international context, however. When he first arrived in the late 1990s, Gerard Houllier, the French manager of Liverpool, alluded to the difficulty of ridding the team of its corrosive drink culture. In other countries, he explained, a typical young player reaching first-team status would become even more professional than before in terms of his eating, drinking and other habits, whereas in England his counterpart would be more likely to celebrate such progress by succumbing to the lure of additional nights on the town.

It has long been the case that continental clubs have concerned themselves with the day-to-day lives of the young men in their care. It started before the Second World War. Jimmy Hogan, writing in *Topical Times* in June 1929, while explaining that professionals in Spain earned considerably more than their counterparts in England, went on to point out how aware clubs were of 'the danger of a man suddenly earning a great deal of money and going off the rails'. To avoid such a state of affairs in Spain, Hogan explained, many important clubs such as Barcelona, Bilbao, Espanol, Real Madrid, etc. introduced the system of players living and dining in the clubhouse on the ground so that they were under the watchful eye of the trainer. He added, curiously, but significantly, 'I don't think this would suit the British player in general; it seems to me a case of the slave's life, despite the fact that it enables a man not only to live a decent life but also helps him to save very much money.'

The Spanish clubs were taking care of young men from the very start of their careers, planning their daily routines, looking at what they ate and how they behaved. As Hogan put it, 'Every club has its youngsters' teams who are reared as professional players.' Perhaps their concern was prompted by the fact that the wages for top players were far in excess of their peers. British players, though paid well, were never earning salaries that threatened to unbalance their social lives.

Micky Burns, Chief Executive of the PFA's education programmes, is trying to revolutionise the education and training of today's young professionals through the adidas Football Scholarship. He has, inevitably, experienced resistance from 'the old school' within football clubs, who to this very day remain unconvinced that education has anything to do with football. 'I come across the old adage from ex-players who were brought up in the traditional way that "it never did me any harm." But times change.'

Burns has talked of the development of the 'whole person' being vital in producing the modern day footballer. 'Today's players need to know more than how to play football to the best of their ability. A 17-year-old can be thrust into the international arena, but has anyone taught him about how to behave when he's representing his country or how to conduct himself in a five-star hotel in Brazil? The answer is no. Yet all this comes with the overall education package which combines social skills with academia, all allied to the football elements.'

Following drink-driving convictions and the Cyprus video controversy, not to mention regular ill-judged appearances in London's more exclusive nightclubs, Rio Ferdinand admitted: 'Since joining Leeds United I think I've come of age, both on and off the field. I now realise just how much responsibility I have, living my life in the public eye. I needed to get away from where I'd grown up. I needed to be on my own and gain some independence, and as a player and a person that has been a huge benefit to me.' What's more, his involvement with the Damilola Taylor Trust and a number of other charities has enabled him to maintain his links with his community in a positive way. 'When Damilola was killed in Peckham, his father got in touch with me through the Professional Footballers' Association and it was all I could do to help. It was terrible what happened and I just wanted to try to put something back into the community.'

4. Handbags at six paces?

'Football's "Love Birds" Get Her Goat'
'The only thing that stops me becoming an out-and-out soccer supporter is that I'm often nauseated by the hugging and fond embracing that occur directly a man scores. Be men on the field, you professional footballers! Leave the "love-making" until you meet your sweethearts.'

Letter from a football fan to Weekly News, April 1957

In the mid-1970s, when the Disciplinary Committee of the FA decided not to accept a recommendation from the Match and Ground committee that footballers who 'kiss and cuddle' should be charged with bringing the game into disrepute, David Lacey in the *Guardian* commented, 'presumably love bites would be another matter'. *Gay Magazine*, meanwhile, telephoned its congratulations to the FA at Lancaster Gate.

Open displays of emotion are now accepted on the pitch. Gazza's tears saw to that. The old-fashioned firm and manly handshake following a goal has long since disappeared beneath piles of squirming, gyrating bodies. Hugging, embracing and kissing are the norm. Even, on occasions, simulations of the sexual act. This is peculiar when off-the-field the taboos concerning homosexuality have locked professional football in a 1950s time-warp.

Until recent times, the subject of homosexuality was simply not mentioned in relation to football and footballers. The 'somewhat male chauvinistic world' of the pro footballer referred to by Lee Chapman has steadfastly refused to join the rest of civilised society in embracing, metaphorically speaking, the gay revolution. The fear of scape-goating and 'mickey-taking', such an integral feature of dressing room banter and team 'bonding', ensured that an individual's sexual identity was kept rigidly within accepted boundaries.

For individuals who are a little different from the crowd, professional football can be a cruelly insular world. There is little room for overt sensitivity in the macho environment of the dressing room, the practice pitch and the bar. Dave Bassett explained: 'On the sexual side of things a bit of banter could well go on. You might find that a player who has been dumped by a bird gets a bit of stick and if a player has a quirky sexuality some of the other players might see that as a weakness that could be exploited.'

Indeed, so susceptible are players to suggestions that they might be gay that reactions are often extreme. When Robbie Fowler made physical gestures at Graham Le Saux during a Premiership match in 2001 suggesting that Le Saux was gay, or indulged in gay sex, Le Saux's response was violent enough to get him dismissed.

It's still a curiosity that the professional football world should seek to exclude the idea of homosexuality as completely as it does. Pro footballers are obviously attractive to other men. Gay magazines and websites regularly discuss the relative appeal of particular players. Their bodies, when they are in their 'working' clothes, are on display in a way that other men's are not, which perhaps increases their anxiety not to be seen as sexual objects.

There is something in the game's steadfast inability to face the issue that reminds one of the objections made by the military to the decision to allow openly gay men and women to enlist. There is also the suspicion that the platoon's (or the squad's) ability to fight could be undermined by the presence of homosexuals. Manager Alan Smith admitted in 2000 that he would have signed a particular gay player (had it not been revealed that the man had AIDS) 'but I would have had to seriously consider the reaction from the rest of my squad, both for his happiness and team spirit. I think it would have been very hard for him to come through it all.'

Perhaps there is a link here with the long-established 'taboo' in football concerning sexual activity on the eve of a match. A manager can exclude females fairly easily along with the distractions they bring. This would not be so easy with a gay player in the dressing room or in the team hotel. Moreover, it has recently been established that home teams win more often because the levels of the sex hormone testosterone are fifty per cent higher when players are about to play a home match, the reaction being linked to a primal instinct among [male] footballers to defend home territory. Perhaps a gay player would act as a destabilising element in such a highly charged environment.

Perhaps, too, in football's hysterical response to the issue, one can detect a latent fear of what passes for 'good clean fun' in the dressing room? That compelling camaraderie that excludes women almost entirely, and which later can so easily be translated into unfeeling abuse of women, as described by Lee Chapman.

It's claimed that there are many gay footballers playing in the Premiership. An Arsenal season ticket holder and chairman of Stonewall, the gay pressure group, claimed in January 2000 that, 'I know of a number of closeted gay footballers but because of the way the issue is treated in this profession they do not wish that to be known'.

In March 2001, the publicist Max Clifford related how the chairmen of two football clubs had come to him 'worried about certain top players', and asked him to set about creating a false (macho) identity for those particular unnamed stars.

The penalties for 'coming out' are severe. Justin Fashanu, who played for eleven British clubs between 1978 and 1993, was gay and in 1990 he admitted it. Many people within the English national game had already found him hard to cope with. In 1981, Brian Clough, manager of Nottingham Forest, bought Justin from Norwich City for £1 million, the first black footballer to command such a figure. At the time Fashanu was in a heterosexual relationship but was soon drawn to Nottingham's gay scene. When Clough learned of his gay leanings, he suspended him. When he turned up for training, Clough had the police escort him from the premises.

Clough claimed that he didn't like Fashanu's 'shiftiness' and his articulate persona 'made it difficult for me to accept that Fashanu was genuine and one of us'. It was peculiar that Brian Clough, with his penchant for kissing all and sundry on the slightest of pretexts, should have been so aghast at discovering Fashanu's secret. Indeed, he likened it to something one consumes, famously asking Fashanu what it was he expected to get from a baker's (bread), or a butcher's (meat) and so why was he visiting gay bars?

Fashanu was a complicated and tragic figure. Bisexual rather than gay, he hung himself in 1998 in a garage in Shoreditch while under investigation for allegedly assaulting a 17-year-old man in the USA. Afterwards, John Fashanu, his footballing brother, told the BBC that he regretted his 'selfish reaction' in 1990 when Justin became the first and only professional footballer to identify himself publicly as a gay man – a reaction that ended all communication between the once-close brothers for seven years. Peter Tatchell, spokesperson for the British direct gay action group OutRage! and who was close friends with Justin in the 1980s, said that Fashanu had been devastated by his brother's public denunciation after he came out, and that Justin had never recovered from the 'betrayal'.

The betrayal cannot be limited to his brother. Fashanu was a courageous man, who fought to overcome many adversities – abandonment by his parents to an orphanage when aged just six, racial prejudice and homophobia. His death was greeted with silence by the game in general, as though it was relieved that a man considered at best an embarrassment was off the scene. In 1994, Justin wrote: 'I have been greatly criticised for coming out in the tabloid press. Many people thought I did it just for the money. I suppose they have never stopped to consider that my world is based around the Sun and Daily Star readers; the football world has that kind of mentality. I genuinely thought that if I came out in the worst newspapers and remained strong and positive about being gay, there would be nothing more they could say. Of course, I was wrong.'

Chapter 7

Football and the Mind

1. The fear factor

'For weeks and weeks I was forced to sit in the stand on match days. Why, I don't know to this day. I became fed up to the teeth. When I was put on the transfer list I'd have been glad to go anywhere for a change. The whole thing was a mystery to me, but it was plain that the club had very little use for me. I kept my chin up as well as I could, but despite myself I became miserable and lost confidence.'

Frank McDonough of Blackpool, writing in Topical Times in the late 1930s

Professional football clubs are curious places. One the one hand, they like to present themselves as institutes of modern enlightenment, where scientifically controlled diets and training techniques are the norm. On the other hand, they also celebrate an occupational culture that uses fear and even violence to galvanise and motivate its workforce.

To be a professional footballer can thus mean being part of a world of uncertainty and manipulation. There are unexpected and mystifying changes of fortune as one struggles to cope with the conflicting expectations and demands of managers, team-mates and fans.

In 1938 an anonymous player wrote of the bullying tactics of managers beneath the headline 'I condemn managers for'. He explained, 'My experience is that it is hell on earth sometimes for players when clubs are having a bad time. I remember one time when things were going wrong for one of my clubs. Our manager was worried. I could understand that – he had to deliver the goods. But he went absolutely the wrong way about bringing an improvement. He started bullying us: treated us as if we were no longer human beings. He made team changes wholesale. The team was chopped about so much we became like tin soldiers. We were knocked down and stuck up again just as the club wished.'

Sometimes the methods employed are so remarkably crude, they border on the manic. Lee Chapman witnessed this extraordinary incident involving Brian Clough in the Nottingham Forest dressing room at half time:

'All the players were sitting down with their heads bowed low, after a disappointing first half. Cloughie approached Nigel [Jemson], and stood directly in front of him. "Stand up!" he commanded. Nigel obediently stood up. "Have you ever been hit in the stomach, son?" he enquired. As soon as he had said no, Cloughie delivered a forceful blow to his midriff. Nigel doubled up in pain and let out an agonised groan. "Now you have, son!" and with that he turned away.'

Clough's unusual approach was tolerated by players because he was successful. When he stepped out of the club into the real world, he found that his behaviour was considered unacceptable. Cuffing two young fans around the ear as they ran on to the pitch brought about legal action for assault. Had it been players he was hitting, the incident might have entered the pantheon of 'Cloughie' legends.

Fights on the training ground, though common, are rarely discussed in public, which is as it should be. Flare-ups between young men involved in an intensely physical sport are inevitable but rarely cause lasting damage. Terry Venables was probably the first player to admit openly that such incidents occur, when he revealed that he had punched 'hard man' Dave Mackay during training at Spurs. Wimbledon Football Club, of course, made a virtue out of training ground 'bundles', claiming they helped build the necessary team-spirit essential for success.

Where managers and players are concerned, however, the abuse is usually verbal. The crude bellowing of Manchester United's Alex Ferguson is generally held up as the exemplar. Many lesser managers clearly feel such techniques work, as with Barry Fry: 'Sometimes I swear at 'em, sometimes I put me arm around 'em and tell 'em how good they are even if they're crap. If they sulk, you lose 'em. I remember Jeff Astle, famous Jeff Astle, playing for me at Dunstable. We were 3–0 down at half time. There was a knock on the dressing room door and a lady brought in a tray full of teas. So I've turned round and kicked the tray of teas all over him. I yelled, "None of you deserve a cup of tea! Get out! You're *****useless, the lot of you!"

'They had to stand on the pitch outside while the other team were having tea and all that. But we won 5–3, and when Astle scored his third he came over to me and went like that. [Fry stuck up two delighted fingers.] I said to 'im: "Jeff, you can do that to me all you like. But this is just what I wanted. I'm thrilled."'

Thus, physical and verbal attacks would seem to be common-place in the tight-knit claustrophobic world of the professional football club, a world in which players are not encouraged to answer back. When they do, fines and suspensions are often the result. Like well-disciplined 'squaddies', they tend to jump to attention whenever reprimanded by 'the Boss', no matter what their age and standing in the game.

Alec Chaplin, who played for Fulham in the 1920s, could still recall some sixty years later how the team would stand in a line in the corridor outside the dressing rooms on the morning after a poor display, no one being willing to enter first and face the wrath of manager Phil Kelso.

The story is told of Dean Saunders, a multi-million pound, 30-year-old Welsh international footballer and 'star' for Aston Villa. Following a morning session at Aston Villa's Bodymoor Heath

MY 10 BIGGEST GROUSES

BY A PLAYER

1—There's not enough money in the game. Ten years is an average life. We ought to be able to retire on savings then.

2—So-called stars are over-fussed. There are eleven men in a team.

3—There are too many " cooks " in most clubs. Managers, directors, trainers, and fans, all tell us how to play.

4—The transfer laws are against the player.

5—Routine training is ridiculous. Each man by physique and temperament is different. Routine often spells boredom.

6—Foreign tours! The directors get a holiday. We get overtime work at close season wages.

7—Too many " private life " rules in clubs. So long as our form doesn't suffer, what has our home life to do with managers and public ?

8—Club favouritism! Certain players can't do wrong.

9—Petty restrictions. We mustn't motor, mustn't ride bikes, mustn't dance, mustn't do any bally thing.

10—Refs. who attempt humiliation as a weapon. Schoolmaster types are noxious.

BY A REFEREE

1—The club report system. There are many sports but lots of " narks." No power at all should rest in the latter's hands. We don't want anyone in our dressing-rooms!

3—Linesmen who play the gallery with their flags ! You know 'em.

4—Those who ask that referees train same as the players. Can we live on our wages?

5—Players who " smarm." Soft sarcasm is worse than downright temper.

6—Stars who howl like the deuce for " protection." The demand is a reflection on our efficiency;

7—Two, three, or four referee fanatics. Again a reflection.

8—Players who don't know the rules. Ignorance is not bliss.

9—Super-critics who don't know the difference between offside and off-license!

10—Other refs. who regard honours as " influence."

BY A MANAGER

1—Directors who try to manage. Pork-butchering isn't football!

2—Players with " five minutes in the game " who can't be told.

3—Self-called stars who want top wages, benefits, week-ends at home, and the town hall. They squeal to pal directors if denied.

4—Fans who just drop in to tell me, politely, that I'm lucky to escape the hands of the Commissioners in Lunacy.

5—Crowds who want First Division football on junior league gates.

6—People who publicly dictate my method. Without my difficulties they " show me up."

7—Scouts who report on players who are too old, badly behaved, or on transfer lists at large fees.

8—Players who tell me how bad other players are.

9—Players who tell me how good they are.

10—Other clubs who put up their prices when they know I'm desperate. Who ask for " mercy " when they want anything from me.

Topical Times,
11 July 1936.

training ground, he was standing near the entrance of the pavilion drinking a cup of tea and chatting to one of his colleagues. When he had drained the last of his canteen brew, he opened the door of the staff kitchen to hand the empty mug to one of the women inside. Just then, manager Brian Little happened to come out of his office. 'Have you just been in there?' he demanded, frowning. 'Er, um…' said Saunders. 'Well, you'd better not have done,' said Little. 'No, Boss,' said Saunders, meekly accepting a scolding for nearly going into the kitchen with the dinner ladies.

For the majority of pro players, their contracts were designed to keep control of their every waking moment. Len Graham's Millwall contract for 1932, for instance, stipulated that he was not allowed to drive or be driven in a car or motor cycle; that he couldn't live in or run a pub; that he was responsible for his own kit; that he had to be indoors by 10.00 p.m. on evenings prior to match days; he was required to sign himself in and out when training; that weekend 'leave' was not allowed; and he was to do as he was told regarding eating and conducting himself in hotels when playing away. Permission for exemptions to any of the above had to be asked for from manager or trainer (see Appendix One).

Some managers like to add their own personal 'rules'. Brian Clough was famous for fining his players for committing a whimsical range of offences. What's more, he would let the players know of their misdemeanours via typed letters on Nottingham Forest notepaper, delivered in crisp white envelopes bearing the Forest club crest. The players dubbed the letters 'red trees'. Defender Kenny Burns was greeted by a 'red tree' at half-time during one game in the 1978–9 season. The letter stated that Clough was fining him £25 for 'breach of club discipline'. What, asked Burns, could he possibly have done? 'Basic,' Clough replied. 'Nobody, but nobody, at my club passes a square ball across the defence.'

This one-way communication system is often closed down completely, however, when awkward decisions have to be made. Managers have been known to sack and demote players with apparent randomness. The sudden switch from being an indispensable member of the team to potential redundancy can be traumatic. Declarations of intent or explanations are rarely forthcoming. The player must deduce the reasons for himself through a series of significant encounters, nods and ambiguous signs.

John Colquhoun of Scottish club Hearts commented on the effect of being dropped: 'It definitely lowers your self-esteem and, even if you convince yourself that there are ulterior motives for it – perhaps that the manager has to play the men he has signed to prove he is a good judge of a player, or that the crowd are on your back, which puts the team under pressure – it still matters to you that you aren't good enough to play. Tripping over your petted lip is the worst kind of signal you can give out when in this position. What manager in his right mind would stick you back in the team if you look as though a chip the size of Arthur's Seat is stuck on your shoulder? Go the other way, be bubbly and bouncy, and the management think you don't care. It is definitely not easy this game within a game.'

Players often find themselves out of favour with an incoming manager, another occupational hazard for the professional. With the rapid turnover of managers at all levels, it can play havoc with a player's career and confidence. Jason McAteer, ex-Liverpool and Blackburn Rovers mid-fielder, admitted in March 2002 that, 'Since I've been involved in the game it's developed into a business that really isn't very nice'. He had loved playing for Liverpool, 'but towards the end it became very awkward. When Gerard [Houllier] took charge I didn't like him. He had burst my bubble but he was always very open about my situation. When I look back now I realise he treated me fairly. He said he only saw me as a squad player, which I found impossible to accept, but at least I knew where I stood.'

He was transferred to Blackburn Rovers when Brian Kidd was manager. However, soon afterwards, Kidd was sacked and replaced by Graeme Souness. McAteer admitted, 'I feared the worst from the moment Graeme took the job. He had a chance to sign me when he was at Liverpool and he didn't fancy me then. The only time we had words was when he took me off for about the fifteenth time. I was playing really well against Burnley, as I had been in the game before that and he took me off after seventy minutes. I called him a few names and then stormed off down the tunnel. It wasn't very professional but it was the last straw. He had named squads and then hadn't stripped me. He did that to me in a game at Birmingham. He could have taken one of the kids for that. At the end of the day, I was a 30-year-old international and he was treating me like a teenager.' McAteer soon moved on to Sunderland.

And being a player at the very top of the game offers no sense of security, either. According to Manchester United's Roy Keane: 'Jaap Stam's transfer from Manchester United to Lazio last year illustrates how little power footballers have in the game. To football clubs, players are just expensive pieces of meat.'

Stam, centre-back at the richest club in the world, international star for Holland and considered one of the best defenders in the world, was suddenly placed on the transfer list by manager Alex Ferguson and sold within a few bewildering days. It was brutal in its speed and somehow typical for the complete lack of explanation from the manager. Stam appeared at a hastily arranged press conferences looking stunned. He told journalists, 'It was a bolt from the blue. I didn't see it coming. I've never wanted to leave this club. I love it here. But when the club tell you they're prepared to sell, you have to start viewing things differently. I don't know who to believe. He [Ferguson] said that I didn't fit into his plans, while other people said it might be the autobiography I wrote. I was happy with my situation at the club. I played there for three years successfully and then in two weeks you're told you're not wanted anymore.' Keane commented, 'What happened to Stam could happen to any of us, and it just goes to show how important it is to look after yourself while you have the chance.'

Both on and off the pitch, the random nature of a professional's life is very stressful. In football, anything can happen at any time. As we have seen, unpredictable managers come and go. Out on the pitch, a player's form can suddenly disappear for no reason. The goal scorer who is used to putting the ball into the net without thinking, suddenly sees the ball fly past the post or the keeper make an incredible save. Nat Lofthouse, the famous Bolton and England centre-forward, once explained: 'You just don't know how it comes. You could say your luck turns. Just like that. One day you go up for a ball and, bang, it's in the net. You've been doing the same thing for months, and getting nothing for it. That's how it was.'

Coping in such a bewildering world can be difficult. No wonder lucky charms, strange rituals and bizarre obsessions are legion in the pro-game.

2. 'There is superstition...'

'This season we depend not upon one mascot alone, for we have been presented with another, which now occupies a place of honour in our dressing-rooms. It consists of a massive bone, picked clean and polished, some say by a terrier's teeth. Upon it is engraved – "Sheffield United's lucky bone. Presented by the cooks of the Hallamshire Yorkshire and Lancashire Regiments Camp, Redcar, 1909. Play Up United!"'

R Evan, Thomson's Weekly News, 1909

" Here's luck to the home team!" Charlie Bisby, the Notts County captain, fixes up a lucky horseshoe on the door of the home dressing-room at Meadow Lane. The players are:— Andrews, Mills, Fenner, Keetley, Ferguson, and Bisby.

According to *Thompson's Weekly News*, 1909 saw the trend for mascots and superstitious rituals become 'The Rage of Football England', with fans sending 'lucky' items of all shapes and sizes to their favourite players. A great deal of the attention centred on Sunderland, who were making good progress in the FA Cup. Billy Hogg, a popular player and captain of the side, set things going by referring to a black cat that had strayed into the ground and which he and the players had adopted. Fans wrote in by the hundreds asking for postcard pictures of the cat, while others sent in items such as lucky three-penny coins to hang around its neck.

The *Weekly News* featured photos of Hogg with the cat, as well as numerous cat cartoons drawn by fans. As the team approached its semi-final clash with arch rivals Newcastle United, the cat took on almost mystical significance. There was even a reported abduction of it by a mystery intruder who stole the lucky three-penny bit tied round its neck!

Hogg recounted letters sent to him, such as this anguished plea from a female fan: 'On the day of its [the cat's] first visit to the field it followed me from the corner of the ground to the stairs at the 1s entrance and, stooping down, I stroked it. It gave three miaows and, strange to say, we beat Bury by 3–1. I feel very anxious to possess a picture of the wonderful cat...'

Hogg was kept busy replying to the cards and letters and might well have felt a certain bitter-sweet relief when Sunderland were finally knocked out by Newcastle in the fourth round after a replay. The final act in the cat saga was a cartoon sent in by a disgusted fan depicting the cat being thrown into the river with a brick tied round its neck.

Newcastle's great rivals during this period, Manchester United, had also gone through their own mascot saga a year or so earlier when the team had been presented on a music-hall stage with a live goat. The goat was looked after by team members for a season or so and paraded at the ground on occasions. It finally succumbed to a glass of beer fed to it one afternoon for a joke. The goat's head was cut off and stuck on a shield and displayed at the ground for years afterwards. In fact, the family of Charlie Roberts, Manchester United's captain, still have the famous goat's head.

Other teams during this period found it hard to compete with Billy Hogg's lucky black cat. Newcastle United's 'lucky' omen was a more prosaic horseshoe. Bradford City had a live bantam cock, as well as a gollywog emblem. Sheffield Wednesday had a pet monkey, Leeds United had a stuffed peacock presented to them in a glass cabinet. Steve Bloomer, then playing for Middlesborough, was pictured with a 'lucky' pigeon on his shoulder. Sadly, as colleague Tommy Watson reported some months later: 'Just at that time we were having a run of back luck and three successive weeks we were defeated. The pigeon died – its grief was so great –and since then we have been absolutely without any emblem of good luck.' He then appealed to fans for a live mascot.

The mania eventually led to Dave Neave of Woolwich Arsenal writing an article in *The Red Letter* in 1909 entitled 'Why I Don't Like Mascots', in which he outlined how irksome the various superstitions of fellow players were. There was an ex-miner who didn't like anyone whistling in the dressing room ('because an accident would happen on the pitch'). There were fans pleading with him to take talismans from them ('Just stick it in your pocket and we're sure to win the tie'). Another player carried a couple of old teeth in his pocket everywhere ('whether his own or his grandmother's, I never asked') and swore by a silver ring obtained from a Northumbrian gypsy. ('Once, while its owner was training, he swung his hand round and the ring came into contact with my face just below the eye and gave me a nasty cut.') Neave was scornful of the lot.

He concluded: 'Mascots – this is my final word – are very fine things in their proper place. By all means stick them up in the dressing rooms as ornaments. But don't depend on them. They won't win matches for you.'

Strange rituals have been a hallmark of professional soccer. Peter Doherty explained in 1948, 'Most of us have our own ideas about preparing for a game. There are those who like to don shirts and shorts before tackling the long job of putting on bandages, stockings and boots. Some even insist on being last or fourth, say, when the team runs out on the field; they feel that their game will somehow be affected if they don't carry out this sort of thing regularly!'

FA Cup runs seem to have engendered more than their fair share of obsessive behaviour. In 1948, prior to a third round tie against Leeds United, Jimmy McIntosh of Blackpool left home in an old discarded shirt by mistake, and for the rest of the run refused to wear anything else. Blackpool reached the final that year – but McIntosh was left out after having played in all the previous rounds!

Manager Barry Fry was famously persuaded to urinate in all four corners of Birmingham's ground in order to lift a 'gypsy's curse'. Malcolm Allison took to wearing a fedora hat during Crystal Palace's Cup run in the mid-1970s. Jack Tinn, manager of Portsmouth, wore some 'lucky' spats, while there have been innumerable 'lucky' suits of all shapes and sizes.

Such activities are designed to alleviate nerves and fear; they are aimed both at controlling events as well as keeping control over oneself and one's emotions. Eamon Dunphy, author of *Only A Game*, has described how the hours before a match are, 'filled with fear and apprehension. Your stomach churned, the shivers of anxiety raised pimples on your flesh, doubt seeped into your soul. The heroes didn't look or feel like heroes in their grim, pensive moments before the dressing room door opened and the noise of an expectant crowd hits you in the face. These were the worst moments of the week.'

The fear felt by the player came in many forms. Fear of the opposition, induced, perhaps, by an over-anxious manager; fear of being unable to live up to the grandiose rhetoric of a manager's team-talk; and fear of the unknown, which frequently had as much to do with confusion in one's own ranks as anything the opposition was likely to fling one's way.

It was a fear just as keenly felt back in the early years of the last century. Jimmy Sharp wrote in 1908: 'The excitement a player feels just as he is about to go on the field before a great match is indescribable. It is the feeling that must have swelled in the breast of the ancient gladiators as they looked upon the crowds that lined the Coliseum; the feelings that surge in the hearts of our soldiers when the order is given to charge into battle. One stands with every nerve strained to the utmost, like a hound on the leash, or like a racehorse pawing the ground before the drop of the starter's flag. The hoarse shouting of the crowd steels one, and the thought, "Perhaps I may be the means of losing or winning this match," makes one feel one's position keenly.'

Such fear is often the means by which players galvanise themselves; they use it to spur themselves on. At other times, however, it can almost destroy a player. Eddie Hapgood, an Arsenal full-back of the 1930s, recalled: 'Arsenal were drawn to play at Walsall in the first round of the FA Cup. In the Arsenal team for that match was a player named Walsh. New to the team, his hands were trembling as he got himself ready to go out for the kick-off. He was duly decked in shirt, shorts and football boots. The part of the equipment lacking was his football stockings. In his excitement, his state of nerves, he had forgotten to put them on. This player stood out in marked contrast to many I have known who certainly didn't forget their stockings; they put them on and took them off three or four times…'

Walsh was dropped following a shock defeat for which he was the scapegoat. He never played for Arsenal again.

3. Playing those mind games...

'Footballers are, as a rule, simple and sincere fellows, thoroughly enjoying the life they lead, healthy, free of the modern taint of automatic psychoanalysis, taking things and the world at their face value. In a rather morbid, gloomy world, it is refreshing to meet men like these.'

*Leslie Knighton, Behind the Scenes in
Big Time Football, 1948*

At the present time, pre-match stress has become a topic for the sports psychologists, who are now moving into the professional game in a significant way. Stephen Smith, an occupational psychologist and a specialist in sport, considers that the key to conquering pre-match nerves, for instance, is to control the breathing rate. This can be done through relaxation techniques, yoga, or visualisation. This is a mental process in which a player imagines or 'visualises' scoring a goal or making a crunching tackle. 'Visualisation is a big part of mental preparation in individual sports,' says Smith. 'Jack Nicklaus, for example, has said that he always has a picture in his head of the shot he is going to play before he plays it.' Which rather dates many of these ideas, which have been common in other professional sports since the 1970s.

Jonathon Males, sports psychologist with the company Sporting BodyMind, felt that the pre-match talks between managers and their teams sometimes didn't help matters: 'The signs of pre-match nerves are the same as those created by any stressful situation. The difficulty is that people react to stress in different ways. Some players become over pumped up, while others may not be pumped up enough. The ideal is for every player to reach his own optimum level of arousal before a match, so that he is psyched up, but not overly so. The trouble is that coaches tend to adopt a team approach to motivation, rather than treating players as individuals.'

This would appear to have been the case where Len Ashurst was concerned when managing Sunderland and Lee Chapman. Preparing for an away match at Stoke, Chapman recalled: 'We were made to warm up in the dressing room by jogging on the spot and then intermittently sprinting flat out while emitting a piercing scream. We had done this since Ashurst's arrival and it had become a standing joke. Unknown to him, the players had begun to utter more and more bloodcurdling screams in an attempt to ridicule the procedure. He obviously took the increased noise as a sign of extra commitment. Unfortunately, I could hold my mirth no longer and started to giggle. His eyes met mine and his look said it all – no one would take the mickey out of him.'

Only recently have clubs and players consulted psychologists in any systematic way. A traditional Anglo-Saxon wariness and scepticism concerning psychology has not helped matters although the profession hasn't completely shunned mental manipulation of various kinds in the past. As far back as September 1909 Middlesborough's Jimmy Thackeray told of the club's radical attempt at instilling confidence into the players by means of a hypnotist:

'The bearded mesmerist has again found his way to Ayresome Park. Last season he paid us many visits and again he has established himself in the dressing rooms and the gymnasium. We don't require to pay for our entertainment at Middlesborough for there's plenty of fun to be had when the old "doctor" comes within the enclosure.' Thackeray described how Alf Common became a favourite subject of the 'mesmerist', 'and the moment he fixes his eyes upon our centre-half, Alf is on his feet walking stiffly towards the "doctor". This was what happened the other afternoon and the rest of the boys rolled from their seats with laughter. For a moment the "doctor" took his eye off his subject and Alf, turning round to us, assured his comrades that he was quite himself by giving us a broad smile and a wink. We have signed the "doctor" on as our mascot for we think he should really be a handy man to cast a hypnotic spell over our opponents.'

The tendency for players not to take such ideas seriously persists. John Colquhoun explained in 1995 the reaction of his fellow players when they were given some group therapy sessions: 'It was very difficult to "let your arms float up to the ceiling as if they were attached to a bunch of balloons" in case Jeremy Beadle popped out of the sauna or, worse, you were the only one to be hypnotised and when you woke up all your colleagues were splitting their sides laughing at you. The result was that we were all peeping out from a half-closed eye to check we weren't the unfortunate getting tucked up. Sports psychology works, but I feel it has to be done on an individual basis. Footballers are far too conscious of what their teammates think to commit to it in a group.'

Most 'psychological' ploys were of the simplistic kind, however. When Arsenal visited Wembley for their first Cup Final under Herbert Chapman in 1930, he took a portable gramophone along, 'with a selection of the cheeriest records he could lay his hands on. The music was started when the players began to strip and so we had players whistling the popular tunes as they prepared for the big game.' Jack Tinn, of the lucky spats and monkey glands, took a comedian along on the trip to tell jokes in the dressing room to keep the players from thinking too much about the game ahead.

Wolverhampton Wanderers were known to have employed a qualified psychiatrist before the Second World War, but often the psychology involved was of the amateur kind. Arthur Campey, Leeds United trainer during the 1930s, noticed that young half-back Wilf Copping was unhappy and homesick and wasn't communicating with the rest of the players. Campsey decided on a course of massage. 'Now I really do believe that massage is the finest training device there is. I think I have done more good with it than with anything else.' Campsey, however, really wanted to get Copping down to the ground so that he could get him talking. 'It took a few gallons of olive oil to loosen him up – in the two senses. But after a bit he began to get pally. He came out of his shell and made friends.' Copping put his decision to stay and play on rather than return to his job in the pit down to Campsey. It's interesting that a later Leeds manager, Don Revie, used to like nothing more than to get his players on the treatment table and give them a personal massage. It was his way of literally getting in touch with his players. Jack Charlton, in particular, has said how much he enjoyed the experience.

As suggested, however, in Britain, there was always been a wariness of things 'mental'. When it was discovered in the early 1980s that Tottenham Hotspur was using a sports psychologist, a national newspaper splashed the headline 'White Coats at White Hart Lane'. Graham Taylor was ridiculed in certain quarters for using a psychologist at the European Championships in 1992 when he was managing the England team. Glen Hoddle had similar problems with his famous faith-healer. It has not deterred Hoddle, however. As manager of Tottenham, he has employed John Syer, a psychologist who stresses that he is part of the coaching set-up rather than the medical team, and helping players achieve positive thought, focus and general improvement being an essential part of his job: 'If a player is going to concentrate for a couple of weeks on a particular skill, say dribbling, then anything that evokes memories of feelings of dribbling well is a support to his efforts to improve.'

Team building and communication are also central to Syer's work. Squad meetings are planned and run with the coaching staff and, on the day before most games, Syer separates 'unit work' with the defence, midfield and attack. After Hoddle has explained the game plan and shown a video of the opposition, the unit meetings give players a chance to talk about tactics and clarify what they want from one another. The aim, he claims, is to strengthen relationships.

'Glenn calls me a team-building expert, not a sports psychologist. He thinks it's important that players talk to each other. The key is for players to give feedback to one another about what they see a team-mate do, what happens as a result and how that impacts on them. Often the player being spoken to doesn't have that information. I'll give you an example from long ago at Spurs. Garth Crooks and Mark Falco were among the strikers and one of them felt slightly guilty every time he ran into the box because he thought he was regarded by the other as being opportunistic or out to get goals first. It turned out when they had the chance to talk to each other that was exactly what the other striker wanted.'

At Middlesborough, manager Steve McLaren has taken the bold step of bringing in a sports psychologist, Bill Beswick, as assistant manager. Beswick has stressed the importance of creating 'a safe, warm and positive environment for players who every day face a great deal of challenge'. He aims to increase their competitiveness by supporting them, understanding their fears, going so far as redesigning the dressing rooms so that there are no areas where players can feel isolated. Unlike Brian Clough and others of a more martial ilk, Beswick aims to raise his team's energy levels by stressing togetherness and understanding. He also helps each player create 'another self', the professional 'warrior', who is given eight key words to learn that characterise the 'other self'.

However, coping with the stresses of playing the game is one thing. Dealing with the opinions and reactions of those watching from the terraces can be quite another thing entirely.

4. The vultures

'Well, ya big nelly! He's no idea. Couldn't punch a tram ticket, never mind a ball... Come on, Cunliffe, get rid man! Look at 'im, fiddling and fumbling about... Get shut of it! Ya can take it home with yer after... Why don't they drop him and play his missus...'

Al Reid, comedian

Barracking, the verbal abuse of players by spectators, has always been an occupational hazard for professional footballers. They are key performers in an entertainment that relies on partisanship to give it its meaning. In February 1908, Jimmy Sharp, under the headline 'Spectators Through the Players Eyes', commented on the Newcastle United fans and their discerning ways: 'Do your best on the field, play to win and they are with you to a man; try, on the other hand, to do a few shady tricks and you will learn just how nasty a crowd can be.'

Chelsea fans, he considered, were a 'better class of spectator' while in Manchester 'the cotton workers are more sympathetic. They are inclined to be blind to the faults of a player and will often cheer on a man who is evidently off-colour.' The fans at Bradford and Sheffield, however, 'yell like factory buzzers'.

Colin Veitch, Newcastle United captain, writing a year later in *Thomson's Weekly News*, was more forthcoming: 'If there is one unnecessary evil creeping into football more than any other it is the pernicious habit which some spectators have developed of persistently "barracking" a player who has had the misfortune to displease them by an unsatisfactory exhibition.' Veitch blamed the problem of such jeering and cat-calling on coupon selling and betting, implying that spectators had money riding on the match and were thus more anxious about a team's performance.

Forty years on, *Soccer*, the players' newspaper, included a small piece on the problem. In December 1947 it noted that Harry Osman had scored his first goal for Bristol City. The report continued: 'It must have been the most satisfying of his whole career.' Osman had been driven from Millwall by persistent barracking, a problem *Soccer* felt was more common than ever. It mentioned two or three other men who had asked for transfers, and added, 'No professional footballer minds in the least the good-humoured barracking which had always been normal in the game – it's the vicious, persistent stuff directed at one player, week after week, which is so objectionable and makes some players ask to be chosen only for away matches.'

Peter Doherty, in *Spotlight on Football*, also written in 1947, suggested that, when a team was playing poorly, 'encouragement, not derision, is wanted to help us back to form. The barracker, whether he writes abusive letters or shouts from the terraces, can cause more unhappiness than he probably realises…'

Herbert Chapman, the great Arsenal manager, agreed. In an article written in 1931 he explained: 'There is much unhappiness among footballers of which the public know nothing. I have sometimes thought that it would be better if they did, for it would give them a fuller understanding of many matters, and lead them to a fairer and more generous outlook on the game. For the football spectator can be, and often is, cruel.'

He recalled an incident that pointed to the incalculable harm which the barracker may do: 'It was signing-on time some years ago. A youth came into my office, and I put the form before him to sign. To my amazement he covered his face with his hands and burst into tears. "It's no use," he said. "I'm no use to anyone in football and I had better get out. I can't stand it any longer. The crowd is always getting at me. I'm going home and I hope I shall never kick a ball again."'

Chapman admitted that he hadn't realised how the crowd had got to the young man, but persuaded him to sign on anyway. The problem persisted and Chapman decided that it would be better if he left and made a new start elsewhere. He then revealed that two great players, David Jack and Alex James, suffered from barracking when they first arrived at Highbury: '…and I shall always think that the dead set which was made against him [James] was deliberately manufactured to hurt the club as well as the player. It was one of the meanest things I have ever known, and one of the finest players it has been my pleasure to see almost had his heart broken. That is not an exaggeration.'

Though barracking occurs everywhere in football, Arsenal would seem to have a continuing reputation for the hostile reception some home players receive at Highbury: Bryn Jones, Don Roper, Horace Cope, John Barnwell and Paul Davis have all suffered but one player in particular who was forced to leave the club on the very eve of its first 'Double' was the first to write publicly about the experience.

Jon Sammels joined Arsenal as an apprentice in 1961 and made well over 250 appearances for the club in a ten-year spell. In 1969, he began to sense that things were going wrong: 'I had a constant feeling of frustration. I went out in matches, tried to do my best and, to my horror, began to realise that the crowd was getting at me. It was a terrible feeling. At the time I was unmarried and had no one to whom I could confide my inner thoughts. I simply went home and worried. It all seemed so unfair. If I had not been trying on the field, I could have understood it, but I had always given 100 per cent. Then came a match against Wolves at Highbury. Even as we were kicking in, I realised I was being booed by a section of the crowd. The noise went on through the match. Every time I had the ball there was a howl. I wanted nothing so much as to get off the field and be finished with it…'

Back in his room he felt everything was crowding in on him. He reasoned that he should have 'snapped out of it' but didn't know what to do. Later he suffered migraine attacks brought on by nerves. He was then injured at a crucial point in the season.

Sammels went to see Bertie Mee, the Arsenal manager, and asked for a transfer. Mee's reaction was to laugh the thing off. 'We had a long chat, the outcome of which was that I should think the matter over carefully. "Let's see how you feel in a few months' time," said Bertie. "If you feel the same way at the end of the season, come and tell me."'

Sammels suspected that he was worrying about too many things: 'By taking on all the club's worries I was being manager of Arsenal in my mind. This was loyalty gone mad. I wanted to give my right arm for the club, and because I was so concerned I could no longer play adequately, so the public put me in the pillory for it. Football is a funny game.'

Though his form improved things got no better for Sammels where the crowd was concerned, and as Arsenal closed in on the 'Double' during the 1970–71 season, Sammels was sidelined. Bertie Mee, he realised, was not going to take the risk of playing him when there was a danger that the crowd might upset the team's progress towards the FA Cup and League Double. Sammels decided he would have to put in a transfer request, but had no one to advise him. He rang Bob Oxby, a journalist, and was advised not to 'rock the boat'. Oxby told him: 'Let's face it, for any Arsenal player to be unhappy at this moment is a big story. It would put you, Bertie and all the players under terrific pressure.'

When told of Sammels' plight, Mee said he would let him leave at the end of the season. After all, he might need him. So Sammels watched as Arsenal triumphed without him. The story of his transfer request appeared in the *Daily Telegraph* on the very day of Arsenal's FA Cup win: 'Perhaps I could be forgiven for feeling bitter. The Highbury crowd made life impossible for me and stole away the prizes which, from the beginning of organised soccer, countless players have striven to earn…'

Only the reticence of friendly journalists on the great night saved Sammels from breaking down, he claimed. 'That night was agony for me. There on the top table was the FA Cup side by side with the League Championship trophy. I was part of the night, yet not part of it. My feelings were so mixed that I had to leave the banqueting chamber.' Sammels was transferred to Leicester City and completed a distinguished professional career.

At the opposite end of the professional scale, the casual abuse received by players at the end of their careers from spectators can appear little more than cruel. John Moynihan in *Soccer Syndrome* recalled that at Chelsea after the Second World War, 'a crowd of males used to come to barrack Johnnie Galloway, an inside-forward who never quite made it in the first team, but made many appearances with the reserves. Galloway rolled round with a big bottom, an elegant passer of the ball, a frequent marksman from outside the penalty box, but his trouble was that he didn't look match-fit after war service.

'His critics hung over the crash barriers wearing their 'spiv' trilbys and "demob" macintoshes and murdered Galloway in hundreds of words. Their merciless baiting would survive the match and go on after Galloway disappeared into the tunnel.'

Such behaviour has been known to contribute to players committing suicide. James Blair, aged 28, an ex-Manchester City player, then playing with Stockport County, became so depressed over his poor form and the reaction from the terraces, that he went back to his home town of Dumfries in March 1913 and cut his throat.

One morning in early January 1930, one of the painters employed on the Dundee FC training quarters at Dens Park was about to start work when he noticed the figure of a man huddled in the corner of one of the rooms beneath the grandstand. Thinking it must be that of some unauthorised stranger who had made his way into the ground, the painter called Mr James Gray, the groundsman. He removed the coat to find that the man was Hugh Ferguson, a popular player with the club, who had gassed himself.

Ferguson, who was 33 years old, had played for Motherwell with great success before being transferred to Cardiff in 1925. He'd returned to Scotland in 1929 but his form had fallen away and he had suffered ill health which had affected his fitness. In his last match he suffered cramp and hadn't played well. According to a *Weekly News* reporter: 'This was seen by the spectators, which was unavoidable. But a section of the crowd, who could or would see no further than that the man was playing a rotten game, let loose their sentiments in barracking and Ferguson heard them. To a man of Hugh's extremely sensitive nature this was extremely painful. There is no doubt but that [the events] that day disturbed Hugh Ferguson very greatly. It depressed him. He might have been able to stand the illness alone but he could not face a jeering crowd.'

The writer added, 'It is not too much to say that he died of a broken heart. He was a kindly, home-loving man – he did not drink and his hobby was breeding pigeons – and he could not bear the thought that he was failing in anything. That crowd may look back now on all that Hugh Ferguson accomplished during his football life.'

Despite the pleas of players and managers down the years, the verbal taunting of players would seem to have become ever more aggressive and threatening. Author Irvine Welsh feels that crowds have a right to vent their feelings on the terraces. Abuse hurled at players, whatever its nature, was justifiable, he felt: 'Behaviour takes place in a context, and the context of football spectating for many people is, has been, and will remain, about letting off steam on a Saturday. I see nothing wrong in roaring "fuck", "shite" or "bastard" at football matches. I always have done, I always will.'

In that context, the treatment meted out to Sol Campbell by his once adoring fans at White Hart Lane is perfectly understandable. Campbell's transfer to hated rivals Arsenal had come as a great shock to the Spurs fans, especially as Campbell had declared his loyalty to Spurs and seemed to be considering staying. He did, however, honour his contract with Tottenham and was, under the new transfer regime introduced as a result of the Bosman ruling, free to leave.

All the same, the behaviour of what would appear to have been thousands of well-educated adults on the day he returned to White Hart Lane wearing the despised Arsenal shirt was remarkable for its elaborate and calculated spite. Organised by the various fanzines and websites, the fans observed a minute's silence, otherwise known as 'the minute of contempt', jeered and booed whenever Campbell touched the ball and released four thousand 'Judas' balloons. One section of the fans turned their backs on their former skipper.

There was some thought given to not playing him but Arsenal manager Arsene Wenger said: 'As a manager you cannot rest a player because you are scared of the abuse he might receive. We have had a brief chat about the situation and I will probably talk to him again just before the game. I will simply tell him to play his normal game and pretend he is against Real Madrid. Like Tottenham, they play in white.'

Campbell repaid the treatment he received by playing one of his best games of the season, and went on to win the Double with his new team. As he put it, 'I'm alive, but it wasn't easy. I was surprised by the reaction but there were passions all over the place. It was difficult. I'm glad I went for it. It was the will to prove people wrong that kept me going. The main thing was to keep on believing in myself. The gaffer here believes in me and so do the players. The players at Arsenal have helped me.'

Campbell is black but there was nothing racist about the crowd's treatment of him. Black players haven't always been so fortunate. Walter Tull, the Football League's first black out-field player, whose rarity value and skill attracted considerable media interest in the early years of the century, seemed to have a bright future. Playing inside-left in a game at Bristol City in 1909, however, he was racially abused by fans in what the *Football Star* called 'language lower than Billingsgate'. The incident was deeply traumatic for Tull and the club. During the following season, he played only three first-team games. The season after that, he was sold to Northampton Town.

As black players began to appear in the professional ranks in greater numbers after the Second World War, the behaviour of fans appeared to have changed but little. Charlie Williams' father was from Barbados and had settled in Yorkshire in the 1920s where he married a local girl. Charlie was born in 1929 in Royston, near Barnsley, and in 1948 he signed for Doncaster Rovers, with whom he would play for some twelve seasons.

'Naturally, the other team's fans didn't like me. They used to shout, they used to chant, used to try and hurt me. And naturally, they tried to get at me through my colour. They used to shout, "You big black bastard!" or "Get that black swine!" and lovely things like that. But if I'd played for their side, I'd have been a grand lad. It did hurt…but sometimes it made me twice the player. It made me determined that nobody were going to pass. I were going to show 'em that I were top man.'

There were few black families in the mining districts of Barnsley before the war, and Williams, with his cheerful approach, was adept at using his 'novelty value' to defuse many potentially unpleasant incidents. 'When I'm told to go back to where I came from, I say, "Well, when's the next bus to Barnsley?"' Being well supported by his fellow Doncaster players, Williams felt no lasting damage was done to him. On the contrary, he was to use many of his experiences as a player as material for his successful comedy act in the 1960s and 1970s.

In the decades following Williams' time at Doncaster, however, the numbers of black players in the game increased dramatically. Cyrille Regis was signed by West Bromwich Albion in 1978 and, along with team-mates such as the brilliant Laurie Cunningham and full-back Viv Anderson (who would, in 1979, become the first black player to represent England at full international level), he was lauded in the press as part of a footballing 'Black Power' revolution.

Like Williams, Regis was philosophical about the bad treatment he received from supporters: 'You just had to learn to absorb those kinds of things. Most black guys, if they get called "black bastard" or whatever, they'll get aggressive. But, personally, I learned to absorb it. I heard it from the terraces a lot, but it was nothing new to me; I'd been hearing it from my school days.'

Like Charlie Williams, Regis detected some irony in the situation: 'I think they were rebelling against me 'cause I'd taken a white guy's place in the team. On the field I can only recall about two occasions when racial remarks were made. At Tottenham, Chris Hughton and I were running for the ball and he's black as well, well, I think he'd got one black parent. Anyway, I heard somebody in the crowd shout, "You black bastard!" I thought I must be mistaken cause he's black too and they're supposed to be his supporters!'

It had never occurred to Norwich City and Nottingham Forest's Justin Fashanu that his colour made any difference until he was in a football trial and a scout said, "We're quite interested in the coloured lad." Added Fashanu, 'And that was the first time I realised they thought of me by anything other than my name.'

He admitted taking 'stick' from fellow players and the opposition in his early days at Norwich City but claimed it only made him stronger: 'At the end of the day, it doesn't matter what colour you are, black, blue, pink, white or green. If you've got a strong enough personality and you want to do it badly enough, you'll get there.'

Danny Thomas, born in Worksop, Nottinghamshire, in 1962 of Jamaican parents, went straight to Coventry City from school to join his brother Val as an apprentice professional. Thomas was more sensitive when his colour was used as a weapon to bait him with. 'Val was the only other black guy on the staff when we started and we used to get it rough from some of the other players. Alan Dugdale was the worst but, in training, some of them used to take it out on me; there was John Craven, 'Kingy' (Bryan King), Jimmy Holmes and 'Hutchy' (Tommy Hutchinson). It was because I was black. I almost took a crowbar to them once. Where the crowd was concerned, '"Nigger, nigger, lick my boots," was the chant I heard regularly. Barracking was nothing new. I took it as a sort of compliment.'

But he was shocked by the reception he received at West Ham United in February 1981, during a League Cup Semi-Final match. Supporters set in motion a ceaseless barrage of racist chants and lobbed the mandatory bananas at him. Thomas was unnerved just once: 'The ball went high into the crowd and, as one guy went to throw it back, he said, "Here you are, nigger!" Then threw it hard at me. I went for him. But fortunately the linesman stopped me.'

Even without the problems that racism brings, however, the increasing cultural significance of the game would appear to have raised the temperature where the question of allegiance to and 'ownership' of the club is concerned. Many years ago, there was an apocryphal tale told about a fan who turned up at his club each week dressed in full home kit hidden beneath a raincoat, hoping that there would come an announcement over the tannoy that the team was short of a player and could anyone lend a hand? He was thoroughly prepared to leap on to the pitch, all ready to play.

The story was amusing because the idea of a fan wearing the team kit seemed absurd unless there was some ulterior motive involved. Once, to wear the team's shirt meant that you were a player. It was a privilege and a professional achievement. It marked you out. Fans could only look on and wish. Now, any supporter with sufficient cash and desire can wear the official shirt. As such, it represents an encroachment by fans into the player's arena. It is a gesture of proprietorship and it underlines just how much more the game and the team means to fans now. It is a situation that places the professional player in a quandary. The emotional stakes seem so much higher.

Serious physical attacks by fans on professional players are rare, however. The murder of Aston Villa's centre-half Tommy Ball in 1924 arose out of an argument over a neighbour's barking dog, while the death threats to George Best in the early 1970s must be viewed in the context of the Northern Ireland Troubles rather than his role as a Manchester United player. The professional soccer player, however, increasingly bears the brunt of a secular society in which football has arisen from its terraces to fill a spiritual void.

In November 2000, threats of physical violence from Liverpool fans moved Gary Neville of Manchester United to call for some sort of protection. He revealed that he had received death threats. His team-mate, David Beckham, had seen an effigy of himself hung up outside a London pub following his sending-off during the World Cup of 1998. There had also been threats to kidnap his son.

Gordon Taylor of the Professional Footballers' Association commented, 'Professional sportsmen are high profile and there are always idiots who threaten people. It's very sad footballers no longer mix with supporters but there's a great danger because there's always someone in a crowd who wants to cause trouble and aggravation. It's not just a question now of clubs looking after players when they're at the ground or training for games. It's a 24-hour process.'

However, Robbie Savage, then of Leicester City, now with Manchester City, professed to enjoying the sense of danger involved: 'All the opposition fans who boo me would swop places with me in a minute. If I do a foul and all the opposition fans shout at me, I just laugh. If I wind them up, I know they can't get me, although Teddy Sheringham said somebody could be killed on the pitch by fans one day. I could be the first!'

Perhaps Savage would think again if professional teams were as exposed as they once were in the years before the First World War. Dave Buchanan of Leyton told of an incident in 1908 when, 'It is no exaggeration to say that my life was in danger'. Buchanan was playing in a cup tie at Brentford, when he injured the opposing goalkeeper. The crowd was incensed and waited for him after the game. The players had to walk from the ground to a brake [an open carriage] that was to take them home: 'All the way along the crowd followed, hissing and booing and shaking their fists.' When they reached the brake, the crowd made a dash for him. Policemen held them back while he threw himself on the carriage floor and his fellow players formed a shield by crouching over him. 'I knew I was safe, but as I heard the screams of baffled rage and heard the stones rattling on the sides of the brake, I felt very miserable indeed. It makes me shiver to think of it!'

STRANGE THINGS HAPPEN IN THE DRESSING ROOMS

New Intimate Stories of the Players
by
ANDY CUNNINGHAM
FAMOUS EX·SCOTTISH & RANGERS FORWARD

Albert M'Inroy.

Elisha Scott.

ON every football ground in the country the players' dressing-rooms naturally are the most closely guarded places of all, for without a check on visitors, they would be swarming with "friends." In consequence, much speculation and rumour arises in supporters' minds as to what really goes on in the dressing-room.

Actually there is no mystery. Before a match, the most cheerful banter and chaff goes on among the players, which, to me, is one of the most pleasing signs of a happy team.

Not all players are alike, of course, in their reaction to chaff, particularly new players to a side, but they soon settle down and become part of the band.

Every footballer has some little fad or fancy. It may be in the method of tying his boots, the order of putting on his outfit, his preference for a special style of studding, or choosing his place in the file in taking the field. Most of these habits are known to the others, and create plenty of good humour.

Alan Morton Always Carried a Gamp

The manager, who is interested in every slight detail regarding his players, also knows of their fancies, and, being wise to the beneficial effect of good humour on the morale of his side, delights in the pre-match hilarity.

Personally, I never once dressed for a match without leaving my left boot to be fixed last of all the preparation. It was a harmless fad, but I got in the end to feel that I would not be comfortable on the field without that rite not carried out.

During the time Albert M'Inroy was with Newcastle United I have never known him take the field without having "just one wee whiff" at a cigarette at the last moment. Willie Robb did the same.

I don't know whether goalkeepers are more nervous than other players, but I remember a young goalkeeper being in a fearful state of nervous excitement before a match. Tommy Ferguson, who used to be one of Scotland's best 'keepers, took part in a league international on Highbury, and, just before kicking off time, was really ill, but he got over it immediately he was on the field.

Alan Morton invariably carried an umbrella

to all the Rangers matches, and we got so accustomed to seeing it that we never had any doubt that we would win our game. But, if by any chance, Alan forgot his gamp and we lost, we naturally blamed him for letting us down.

It is not the first time he has been ordered by the rest of us to go home and get his umbrella, or buy a spare one, which, I believe, he once did.

Shortly after the war, Rangers were playing Liverpool at Anfield in a friendly—a benefit, I think, for the trainer. We were down at the ground very early to have a look round, and, in going into the Liverpool dressing-room, we found Elisha Scott getting himself ready for the match.

Naturally we were surprised, and asked Elisha if he were going to have a game on his own, or a bit of practice.

"Oh, no," he remarked, "I always take plenty of time to get myself fit and all my gadgets on."

M'Inroy Had to Have His Smoke

Most players like to dawdle over their dressing, and it was no uncommon experience at Ibrox for Geordie Livingstone to be rushing around at the last second with the remark that there was a match on, or that the players would soon be coming in for half-time.

Seldom was one of the Rangers addressed by his proper name—we all had nicknames. They would have been confusing to a stranger were he to hear Sandy Archibald being addressed as Harry, Muirhead as Horace, myself as Sam, wee Alan as Johnny, or Arthur Dixon as Joe, &c. That was carried out on the field also, not with any idea of misleading anyone, but simply as an expression of the friendly spirit prevailing in the team.

When a side has suffered a bad defeat, a humorist in the bunch is invaluable to take away some of the gloom inseparable from a losing feeling. I don't mean, however, one of the type which does not feel the sting of a defeat and who can laugh unconcernedly as if the prestige of the side did not matter.

Most players feel the sting of defeat deep down. Some do more than others, I admit, and it has been my experience to see young players in tears over a beating. That, however, is taking too serious a view of the game, but it is a spirit much more to be commended than that of total unconcern.

I do not think there is any club which, at one time or other, has not been the subject of gossip, scandalous stories, supposed to emanate from the dressing-rooms. Personally, I take all these stories with a large grain of salt, because, knowing footballers as I do, I have found little ground for belief in such scandal as one hears, particularly when a side is having a bad spell.

It is a source of wonderment to all managers and players just where these yarns arise, but I am sure if the originators of them could

foresee the harm they do, they would be chary of loose talk.

As a contrast to the closely-guarded atmosphere of dressing-rooms in this country, should see the free and easy access to players' quarters on the Continent and America. Having seen these, I am all for our own method.

In New York, and other American cities where I played, the dressing-rooms, before and after the matches, were in a state of pandemonium. Players could not find room enough to get dressed or undressed without a gang cluttering up the place.

It may be been excusable, inasmuch as they were a touring side from home, and, naturally, the folks wanted to hear and see as much as possible. But it was very uncomfortable for the players.

One can imagine the influx of people a private dressing-room on this side were it a prohibited place. What an opportunity story-telling such access would provide.

A few years ago I made a suggestion to the shareholders of Newcastle United that they come along any time during the training to see just what dressing-rooms were like and what went on during a normal day's work.

Elisha Scott—Football's Earliest Dresser

I was delighted that a big number of them accepted the invitation, and, after an interesting morning being shown round, went away pleased with their experience, and expressed themselves as pleasantly surprised at having seen "inside" for the first time in their lives.

Dressing-rooms are now palatial compared with my early junior days. Our junior "pavilion," as we called it, did not boast water, cold or even cold, which had to be got from a nearby stream.

The stories one hears of players before kick-off in big matches being so excited they cannot lace their boots are exaggerated although I have known of one such case—a Scottish-English league international at Hampden. Andy M'Atee was our outside-right, not even the presence of his clubmate humorist, Jamie M'Menemy, could get out of his stage-fright.

Playing at Home (with the Girls)

'When Alf Common joined Sheffield United [in 1901] he had a job as well and was thus drawing two pay packets a week. Manager Nicholson persuaded him to let him save half the football pay and the bonus. Sometime later, when the Sheffield team stepped out of the train at Sunderland, Common, as the youngest player, waited behind to help the trainer with the 'skip'. While he waited, his eye fell on the advertisement of a house for sale that night. He read and re-read it, and then asked Mr Nicholson to buy it with the wages he had saved. After the match next day, young Common went to his own home. "They're selling this house, I see," he said to his father.

"Yes," was the answer. " It was sold yesterday. I wonder if we shall have to go?"

"You won't have to go, Dad," Common said. "I've bought it."

You need to have been poor to know what that meant to the old people! They lived in that house for thirty years.'

Leslie Knighton, Behind the Scenes in Big Time Football, 1948

THIS WEEK :-
PETER DOHERTY—
Home lover
and Handyman

The HUMAN SIDE
of the
PLAYERS

Topical Times,

7 May 1938.

1. Homes for heroes

Finding somewhere to live would always play a big part in a professional's life. The short nomadic careers of pro footballers differentiated them from other workers at the end of the nineteenth century. From early on in the profession's history, the majority of players didn't work in their native towns, but were signed by teams often great distances away. Moreover, being liable to a sudden transfer, there was no certainty as to where they would reside for the duration of their playing careers.

The first professionals, being predominantly Scottish, probably made the biggest 'leaps'. Many made a success of moving south. They stayed, opened businesses, and went on to coach and manage. Many, however, returned home after a short while. The separation from families and friends, the general uprooting of their lives and the harsher realities of professional football as an employment prompted them to up stakes and leave, sometimes before their contracts ended. The numbers of men returning to Scotland to be 'whitewashed' (reinstated as amateurs after having played professionally in England) gives an indication of the problem. After the 1890–91 season, 115 Scotsmen applied, along with another 73 the following season.

Some Scotsmen were luckier. Alec Chaplin joined Fulham from Dundee Hibs in 1919 and for a time lived in Acton Vale before moving into the famous Cottage building in the corner of Fulham's ground. It wasn't, he claimed, a particularly good house, but it was extremely convenient. There was a tea-room where his wife occasionally made tea for the team and a billiard table, which he had responsibility for maintaining. He lived there for ten years and considered himself luckier than many other Fulham players at the time, many of whom were in digs and who only saw their families occasionally during the season and in summer when they went back home.

A high rate of occupational mobility would remain a feature of a professional footballer's life. Exactly where a player lived was often determined by the club that signed him. Such stipulations might include places where they could *not* live. Len Graham's Millwall contract of 1932, banning him from living on licensed premises, was not uncommon. Neither was the clause in many players' contracts insisting that they move to the town where their club was situated. This could cause difficulties when the player in question was happy where he (and more important, perhaps, his wife) was.

Frank Barson, who lived in Sheffield, had only been at Aston Villa for a season, having been signed from Barnsley for £2,850 in 1919, when he began a running battle with the directors over their insistence that he move to Birmingham. Barson originally signed for Villa from Barnsley on the understanding that he continued to reside in Sheffield where he had a small business and a house. When it came to re-signing, however, the directors told him to move to Birmingham. He pointed to the fact that a number of other players with Villa resided elsewhere but the Villa directors were adamant.

Barson protested to the club secretary, and thought the matter was closed when he was offered a new contract, which he signed. However, when the directors later reiterated their demand that he move to Birmingham, Barson and Clem Stephenson, another player angry at being asked to move home, took the drastic decision to boycott a league match. Instead of travelling to play at Bolton Wanderers, they stayed at home. Villa lost by five goals. The two men were summoned to a board meeting and suspended for two weeks and again told to move house.

FAMOUS FOOTBALLERS AT HOME

A charming study of Neil Ha[...] Partick Thistle, with his wife [...] youngest child.

C. Dawson, Preston North End, and Mrs Dawson.

George Harrison, of Everton, and Mrs Harrison.

Tommy Meehan, of Manche[...] United, with his wife and baby

PRINTED AND PUBLISHED BY D. C. THOMSON & CO. LTD, 12 FETTER LANE, FLEET STREET, LONDON, E.C.4.

Barson stubbornly continued living in Sheffield, his stance being tolerated, perhaps, because he was a valuable player. His career at the club ended, however, in 1922, over another argument concerning club regulations. Manchester United, the club who bought him, wisely allowed him to remain living in Sheffield.

Previous page: *Topical Times,* 3 April 1920.

One can understand why some clubs insisted that their players resided locally, particularly before the days of motorways and high-powered cars. Barson's struggles, however, underline just how much of a problem housing could be for a player. Only valuable players could hold out if the directors insisted, although the public dressing- down Manchester United manager Alex Ferguson gave David Beckham when he missed training in February 2002 is an example of such tensions continuing to the present day. Beckham decided to stay at his home in Hertfordshire to look after his sick son. Ferguson felt the incident highlighted his major concern that a daily 350-mile round-trip between the Beckham household and Manchester United's Carrington training ground was a waste of vital energy. When a player isn't training or playing, Ferguson felt, he should be resting. Although he was unable to discipline Beckham for where he chose to live, he dropped him for the next match in order to make his point.

The housing of footballers, though always crucial for the men and their families, became a public issue after the Second World War. The bombing of major cities, especially London, had reduced the housing stock considerably, causing major problems for everyone. In the *Sunday People* of 24 November 1946, the headline 'Problem of the Homeless Footballer' highlighted what its author, Dave Mangnall, considered 'The Game's Biggest Headache Today':

'Behind the glamour and the clamour of the world's greatest game is often a bedrock of loneliness and fear. Behind the current cascades of cash falling into league clubs' bursting tills and pools promoters' bulging pockets is a seamier side to an entertainment industry which still ranks among the poorest paid on the earth....

'How does he live, this quiet, modest, generally underpaid fellow who earns during the few years of his playing life £10, £8, £7, £6, £5 and less per week? What do you know of the men behind the money? Their home life, their personal happiness, their worries, their difficulties, their stakes in the future? Well, I'll tell you. NOTHING. Nothing at all.'

Opposite page:
Topical Times,
6 June 1931.

Dave Mangnall, the manager of Queens Park Rangers, revealed: 'I've got good players, but – and here's my point – you can't keep men happy when they're homeless. Seven of my boys are either separated from their wives and families or have no homes at all. It is, in many ways, a tragic situation for a club with but one chance in twenty-two of going up to the Second Division, but I happen to know that it is not peculiar to Rangers alone.'

Mangnall gave one or two examples. His left-half, Ivor Powell, was earning the maximum £10 per week (£12 with bonus) 'yet his present circumstances take all the shine off his money. He cannot find a home in London. His wife lives in Blackpool with her parents while Ivor lodges at a restaurant in Shepherds Bush. Out of his salary he has to send about £6.10s home, feed and clothe himself as well as pay tax and also spend nearly three pounds every other weekend on the rail fare to Blackpool. And I don't suppose he'll mind my telling you that they are expecting a little Ivor soon.'

Danny Boxshall, who had served six years in the army and been awarded the Military Medal, lived with his wife and child in one room in Harrow. John Barr had 'digs' in London while his wife and child quietly bore their enforced separation in Scotland. 'They can't find a home for the three of them in London and he's a £7-a-week reserve. £3.10s goes to his wife; £2 to lodgings.'

MASTER MATCH

THE FOOTBALLER'S SON
46

Clearly, houses would come to play a part in many a transfer deal. In this same year, it was revealed that Charlton Athletic were ready to buy an £1,800 house for the Scot Tommy Walker if he signed for them but he turned them down and went to Chelsea instead. Such experiences encouraged clubs to invest in houses, many eventually owning between fifteen and twenty, which were offered to players, usually for a reasonable rent. Derby County, like many clubs, owned almost a street of houses, which encouraged footballers to 'cluster'. Tim Ward returned there to play after the war and rented a house with a bathroom and inside toilet for 25s a week. A sensible player would try and establish the right to buy the house he rented in his contract, or maybe make an agreement that the house would be sold to him for a nominal fee at the end of his career.

Buying a house before the 1960s was not a common event, however, either among footballers or the populace in general. Home ownership was rising, but was nowhere near the levels it would

Behind the Scenes with Football Favourites

TOM WARING as he appears on the field—

—A PEEP AT THE WARING FAMILY, with baby in the limelight and Aston Villa's centre-forward in the background.

ROBERT GURNEY, Sunderland's leader, shows his ability with the hedge scissors while Mrs Gurney cheers him on—

—GURNEY shoots for goal.

PRINTED AND PUBLISHED BY D. C. THOMSON & CO., LTD., 12 FETTER LANE, FLEET STREET, LONDON, E.C.4.

reach post-1980s. Only players at the top of the profession considered the idea. When Bobby Charlton helped win the World Cup for England in 1966, he and his wife lived in a detached house in Flixton, a pleasant suburb in Manchester. Charlton explained, 'We had no mortgage. It was very unusual for players to buy their own houses but we wanted our own and had to make sure we paid for it.'

In fact, a majority of the World Cup winners of 1966 were living in their own homes. Martin Peters' Ilford home had cost £3,000, Geoff Hurst's semi-detached house in Hornchurch had cost £5,000, while Bobby Moore and his wife Tina lived in a four-bedroomed detached house in Chigwell, well within the Hurst price range. Jack Charlton had had a house built for him in Leeds for £5,000, while George Cohen's was the most expensive: an £11,000 detached four-bedroomed place in Worcester Park, Surrey. Cohen, however, was already a businessman. The team were on wages ranging between £45 and £70 a week, before bonuses, which Roger Hunt considered, 'a comparatively decent wage then – double or treble the national average. I had a nice house and a good lifestyle in my early 20s.' Only two of the team lived in club-owned houses: Gordon Banks and Ray Wilson. Nobby Stiles lived in a semi-detached house he had bought from his club, while Alan Ball, unmarried and aged 20, was in digs in Blackpool.

In recent years Premiership clubs, keen to promote the notion of glamour brought by star names, and increasingly desperate to secure top players, have offered to provide them with houses. During David Ginola's controversial move from Spurs to Aston Villa, it was widely reported that the French winger was demanding a six-bedroomed house from the Birmingham club, as well as £63,000 a week in wages. Ginola's agent denied such claims, but there have been many other cases of clubs entering the property market on behalf of their players.

It has been claimed that one of the reasons Crystal Palace teetered on the brink of bankruptcy recently was the club's habit of renting substantial south London properties for their players, in some cases complete with servants. Chelsea, of course, have a number of luxurious apartments that have been built at Chelsea Village, the property complex surrounding the ground, which are occupied by first-teamers, Jody Morris among them. The club has an interesting track record where property is concerned. In 1991, it was fined a (then) record £105,000 by the FA after one of its companies was discovered to have bought defender Graham Roberts's Scottish house from him for £100,000 over the market value when he joined the club from Glasgow Rangers. Other clubs have, in the past, used similar practices. In 1992, the Inland Revenue discovered that Tottenham Hotspur had given undisclosed 'loans' to Paul Gascoigne and Chris Waddle to buy London houses when they joined the club.

2. Upwardly mobile

'A man used to be able to sit on the bus next to his hero, walk to the ground with him, touch him, see him riding a bike away from the ground. Our centre-half [at Barnsley] used to get on the bus two stops from where I got on. He used to have his boots round his neck.'

Michael Parkinson, talking in March 2002

Michael Parkinson's comments bemoaning the fact that players and fans had become 'disassociated', that when he was a boy in the 1930s and 1940s, players lived in the same streets as the fans, was true, but only up to a point. The vast majority of professional players still do live in close proximity of fans, though few now use public transport to get to the ground. Professional players have, however, often chosen to live far from their roots and they have often found themselves stepping out of their original class milieu. From the earliest period of pro football, many players were taking a step up the social ladder, and the location of their new houses reflected such movements.

Billy Meredith, who played for Manchester City in the 1890s, was one of the top earners of the pre-First World War period. He had been born into a poor mining family in Chirk, North Wales. When he first moved to Manchester City, he lived in lodgings close to the Hyde Road ground. Then, when he married and had children, he moved to a rented house in Nut Street, near Belle Vue Pleasure Gardens. This was a simple terraced house without an inside toilet but with a tiny garden. Upon joining Manchester United, however, he moved to the suburbs, closer to the Old Trafford ground. He rented a comfortable semi-detached house owned by the club. It had an

Tom Reid,
Manchester United,
with fiancée
Frances Hutchinson.
Sports Pictures,
8 June 1929.

indoor toilet, a bathroom and a garden. These conditions were very different from those in his home village of Chirk, to which he returned each summer for a holiday. He eventually established himself permanently as a publican in Manchester, where he died and was buried. His was a common journey among players.

Between the wars, many more leading professional footballers began to enjoy comforts and lifestyles that set them apart from their working-class roots. Fred Keenor, another Welshman who played for Cardiff City, developed a passion for middle-class recreations such as motoring and shooting. The maximum wage may not have made Keenor rich but that, together with the money he earned from product endorsement and the free time a professional player enjoyed, enabled him to develop tastes that were hardly typical of his background. To emphasise the move upward, he had a house built, in a select part of Cardiff, which he designed himself.

Alex James, who moved to Preston North End from Scotland in 1924, is another good example of a working-class player who wholeheartedly embraced an aspiring middle-class lifestyle. Once established in London with Arsenal, he lived in a comfortable, club-owned house in the pleasant and solidly middle-class suburb of Barnet, North London. Scotland then offered him little more than a holiday golfing jaunt.

Today, however, players at the very top of the scale, though they still move around the country, do appear to have retreated behind the walls of an array of exclusive housing complexes. What's more, various 'footballer belts' have taken their place alongside the stockbroker belts in popular folklore. These choice locations are often situated close to club training complexes, a stipulation in many players' contracts. In February 2001, for instance, no fewer than five pro players could be found clustered on a small purpose-built estate on the outskirts of Warrington, Cheshire. Along with Carlo Nash, a Manchester City goalkeeper, there were two Everton players, one Blackburn Rovers player, and an ex-Liverpool player.

Wilmslow, Cheshire, is another favoured location. As an estate agent brochure explains, 'For any footballer playing in the North-West there has only ever been one credible place to live. Just one address that can properly reflect your wealth and success: Wilmslow, the small glitzy stretch of stockbroker belt just south of Manchester. Jet-set Wilmslow provides all that a Premiership player could wish for: large modern houses on modern estates; airport access for those international fixtures, a surplus of shops selling expensive knick-nacks and accessories. There are, of course, plenty of other footballers to keep you keep company: the Beckhams, the Nevilles, and Manchester United manager Alex Ferguson among them.'

Other chosen Manchester United enclaves are Hale Barns and Alderley Edge. Liverpool players are said to favour Birkdale, near Stockport, close to various golf courses; Leeds United men cluster on the outskirts of Wetherby, near their purpose-built Thorp Arch training centre; Derby County players live on a new estate to the south of the city built by the club's vice-chairman, while Aston Villa players house-hunt in such locations as Tamworth in Arden, close to their Bodymoor Heath training ground.

Opposite: *Topical Times*, c. 1930.

Premiership players would seem to be spoilt for choice and advice concerning choosing the right location. Their 'house' journal, *The Players' Club*, contains regular features on buying homes as well as lavish advertisements extolling the virtues of such venues as The Knoll at Lostock, near Bolton ('eleven detached executive houses, starting price £1–2m each'); the Regency Place, also near Lostock ('a select development overlooking Regent Park Golf course'); the Atrium in Oxted, Surrey ('no ordinary house' at £700,000); or Totteridge Village, London N20 ('price range between £1.45m–£1.65m').

Cala Homes ('Homes Fit For Champions') profess to understand players' needs: 'A player's lifestyle is demanding enough without the hassle of finding the right place to make a home. At Cala, we understand your priorities – peace, quiet, security, comfort, style, good roads, links and enough space to relax and unwind.'

Another firm pitching for business emphasises safety and security: 'We always plan our houses in such a way that there are no blind spots between them – no brick walls or twisting pathways which can interfere with vision or provide a hiding place for strangers. Every plot is fenced for added security and even our landscaping is created in such a way that strategic positions are always clearly visible for home owners and visitors.'

Players are also warned that buying an exclusive millionaire-style home is no guarantee of peace and quiet and are advised to check whether their neighbour will be coming and going via helicopter. Moving up the social ladder clearly brings many unseen problems in train.

3. Through the keyhole

'[Bobby] Moore sees the Georgian-style house, which he spent something like £80,000 on building and which numbers among its features a spiral staircase and a bar that wouldn't look out of place at the Waldorf Astoria, as the realisation of a dream. "It's game, set and match for us," he says.'

Hugh McIlvanney writing in the Observer Review, 1975

FOOTBALL NOTABILITIES *at* HOME

TEA-TIME AT WEST HAM
Victor Watson and family

ERIC BROOK (Manchester City)
acts as accompanist to his
wife and daughter

LISTENING-IN AT WIGAN
Jim Sullivan (Rugby League star)
and Mrs. Sullivan

It would be many years before the popular press thought it worth its while to take a peek behind the front doors of the stars. When it did, what was revealed seemed reassuringly normal. The domesticated inter-war professional footballer would be the model recommended by managers to their teams in the decades to come.

In 1938, Peter Doherty and his wife were one of a number of football couples featured in a short series in *Topical Times* entitled 'The Human Side of the Players': 'The house is the home. That's the Doherty slogan. Mrs Doherty is very proud of their wee house. Peter is a smiling and willing "improver". As a youngster, Peter served a bit of time in the building trade. He knows a bit about everything to do with houses. Peter has put new tiles in the fireplaces, bathroom and so on. How it became done is very illustrative of the easy grace of the life in the Doherty household. Mrs Doherty mentioned that she had tired of the tile colours of the dining room. Peter agreed. Next day he came home with a lot of tiles, plaster and whatever else is necessary for tiling. Then he took the old ones out, put the new ones in. Most married men would have hummed and hawed, and discussed the matter. Peter never gets excited. New tiles wanted? New tiles it is. Same with paper on the walls and so forth. He just takes it in his stride. The result is a credit to Peter's work and his wife's good taste. Their home is very wonderfully papered and furnished. The taste is faultless.'

Such journalistic politeness seems even further away in time than the sixty-five years that have since passed. Today, the mockery of footballers' domestic pretensions has reached epic proportions. Indicative of how the press perceive the footballer's home today is this paragraph from the property pages of the *Daily Telegraph*: 'They are not too hard to spot. The expensive, limited-edition sports car sitting next to the top-of-the-range people-carrier on the gravel drive offers the first clue. His and hers initials lovingly picked out on the wrought-iron gates or carved into the fake-Tudor beams give another. Sneak up to the leaded windows of the living-room, and behind the ruched, pink silk curtains you can spy the biggest television screen this side of a NASA control room and a £10,000 Bang and Olufsen music system. The club badge on the patio or decorating the bottom of the swimming pool should provide clinching evidence as to the type of person who lives here.'

The houses and furnishings which footballers buy today command huge public attention and it seems to be an unquestioned fact of life that their taste rarely rises above the most clichéd. Carlo Nash apparently liked the £480,000 show house he was viewing so much he wanted to buy it exactly as it was. This included steel-tipped chopsticks on the dining-room table, a trumpet and some fading Boosey sheet music in the spare room; with monks chanting on the multi-room sound system. 'It's great. The master bedroom is just like a suite in a hotel,' he enthused.

The house was described in the brochure as 'Classical or faux Georgian' in style, the garden being a 'strategic open space' where there was a gazebo, some decking, a few shrubs and a tiny lawn. 'So long as it's got enough space for a barbecue and some sunbathing in the summer, I don't mind,' said Nash.

Meanwhile, a photographer who made his living 'snapping' footballers was quoted as having 'trailed around enough of their houses for *Hello!*-style shoots to profess being overwhelmed by the sight of so many gold candelabras and gaudily painted porcelain dogs'. He continued, 'Usually, you're confronted with something that's rather naff, just like a developer's brochure. Aside from a crowded trophy cabinet, a Gameboy on the floor and a snooker table, there is little personality.'

Sniggering at a footballer's furnishings and the accompanying lifestyles has become something of a spectator sport. The new-found wealth, glamour and status of the average Premiership player produces longing and contempt on behalf of the fans in equal measure. He may earn £25,000 a week and be able to score from thirty yards, we mutter, but my God, did you see his coffee table? Premiership players who have eagerly embraced *Hello!*-style publicity (and cash) can't complain. But there is a parallel here with the treatment meted out to 'Essex man and woman', those working-class people who have made a determined effort to move away from their roots, losing their cultural and aesthetic bearings along the way. They encounter two sorts of middle-class scorn: from the left for their 'betrayal' of their class; from the right for their hopeless presumption.

If they do it with officially approved style, of course, they receive approbation from all sides. In 1991, it was written of ex-footballer/TV presenter Gary Lineker in a Sunday newspaper profile 'Where most [footballers] in the South East favour nouveau riche dwellings in Hertfordshire or Essex, Lineker owns a five bed-roomed Georgian terrace worth £800,000 in St John's Wood, prized no doubt for its proximity to Lord's cricket ground.'

However, the choice of house and contents by players at the very top will often have been made with an eye to the near future. The transient nature of a professional's life (when he can be bought and sold as quickly as it takes his manager to pick up the phone and talk to his agent) suggests that something immediately saleable will be an investment. Thus, why spend time making the house distinctively yours when, six months later, you could be playing for a team on the other side of the country or even the world? As the David Wilson Homes blurb puts it: 'The beauty of purchasing a David Wilson home is that [the player] can easily part exchange their old home for a new one, making the process easy and hassle free.'

Buying a home 'off the peg', as Carlo Nash appears to have done, also suggests a need to establish something instantly, so that the routine of playing and resting can be established swiftly. A week or two of physical dislocation can result in a dip in form and thus the loss of one's place in the team. Players' fortunes change from week to week. Tranquillity away from the stadium has to be established without too much fuss.

And many players are extremely young, with little or no experience in actually building a home. Dwight Yorke, for instance, went from a small bathroom-less bungalow on a dirt track in the West Indies to a £1 million mansion in Cheshire in the space of a few short years. Born in 1971, the eighth of nine children, he was brought up in the village of Canaan in Tobago. The family's house, built from concrete and breeze blocks, had two bedrooms, a living-room and an outside kitchen. There was no bathroom or lavatory, simply because the only water available came from a standpipe at the end of the road.

After signing for Aston Villa as a 17-year-old, Yorke arrived in Birmingham in December 1989. He spent six weeks in city-centre digs before moving to Shustoke, a remote village in Warwickshire. His new accommodation was in a pretty, sixteenth-century cottage, complete with wooden beams and period furniture, the home of Sheila and Bryn Dudley, one of a number of couples who look after young Villa players. Three years on, and Yorke bought a house in Walmley, near Birmingham, for £95,000, followed by a bigger one for £200,000. After his transfer to Manchester United in 1998, Yorke lived for four months in a succession of luxury hotels before buying a new £600,000 house in Bramhall, the heart of Cheshire's stockbroker and footballer belt. It was described by Hunter Davies in his official biography of Yorke as 'brand-new, brick-built, long and low. Beverly-Hills posh'; it also had the 'trademark' high-security gates and three cars in the drive. 'Every room on the ground floor seemed the same – white carpets, white walls, expensive pieces of marble, glass, polished wood, all of it unused, unlived in,' wrote Mr Davies. 'Upstairs, I didn't count the bedrooms, probably four or five, all with white carpets, devoid of any personality.'

It's hard to know what Davies was expecting. Not all comment is so disparaging, however. In a recent series on Sky TV looking into the lifestyles of the 'Soccerati'– young, talented and wealthy Premiership players – viewers were taken round the purpose-built bachelor 'lad-pad' of Blackburn Rovers' Matt Jansen. The modernist city-centre apartment had a roof-top hot tub, where Jansen could soak himself beneath the stars listening to his 'tunes' on 'surround-sound', a huge 'lazy boy' chair (bought when he saw it on the TV series *Friends*) and a grand piano that had to be hoisted up at great expense so that he could learn to play 'tunes for the lads to sing along with'.

As Jansen sat in front of his computer (which he could barely use except to surf for holidays and properties to buy), various top football journalists fell over themselves to laud him as a perfect example of the new 'intelligent' player living the wealthy 'lad' lifestyle yearned for by thousands of young men up and down the country. The question of his personal tastes never came into it. The contrast between Jansen and the Soccerati series' front-man, George Best, was almost painful to see. When Best had tried to make the quantum leap from traditional bed-sit footballer digs to owning his own home back in 1969, the experience had been a chastening one. Mocked and derided for his taste in architecture, not to mention house-hold fixtures and fittings, and driven to distraction by the intrusive behaviour or fans and press alike, Best was forced to beat a hasty retreat to his original landlady and remained with her until the end of his playing days.

4. Footballers' wives

'To be the wife of a famous footballer. To share a name that is constantly on the lips of thousands of admiring, idolising people. To taste the very same cup of victory and success that he drinks – yes, and the often bitter cup of disappointment and defeat. This, surely, is to be one of the most enviable among women?'

Mrs David Jack, writing in Thomson's Weekly News, 1928

World Cup wives of 1966: Mrs Ray Wilson.

Matt Busby, Best's manager at Manchester United, always put Best's failure to settle down to not having had a wife at home to make the supper and ward off the groupies. Best did make an attempt at marriage, to a blonde Danish girl he met on a pre-season tour. Rather ungallantly, he commented in one of his biographies, 'You could say I fell in love with a pair of knockers.' Dwight Yorke's courtship of Jordon, the pneumatic nude model, suggests the two men shared tastes both in house styles and female figures. What's more, the two blondes certainly fit the contemporary template for the 'Footballer's Wife'.

Footballers' weddings were the object of attention in the press from very early on in the professional game. Exactly who pro players married, however, was rarely considered newsworthy. Players hadn't started moving in show business circles to any great extent and wouldn't do until the 1970s. If they had done, they would have found stage and screen actresses earning money far in excess of what even a top player earned. Thus, they found their partners, like most other working-class men, at local dances, at the cinema, in the local grocer's shop or even in the workplace. Alec James married the daughter of Raith Rovers' trainer Dave Willis. Some players set their sights higher.

In 1912, Thomson's Weekly News reported on 'a pretty romance of the football field' involving Walter Aitkenhead, Blackburn Rovers' inside left, who was to wed Ethel Cotton – daughter of Lawrence Cotton JP, one of the club's directors. Cotton was a wealthy industrialist and Aitkenhead eventually became his personal secretary, inheriting the business when Cotton died.

Sweeping a club director's daughter off her feet would be a staple of much football fiction during the inter-war years. In reality it could produce a local sensation. In February 1933, Neil Dewar arrived at Manchester United from Third Lanark for a fee of £5,000. He scored fourteen goals in thirty-six appearances, and was then suddenly transferred to Sheffield Wednesday in December the same year. Some months later, it was announced that he had eloped with Betty Thompson, aged 19, daughter of Manchester United director AE Thompson. In November 1934, Betty had a baby daughter.

World Cup Wives of 1966: Mrs George Cohen.

Though players were hardly pin-ups in these early years, they were still valuable in matrimonial terms. The magazine, Football Answers, in February 1920 gave the following assessment of the professional player: 'The footballer is usually a presentable fellow, clean, manly, good-tempered. Also, he is a bit of a catch as a sweetheart. As a bachelor, at least, he has money to burn on chocolates, picture palaces and the like. If he is worth having as a sweetheart, he is equally so as a husband – a healthy life, good, regular wages, a benefit to look forward to and a good chance of starting a business of his own or well-paid employment as a manager, coach or trainer when he retires. Undoubtedly, the average footballer is something of a matrimonial catch these days.'

So much so that their names were occasionally used by unscrupulous characters intent on seduction. In March 1924, Victor Wright of Tower Gardens Road, Tottenham, was summoned at Enfield by a Ponders End girl in respect of an affiliation order. Wright was alleged to have impersonated Charlie Walters, the Tottenham Hotspur centre-half, telling his victim that he was going to have his benefit match soon and would then marry her and take her to South Africa. When she read in the papers that Walters was engaged to be married, Wright said, 'Don't believe all you read in the papers.' On another occasion, she went to see Tottenham play and told Wright that she did not recognise him on the field, as his hair seemed different. He replied, 'I always shampoo

World Cup wives
of 1966:
Mrs Bobby Charlton.

my hair before going on to the field and dye it when I come off.' Just prior to having Wright's child, the girl went to the Spurs ground to confront the innocent Walters, who had to employ a solicitor to sort the confusion out.

Occasionally, a popular player's wedding caused a minor sensation. When Ted Sagar of Everton got married in 1932, it was reported that, 'A number of women attempted to kiss Sagar as he left the church. He was rescued by stewards and compromised by kissing a little girl who presented him with a horseshoe tied with Everton colours.'

There were regular reports from players on honeymoon, and bridal pictures aplenty, but the coverage of wives as such was minimal. There was a tendency, however, in the popular sporting press to present the home lives of the football stars as near perfect examples of marital bliss. Typical of the genre would be the 'Human Side of...' series in *Topical Times* in the late 1930s. The home life of Millwall's Dave Mangnall, according to the journalist, 'means a lot to him. His tall, fair-haired attractive wife Anne and two-year-old son Dave, junior, are the magnets that make the fireside his natural rendezvous most evenings of the week.' Anne had been a nurse but had married Dave when he moved from Huddersfield to Millwall. 'A quiet evening at home, rendered even more pleasant if the wireless has a brass band concert to offer, is the delight of both.'

Only when players and their wives found themselves in court did one get a glimpse of a less than idyllic picture. 'Pongo' Waring, the great Aston Villa striker, broke down in tears when his wife collapsed giving evidence in a Birmingham Police court during an action concerning Waring's maintenance arrears in 1936. Then there was the uncontested divorce granted to ex-Manchester City player Jimmy Broad's wife in 1935, the other woman involved being the player's 'digs' landlady.

The footballer's wife was usually silent during the inter-war period. In 1929, however, on the eve of her husband's record transfer to Arsenal, David Jack's wife talked about her life. She reminded *Weekly News* readers of the reality of a player's life: 'There is no security of tenure for him; loss of form or a damaged limb might mean the abrupt termination of his activity on the field.' With no pension forthcoming, 'all this is a source of serious concern for the thoughtful wife'.

Clubs, she felt, were generally kind and considerate to wives for very practical reasons. 'The majority of first-class clubs like to see their players married for the very reason that it increases their sense of responsibility and makes them more willing to settle down with one club.' Wives also performed an important supporting role in controlling their husband's diet, and aiding in his recovery from injury. She might also work with the club manager to keep the player concerned disciplined, pointing out that a manager sometimes used the wife to bring pressure to bear upon a player who might be causing 'difficulties'.

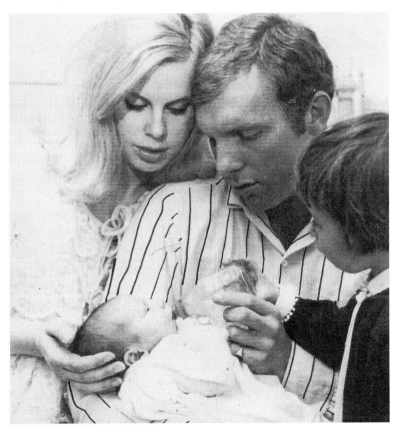

Bobby Moore, wife Tina, baby son Dean and daughter Roberta, 1969.

Moving to a new club was particularly unsettling, however. 'We were very happy at Bolton. We had settled and made many friends in the town. When I heard rumours of my husband's possible transfer to the Arsenal club I was secretly much perturbed.' When the move was confirmed, she felt the ground had vanished from beneath her feet: 'Oh! The severing of old ties, the disheartening search for a suitable house in London, the lonely feeling that the capital and its vast suburbs inspired in me! I felt adrift, outcast. My enthusiasm for football temporarily faded.'

In spite of such difficulties Mrs Jack still felt that marrying a footballer gave a woman the chance to involve herself in her husband's day-to-day life in a way that was usually denied to the majority of women. When a player's career ended, he was often in his early 30s and life after football could be difficult. Before the era of massive salaries and pension-plans, many players started small businesses while they were still footballers and so the wife was often involved in establishing and running the business when the player was away.

In 1958, Marion McDonald, wife of the Burnley and England goalkeeper, explained: 'We decided to go in for a small-holding around Guildford way when Colin finishes with football. We think we could manage about twelve acres. So Colin is studying small-holding. A few weeks ago we bought fifty hens. Colin built the hen-house himself with some second-hand timber. He's made a grand job of it. The only snag is I'll have to feed the hens while he's away.' Mrs Ronnie Clayton, wife of the England and Blackburn star, revealed that since they had taken on a newsagent's shop, which she had to look after when he was playing, she'd lost two stone in weight.

Another unusual aspect of the footballers' wives lives was the fact that footballer husbands were around the house a lot. Before the 1960s and 1970s, the routines of working-class life were set by the factories and offices in which the vast majority of men were employed. They went to work in the morning and came home in the evening. Women, if they weren't working themselves, looked after the home. For most of the week, the couple were apart. In a football household, the player went out in the morning but was back by lunchtime. In the afternoons there would be more training, but only for a couple of hours. As players had to conserve energy and avoid injury, relaxing at home was considered part of the job. Women had the opportunity, therefore, to spend much more free time with their husbands than the average working-class woman. In a series of interviews with ex-players and their wives conducted in the late 1990s, however, Brian Gearing of the Open University discovered other aspects of life with a footballer. One wife remembered: 'It was a lonely, lonely life…playing football over Christmas and bank holidays. But during the week he wasn't here either…he was at the YMCA playing snooker.'

Clare Williams, married to Paul 'Willo' Williams, much-travelled Northern Ireland international of the 1990s, suggested, 'Football is like no other job that I know. Imagine a 10.30 a.m.−1.00 p.m. working day. No rush hour traffic, always home for *Neighbours* and, on game days, a pre-match lunch thrown in. When I first met my husband I thought, "Great, someone fit to join me in the gym, play racquetball, go swimming." What I didn't bargain for were the afternoons crashed out on the settee recovering from a hard morning's training. The most energetic activity might be a stroll around the golf course (using a buggy!).'

Alan Ball's wife, Lesley, recalled in an interview in June 2002 how she had to accustom herself to loneliness, to centring her life on the couple's children, to the continual moving as they followed Alan from Everton, to Arsenal, to Southampton and on to the North American Soccer League. If she had a problem, she solved it herself, 'because he had to concentrate on his football'. The rewards were a middle-class lifestyle.

Clearly, how opportunities were used depended on the couple involved and what they chose to do with their lives, but it was a different life, with its generous amounts of free time combined with more than sufficient disposable income, and it set footballing families and households apart from the rest.

Charlie Williams and first wife Audrey in 1957.

Football Notabilities at Home

ROY KINNEAR, the Wigan Rugby League player and Mrs Kinnear, pose for their photo after a motor run

AUSTIN CAMPBELL, Huddersfield Town, and Mrs Campbell

BILL IMRIE, Blackburn Rovers, with Mrs Imrie and baby

The potential effect that a footballer's wife might have on a player's career first came into head-line prominence, however, in 1950, when a number of top players were tempted to Colombia by promises of lucrative contracts and lavish accommodation. The football side of the saga is familiar but much of the real drama was of a domestic nature, with the wives very much to the fore.

Previous page:
Topical Times,
c. 1930.

Neil Franklin, the England centre-half, was one such player who went as far as signing a contract and settling in Bogota with his wife. When she became pregnant she decided she wanted to have the baby in England. The club agreed to pay for the trip and Franklin accompanied her to New York. He suddenly decided to return to England with her and never went back to Colombia.

Because of the secret nature of the enterprise, Welshman Roy Paul's wife wasn't told of his decision to go and, when informed by journalists that he was in South America, her comments didn't auger well: 'I'll certainly join Roy when he sends for me, but I know I won't like it. Gelli (in the Rhonnda) is good enough for me,' she declared, while her mother, on hearing Roy might have to work his passage back on a cargo ship, the deal having fallen through, said: 'And I hope they make him scrub the deck from end to end. That will teach him to fly off to the other side of the world without saying a word.'

Trevor Ford of Cardiff and Wales later claimed that he had been giving serious consideration to the offer when he received a cable from his wife urging him not to sign but to return home immediately as their son was ill. He later commented: 'Like so many players, I was influenced in my decision to come home by my wife. Thank goodness nobody accused me of hiding behind my wife's skirts. This is the charge that is frequently levelled at soccer players nowadays. Fans sneer: "Look at 'em! Full grown beefy blokes sheltering behind their wives' petticoats." In nine cases of out ten this charge is as ridiculous as it is unfair. I've heard veterans of an earlier era talk of how the great Jimmy Seed went to Tottenham and moved into mean digs until accommodation could be found for his wife. Today's wives won't let their husbands move until a house is provided…'

Significantly, the only player to make a success of the venture in Colombia was Charlie Mitten, whose wife later said that it had been a wonderful experience: 'We had everything we wanted – a lovely villa, two maids and a gardener…'

5. 'Trophy' wives

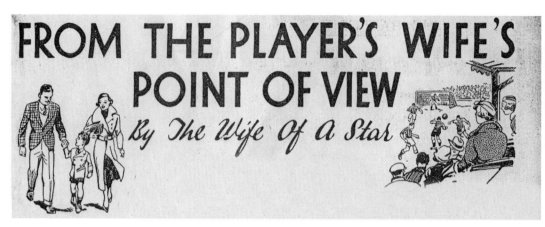

FROM THE PLAYER'S WIFE'S POINT OF VIEW
By The Wife Of A Star

Topical Times,
7 May 1938.

'My wife, whom I married shortly after leaving Blackpool, hails from that town and is rather reserved by nature. When I told her I intended to write about her in this book, she was violently opposed to the idea. "You're discussing football," she said pointedly. "Stick to it. Soccer fans are not interested in a player's domestic life."'

Peter Doherty, Spotlight on Football, 1947

Shelly Webb, wife of ex-England, Manchester United and Nottingham Forest star Neil, interviewed fourteen footballer's wives for a book in 1995 and the picture they painted was of chronic insecurity, constant upheaval, boredom and loneliness. Echoing Mrs David Jack in the late 1920s, she found that wives were still coping with the same fundamental difficulties. These are primarily the invasion of privacy, frequent uprooting due to transfers, the time spent apart, the difficulties caused by player injury or bad form and, finally, adapting to the realisation that the player's football days may soon be over at quite an early age.

The only significant difference between the experience of being a footballer's wife in the 1920s and that of now concerned the behaviour of other women. The worst hazard, Webb felt, was the 'pack of female groupies who swarm around soccer stars wherever they go. You can be out for a quiet meal with your hubby and they come up and proffer a piece of flesh for him to sign. Then they sidle up again and drop their telephone number in his pocket and you are sitting there with him. I hate to think what happens when you are not there.'

Lee-Ann Baker, wife of Wimbledon midfielder Andy Roberts, agreed: 'There are so many women out there that we call the "goal diggers". They don't care if you are sitting right next to your husband wearing matching wedding rings. They'll dance sexily right up to him and give him their phone numbers. The last thing you want to do is go to the loo. When you come back they will be swarming all over your man. It's a privileged life but you have a lot to put up with.'

The attractiveness of professional footballers for the opposite sex did not begin in the 1960s with George Best, of course. Collecting cigarette card pictures of professionals was, however, a young man's hobby and little attention was given to the footballer as pin-up. In 1904 an *Umpire* poll for Best Player put Billy Meredith ahead of Steve Bloomer, but this was in purely football terms. In November 1911, *Thomson's Weekly News* announced the result of a 'great referendum'. Readers had voted for the 'trickiest player', 'the greatest general', 'the most popular player', etc. To the surprise of the editors, Jimmy Turnbull of Bradford was voted the Best Looking Player. ('There's honour for you James! Bob Crompton follows hard at his heels but, curiously enough, the majority of the ladies fancy the Park Avenue pivot.') It was assumed by the editors that it had been women voting for him, of course. However, such opinion polls were rare in pre-war days. Sex appeal, or the admission of such, was clearly something of a taboo but here were young, fit, healthy, reasonably wealthy men appearing in public dressed in scanty attire.

Charlie Roberts, the popular captain of Manchester United and famous for wearing extremely short shorts, recounted a peculiar episode that occurred in 1908 after a controversial fourth round tie at Burnley. The Manchester United team found themselves facing an irate crowd outside the ground: 'After I dressed I was informed that a large crowd of factory women were waiting for me outside and that it would be best for me to leave the ground by another exit. I left the ground quietly with some of the Burnley players at the top entrance to the ground and as I looked

THE BEST DRESSED PLAYERS

TED CATLIN (Sheff. Wednesday) —Likes his materials hefty and very much built to order.

HARRY HOLDCROFT (Preston North End)—Always spruce but conventional.

GEORGE AINSLEY (Leeds Utd.) — Unconventional, comfortable and colourful.

BERRY NIEUWENHYS (Liverpool) —Subdued good quality material. Always looks well cared for and well turned out.

FRANK SWIFT (Manchester City) —Has a good eye for blending the colours.

LEN BUTT (Blackburn Rovers)— Bright dresser, likes light, colourful effects.

BOB STUART (Middlesbrough)— Crisp and dapper.

PERCY GROSVENOR (Leicester City)—Sophisticated taste.

down the street I could see all the womenfolk outside the players' entrance where our conveyance stood. I walked into town and to the hotel for tea without even being recognised but I understand a funny incident happened as the rest of the players left the dressing room to get into the brake that was to take them to the hotel. As soon as they emerged, cries of "Where's Charlie?" were heard. At last someone cried out, "That's him!" and poor Alec Bell was mistaken for me and in the bit of a scuffle that followed, one of the factory lasses put a huge dummy tit into Alec's mouth and as he mounted the steps with it between his lips – he kept it there for the fun – the women yelled with delight. It evidently pleased them to see me, as they thought, with a dummy tit in my mouth. But what I actually had in my mouth at the time was a good cigar.' Exactly what significance the dummy tit had was never explained. Roberts, with his David Beckham hairstyle and 'Jack Johnson' nickname (after the then World Heavyweight Boxing Champion) was clearly the object of some kind of mass female fascination.

Previous page:

Topical Times,

25 March 1939.

A more traditional approach was the letter received in November 1909, by George Holley of Sunderland. Holley told *Weekly News* readers: 'As soon as I had lifted the envelope I knew the message had been dispatched by tender hands for the sweet odour of perfume quickly rose to my nostrils. I blushed and hastily tore the envelope open, extracted the message and there rolled on the floor a sweet little charm in the shape of a glass pendant into which was set a neat little spray of "lucky white heather". What did it mean? I then read the message: "Dear Mr Holley," the writer began, "I send you this little charm in the hope that, if you wear it, it will help you to go through the football season without being kicked. It is lucky white heather." No signature was attached, the young lady in question saying she would be easily recognised as she sat at the front of the pavilion and would be wearing a similar charm.' Holley didn't say if he spotted her or not.

As we have seen, with their relatively limited income, players, no matter how physically attractive they might be, could never aspire to winning the hands of music-hall or film stars. When Gracie Fields was introduced to Arsenal players in the early 1930s, she failed to recognise Alex James, probably the most celebrated player in the country at the time while the closest James

would have come to a female film star would have been as a paying patron in his local cinema. His wife, in fact, was the daughter of his trainer at Raith Rovers whom he'd met when he was still
a relative unknown.

The footballer as matinee idol was slow to develop, but it was
given a boost by the large number of players who joined the RAF
during the Second World War as Physical Training Instructors, and
thus automatically earned a Warrant Officer's stripe. Changes
occurred as a result. Arsenal's swashbuckling Denis Compton, the
original Brylcreem Boy, was often seen with a starlet or two on his
arm. The debonair England captain George Hardwick, through his
close friendship with actress Dora Bryan, found himself escorting
some of the most attractive leading ladies of the post-war period to
dinner, including Kay Kendall, Shirley Eaton and Margaret
Lockwood. Football's equivalent of Clark Gable, however, had
already met his wife, Joy, an ATS girl, at a war-time dance on the
Isle of Sheppey.

Billy Wright's marriage to Joy Beverley, one of the popular
singing trio the Beverley Sisters, appeared to mark a step up for the
footballer as celebrity husband. Though it was hardly Joe DiMaggio
and Marilyn Monroe, the marriage was one of equals in that both
were successful in their respective spheres. By the 1960s, thanks to
George Best, the women who became involved with top players
were beginning to receive more attention and some of his potential
spouses were celebrities of a kind – a series of Miss Worlds, the
actress Sinead Cusack. As we have seen, the woman he actually pro-
posed to, however, was a blonde called Eva whom he met on a football tour of Denmark.

In May 1976, when the porn star Fiona Richmond threw off
her clothes and jumped into the Crystal Palace team bath along
with manager Malcolm Allison, most of the players, including
Terry Venables, jumped out and headed for the changing rooms.
A tabloid photographer had been taking photos that, according
to Venables, were to cause no end of trouble with their wives. It
was a glimpse of things to come. More pertinent, however, was
Fiona Richmond's comment afterwards: 'I think Malcolm's done
a great deal for football. At least he's colourful. He shoots his
mouth off but he's very open and honest about what he does. And
he gets other people interested. As a woman I would never have

normally taken an interest. I don't find footballers particularly attractive.' They were, she felt, 'a draggy lot…'.

Ten years on, and Peter Stringfellow couldn't get enough of them into his fashionable night club. The young wealthy footballer had become an essential member of a new glitterati consisting, it would seem, of female soap opera stars, minor pop singers and *Sun* newspaper Page Three girls, as the new money generated during the early boom years of Margaret Thatcher flooded into certain young people's pockets. As Jenny Blyth, the Page Three consort of West Ham and Celtic star Frank McAvennie put it: 'It was bottles of Bolly all the time. Everyone had money.' The couple were, as she put it, the 'Posh and Becks' of their day.

It was as if the professional footballer as celebrity had at last entered a sphere where he and the women he consorted with were equally newsworthy, if not quite as talented. Apart from one or two celebrated individuals such as pop stars Victoria Beckham and Louise Rednapp, fashion model Coraline Ginola (wife of Aston Villa's French star David Ginola), and actress Leslie Ash, Lee Chapman's wife, the women involved are rarely superstars. A surprising number, in fact, are 'soap star' actresses from popular series such as *Hollyoaks, Brookside, EastEnders, Emmerdale* and *Grange Hill,* as well as TV celebrities such as Ulrika Johnson and Dani Behr, or 'models' like Caprice and Jordan. Nevertheless, their appearance confirms that footballers now move in more glamorous circles than before. Louise Rednapp felt, 'I definitely think it helps if you're both used to being in the public eye. Whereas Jamie and I both understand the pressures of each other's jobs, you can imagine the problems of being married to one of the Spice Girls if you were a joiner, for instance?'

This suggests that most of the wives of today's top footballers face new pressures because there is little evidence to suggest that they are any different in social or occupational terms from footballers' wives of ten, twenty, or even fifty years ago. A recent survey of wives and regular partners revealed an assortment of ex-telesales operators, lap dancers, PR consultants, clothes shop assistants, supermarket check-out girls, bank-clerks, clerical assistants and the ubiquitous hairdressers.

Hypothetically, to move from a hairdressing salon in Wigan to a millionaire's mansion in Alderley Edge is a big leap for a young woman. How does she respond? What is she supposed to look like and how should she behave? Many young women appear to be as ill-equipped as their husbands to cope with such transformations. They, like their husbands, have no training in what to do, either with their time or their money. Their every slip, however, is pounced upon by an avid press.

At the very top, dealing with the publicity fall-out of their husband's career brings difficulties. One player's wife said she had great difficulty in judging who were truly her friends, noting that people's attitudes changed drastically towards her once they knew that she was the wife of a professional footballer.

As a profile in the *Daily Telegraph* rather unkindly put it: 'They may drive Bentleys and bathe in L'Air du Temps and share a taste for housing with the Duke and Duchess of York, but the fact remains that most football wives, like their million-pound-a-year husbands, come from lower-working-class backgrounds, are poorly educated, socially awkward and more dependant than most of us on the support of the families they grew up in.'

It doesn't help that they have also become the subject of a TV 'soap', *Footballers' Wives*. Drawing inspiration from Birmingham City executive Karren Brady's 1990s sex 'n' shopping novel, *Trophy Wives*, and evidence from some highly selective interviewing of real wives, it has proved wildly successful but has led to much snobbish comment. Richard Williams of the *Guardian*: 'There's nothing too bizarre [in the programme]. It all seems horrifyingly easy to believe. They [footballers and their wives] see themselves as the new rock and roll royalty. It's true that the culture it depicts is relentlessly banal. But that's the way most people are, not just footballers.' The programme, he claimed, has 'everything to do with [football's] sleaze and excess as an ailing spectacle at the bottom of the cultural food chain'.

Back in the real world, most footballers' wives are still trying to deal with the traditional problems associated with their calling: exclusion from that male world of dressing-room banter and juvenility; being on the sharp end of painful readjustments when their spouse's career winds down; being on the blunt end of physical abuse when alcohol and ego run riot; 'holding the fort' while he is on tour, on the team bus, on the town. Many wives have great difficulty in establishing their own identities. As one put it recently, 'You're expected not to have a career or life of your

55

Topical Times, July 11, 1931.

A Football Notability On AND Off The Field

A wedding-day photo of JOE BERESFORD, the Aston Villa forward, and his bride. Joe was married this year.

Beresford on the ball.

own. The manager isolates you, takes the players away to hotels at weekends and on holidays and the wives are never included. Imagine your children coming home from school crying, upset about the things that were being said about their father.'

Perhaps the introduction of Sven Goran Eriksson as England manager presages a change in the way women will be treated in future? Prior to the 2002 World Cup, the twenty-three players, their wives and girlfriends spent a five-day 'working holiday' in the five-star luxury Jumeirah Beach Club in Dubai to 'encourage the families to bond' before the competition. Eriksson commented, 'In football today, you have to treat the family in a good way. If the wives are not happy, you have a problem, because life becomes difficult.'

No such bonding occurred prior to the 1966 World Cup. Even when the Boys of '66 returned in triumph to the Royal

Garden Hotel in London for the victory reception, their wives found themselves sidelined. Alan Ball's wife, Lesley, recalled: 'We weren't invited to the reception. It was all male. We held our own little celebration in one of the fast-food restaurants in the hotel.' And the FA's commemorative gift to the loyal spouses to mark the historic win? 'If I remember correctly it was a pair of scissors. It was 1966. That was normal then.'

Chapter 9

When the Cheering Stops

*'A little lad was boasting to his mate at school.
"My Dad's got more than a hundred medals
for football."
"What is he, a striker?"
"No, he's a pawnbroker."'*

Charlie Williams

The fate of professional players after their playing careers have ended has always proved fascinating to football fans. Perhaps it's simple curiosity, a desire to see how an old favourite is faring. Or perhaps it's something else, a voyeuristic trip into the abyss? Rags-to-riches-to-rags-again stories have always held a grim satisfaction and, where footballers are concerned, there seems to have been no shortage of fallen idols: once proud stars found making tea on building sites.

Herbert Chapman, who played professionally before the First World War and later managed both Huddersfield Town and Arsenal, recalled in 1931: 'In my days as a player, football was regarded as a

SIX FAMOUS PLAYERS TAKE YOU INTO THEIR CONFIDENCE

When I Finish With the Game

BACK TO MY OLD TRADE !

I SHALL go back to my old trade—electrical engineering.

It seems a pity that the many years I spent learning the trade should be thrown to the winds.

by

REG. SMITH

(Millwall outside-left).

I prefer to get away from football. Not that I don't love the game. I do. But too many pro's have the idea of keeping in the game when they stop playing. One more may be just one too many!

I don't intend to be that one!

I get plenty of practice in my old profession. Just recently our Manager, Mr Hewitt, commissioned me to assist in the re-wiring of the offices at the Den.

That was a pretty big job and kept my leisure moments fully occupied for many days. In addition I still get little jobs here and there for friends. It all helps!

THERE'S NOTHING LIKE FARMING !

WHEN I finish with football I want to get back to the land. Farming is the job of my choice! When I was a lad I used to help on my granddad's farm back home in Scotland.

Whether I was milking cows, hay-making, or

by

BERT JOHNSTON

(Sunderland centre-half).

cleaning-out the stables I enjoyed every minute of it. I was out in the open-air and had the satisfaction of doing what I think is the most honest-to-goodness job in the world.

An uncle of mine has a farm in America. In letters he has told me once or twice that he will find me all the work I need if I ever decide to cross the Atlantic to visit him. I'm keeping that invitation in mind!

NO INSIDE JOB FOR ME !

AN agent for an insurance company. That's what I want to be when I wrap up my football boots for good.

I've got one qualification—I drive a car.

by

HARRY CANN

(Plymouth Argyle 'keeper).

And I'm studying insurance matters in my spare time. I'd like this job because I would be outside most of the time. I'd never be able to settle down at an inside job.

Before I began playing football I was a slate-splitter at a stone-quarry in Cornwall. But that job doesn't appeal to me at all now!

I Want to be a Manager !

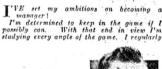

I'VE set my ambitions on becoming a manager!

I'm determined to keep in the game if I possibly can. With that end in view I'm studying every angle of the game. I regularly

by

GEO. AINSLEY

(Leeds United inside-right).

attend the Leeds Instructional Course during the summer to get an insight as to what goes on in the coaching direction.

I want to feel that I have a sound knowledge of every phase of the game. For that is the only way I think a man can become a success in the game to-day.

I don't think managing to-day is simply a matter of sitting in the office buying and selling players and selecting the team.

It's necessary to be able to understand and take an interest in all that the players are doing.

I spend most of my spare time studying and giving lectures to clubs and school children in Leeds. All this has a bearing on later development.

Manager George Ainsley—that'd look swell !

THE JOB I'M SUITED FOR

WHEN I'm paying my bob at the turnstile it is going to come out of my wages as an electrician. I served my time as an

by

DON DEARSON

(Birmingham half-back).

electrician. Still think it is the job I'm most suited for.

If I can take a wireless set to pieces or fit an electric bell to a door I'm in my seventh heaven. Now I'm learning the office side of the electrician's business, too.

I work occasionally in the office of Mr Wiseman, one of our directors, who has a plumbers' business.

I'm studying Shorthand Because—

I WANT to be a clerk. That was my job before I began playing. Regular hours—knowing exactly what you've to do and when to do it—steady wage. That's my idea of security in life.

When I was clerking at Boston, my home-

by

REG. TOMLINSON

(Southampton centre-forward).

place in Lincs, I only had one grouse. I only got one Saturday afternoon off a fortnight and was only able to play football half as often as I'd have liked! When I'm older that won't affect me!

I'm a pretty good book-keeper, but I can't write shorthand. I've discovered since that shorthand is useful in any sort of office job, so I'm studying it in my spare time.

career with a dead end, and I remember the hard luck stories that used to be told of the old-timers who hung about the entrance of the dressing room on match days, hoping for help. A few seasons ago, before an away match, one of these old timers, with hair turned grey, made an appeal to us for assistance and, as has long been the custom, we had a whip-round for him. Afterwards, when we were travelling home at night, the tragic plight of the old fellow was discussed, and a young player with some imagination remarked, "Is that the end? Is that what we all come to?"'

Chapman considered that there were many attractive possibilities available to players in the 1930s, 'provided a man has fitted himself to exploit them…' and that, 'anyone who has to hang around dressing rooms cadging half crowns has only himself to blame'. Football, Chapman declared, could not be held responsible for such men. 'There are, of course, fools in football, as in every other walk of life. I might tell of the letters I receive from players who have grown too old for the game, and who have been thrown on their own limited resources. Pathetic, even tragic, appeals are made to me to appoint them as scouts, or to find them employment as coaches.'

Chapman was of the opinion that players should have a trade, that they should work at something outside the game. 'I am always glad when any player of mine wants to work. In the first place it is an assurance to me that the man who makes this demand has intelligence. He is thinking about the future and what his position will be when his playing days come to an end. I am happy to say that we have several players with the Arsenal who either work or who are fitting themselves to work when they must inevitably find another means of earning their living. I wish there were more.'

Before the First World War, the plight of players who had no 'second string to their bow' as Chapman put it, was already causing the newly re-formed Players' Union concern. Indeed, it was one of the main reasons the Union had been resuscitated. Walter Bull, an officer of the Union, wrote in 1909, 'At every meeting we get appeals from old players, or their families, and already we have not been backward in our grants. I recall the pathetic case of an internationalist, whose name was once a household word. He broke his leg in the middle of his playing career. Although he was a steady chap he had not much money saved and he was left alone with a wife and one or two children to provide for as best he could…'

The principal concern for the Union was with players who had injured themselves so badly that a return to their former employment was impossible. As most players were from a manual working-class background, physical fitness was often crucial if they were to resume as miners or factory workers. In effect, some unfortunate men had become redundant twice over. With the profession of football only fitfully recognised by government agencies dealing with sickness and unemployment benefit, and with insurance policies paying trifling amounts to men invalided out of the game, ex-players were often faced with an almighty plunge in earnings.

As an example, Tom Holland of Millwall was plagued by an injury to his knee and, at the beginning of the 1913–14 season, he was not retained because the club could no longer use him. Holland, previously on some £5 a week as a player, had to take work as a cotton operative at 25 s. per week when his playing career ended.

In 1913, a writer for *Football Players' Magazine*, the monthly publication of the Players' Union, recognizing that many players had no previous industrial training, recommended that it would be 'desirable for all players to follow ordinary employment during the week' to ensure that they could acquire other skills. Young men often spent their prime working years playing football so that when they returned to the world of non-football employment, they were forced to compete against younger and better trained workers. He thus urged young players to obtain written permission from their clubs to continue at ordinary work while they were engaged as footballers.

The problem was that many players who sought regular employment in addition to their football work often found obstacles put in their way by club directors who were concerned that outside jobs could affect attendance at practice and training sessions, not to mention endanger the physical health of men they were paying hefty wages to. There was no pattern to it, however. Some clubs allowed men to work, some did not. Others banned certain sorts of work, others seemed not to mind what a man chose to do outside of football hours.

The *Bolton Cricket and Football Field* reported in January 1909 how Sammy Frost, who'd helped Manchester City win the FA Cup in 1903, was forced to recognise how ill-prepared he was for work other than football after recurring knee ailments rendered him expendable by Millwall FC, his last club. Frost admitted that he 'knew no trade or industry, having been a footballer all my life, so that he was 'an unskilled labourer in an already overstocked skilled market'. Manchester City, the club with whom he'd spent the best part of his career, had insisted that its professional players give up their original trades. One of Frost's more illustrious team-mates, Billy Meredith, had been particularly angered by the club's insistence that he cease travelling to and fro from Chirk to continue his job as a miner.

Not too many professionals before the First World War were fortunate enough to avoid having to return to the mines or factories. 'The luckiest and longest-headed,' observed one writer who was not inclined to sympathise with players, 'manage to get themselves set up in public houses, and so long as they limit themselves to selling the drink they do well; but, of course, they form a very small proportion of the whole number.' Several of the first generation of professionals in Lancashire kept pubs while still playing, as it was often part of the deal that had taken them to the club in the first place. An advertisement for a 'first class forward', which appeared in the column of the *Athletic News* in 1890, stipulated that the successful applicant would be 'required to act as manager of a fully licensed house, the headquarters of the club...'.

In 1886, the Blackburn Rovers player, Hugh McIntyre, considered to be one of the very first professionals, was landlord of the Castle, a pub in the town, while another Blackburn player, Fergie Suter, also a candidate for the 'original professional', was landlord of the County Arms in the same town in the 1890s. About half the great Sunderland team of the 1890s were thought to be public house landlords. Billy George, the Aston Villa keeper, was given permission by the club to keep an outdoor beer-house in 1903. Similarly, Harry Stafford, captain of the Manchester United team around the turn of the century, later became licensee of one of the public houses owned by the brewery whose chairman was also chairman of the club.

Becoming a publican was, perhaps, inevitable where clubs such as Aston Villa and Manchester City were backed by brewers. They often had their original headquarters in public houses. Manchester City's was the Hyde Road Hotel, and Billy Meredith, their most famous player in pre-First World War days, would be a publican in the city for twenty years or so after he finished playing, even though he was teetotal and his brother, a Methodist preacher, insisted on crossing the threshold singing temperance songs.

However, there were only so many public houses to go round, and normally only high profile men were offered them, their name and reputation being an attraction to customers. There was an increasing tendency, however, as time went on, for clubs to ban players from taking licensed premises. Len Graham's Millwall contract for 1932 even banned him from living on licensed premises. Firm evidence as to what men did after their football careers were over is hard to come by. Occasionally, however, one is afforded a glimpse.

In the summer of 1908, the *Athletic News* investigated what had happened to the players of the all-conquering Preston North End team of the late 1880s and the Sunderland 'team of all the talents' of the 1890s. Of the twelve former Preston players, three had died, two were in football management, one was working as a coal miner in Scotland, one was a solicitor and one had migrated to South Africa. The remaining four were said to be 'living' here and there. Of the ten ex-Sunderland men listed, two were dead, two kept pubs, one had a 'large shop' in Newcastle-on-Tyne, one was in farming, one was an electrical engineer, one was employed at a printing works, one was in football management and another was 'living on Tyneside'.

In 1930, a similar survey of Manchester's two pre-First World War Cup-winning sides – City of 1904 and United of 1909 – revealed that City could boast one electrician, four publicans, three men still in the game as coaches or trainers and one land surveyor, while two were dead. United had two men working in manual trades, four who had built up their own businesses, three who were in pubs, one who was still in the game as a trainer and two who had died.

Three of the above had done particularly well for themselves: Jimmy Turnbull was a wealthy pawnbroker, Harry Moger had built up a flourishing bookmaker's business, while Charlie Roberts had established a wholesale/retail tobacconist business that would continue into the 1980s.

Finally, in 1936, *Topical Times* ran a series which looked at the fates of men who'd been in Cup Final teams between 1910 and 1915. Fifteen were dead, thirteen were in manual trades, eleven were either coaching, scouting or managing, sixteen had pubs or sweet-shops, three had substantial businesses while one, Charles Buchan, was a journalist.

SPORTS PICTURES
and
FOOTBALL MIRROR

No. 287. [Registered at the G.P.O. as a Newspaper] For West Ending SATURDAY, SEPT. 27, 1924. [Phone Central 5174] [20 Pages.] Two Pence

FORWARD! THAT'S HIS MOTTO.

Stanley Seymour, Newcastle's famous wing forward, is a keen business man. He realises that a footballer's playing days are very limited and, wisely, he gives practically every moment he can spare away from St. James's Park to fostering his tobacco and confectionery store. (*Excl.*)

While it's true that many of these men could be considered 'stars', the wage 'cap' had restricted the amount that even top men could earn and, though less than a third of players actually received the 'Maximum', the spread of wages from the top men to the journeymen was not particularly wide. Thus, the post-football careers of these men could be said to be typical.

Players whose careers fell during the inter-war years would seem to have continued in this uncontroversial vein. In 1939, beneath the headline, 'Where are the Boys of the Old Brigade?' Tommy 'Boy' Browell, a legendary player with Manchester City in the 1920s and 1930s, cheerfully posed as the bus driver he then was for Lytham St Annes' Corporation. In the same year, the same paper carried an article, 'When I Finish With the Game', in which players talked of what they were planning to do when they hung up their boots. Reg Smith of Millwall, Don Dearson of Birmingham City and Reg Tomlinson of Southampton talked of going back to their old trades: electrical engineer, electrician, and clerk respectively. Harry Cann of Plymouth Argyle revealed he was studying to be an insurance salesman; George Ainsley of Leeds was attending summer courses at Leeds to become a coach; while Bert Johnston of Sunderland was considering farming, as it was in his family.

After the Second World War, however, there was much breast-beating in the popular press about the 'destitute footballer', the man thrown on the scrap heap, cruelly abandoned by 'the game' and condemned to a life of humiliation and penury. Jimmy Guthrie, the Players' Union secretary at the time, was waging a campaign to force the Football League to release monies from its Jubilee Fund to pay pensions to men forced out of the game by injury or disability.

In September 1948, the sad case of Arthur 'Boyo' Evans was highlighted in the *Sunday People*. Evans had been a promising young player for West Bromwich Albion until his sight had failed. At 24, he had no way of supporting himself and his wife. The club, having released him, paid him his accrued share of benefit – £350 – and said they'd try and look after him, 'under the laws of the game', while the League Secretary commented that they'd consider his case, 'if an application is put into the League'. Guthrie considered his treatment a disgrace.

Some months later, in the same paper, Jim Dillimore, an ex-Millwall player, was pictured playing a mouth organ outside Millwall's ground, and busking for coppers 'from the crowds who no longer recognised him…' according to reporter Alan Hoby.

Dillimore had played in an England international trial before the war, scored the winning goal and looked set to be a big star. The following week, however, he broke a leg. The following season, after five years with Millwall, he was given a free transfer, but no benefit. He moved to non-League Weymouth and thence to Chatham, where he managed to break his other leg. His last match was the unemployed men's final at Wembley. In 1948 he was drawing unemployment benefit of 37s 6d a week and held a Disabled Person's Card. He applied to the Football League for help and Fred Howarth, the League Secretary, wrote back to inform him that only those on 'active service' in May 1938 were eligible for funds. Dillimore was also turned down by the FA Benevolent Fund.

Dillimore was quoted as saying, 'And to think I gave up a safe £6 a week job to earn £5 a week from professional football! I was disabled as a result of playing professional football and I reckon I am entitled to something from the game I still love and gave so much to…'

(Dillimore was something of a professional busker, however. Originally from Barking, he regularly entertained the crowds queuing to enter the Vicarage Field by playing an accordion.)

Over the next few years, various footballing 'legends' suffered the ignominy of having to appeal to the sentiments and generosity of football fans to rescue them from the sorry states into which they had fallen. These cases seemed to suggest that the higher the footballer reached in fame, the less equipped he was to manage his withdrawal from the game. The long and rocky career of pre-First World War player George 'Gatling Gun' Hilsden was a case in point. Playing for Chelsea and West Ham, he earned the top wage

George Mee, the singing footballer of Derby County, rehearsing some of the songs he puts over so well at Blackpool (c. 1934).

and took a benefit in 1912 of £200. He was also able to earn extra money by writing newspaper articles and, while at Chelsea, he was on a lucrative bonus system whereby he earned £1 for every goal he scored.

However, as his biographer, Colm Kerrigan, put it, 'He developed a taste for the good life,' and saved little. After being gassed during the First World War, he wasn't retained by West Ham and in 1921 was spotted working on a building site somewhere in London, making the tea. In 1924, he appeared on the music-hall stage in 'The Football Match', a Fred Karno comedy show from before the war revived by comedian Sandy Powell, but in his latter years he lived in the East End, scraping a living in various ways. One of his escapades during a bleak period was to go around several East End pubs raffling boxes of chocolates but arranging for the prize to be won on every occasion by his wife, who just happened to be on hand to draw the lucky number. Hilsden died in 1941 in Leicester. Four people attended his funeral, which was paid for by the FA. No stone marks his resting place.

Alex James, who was at the height of his fame a decade or so after Hilsden, was probably the first top professional footballer to make a concerted effort to cash in on his name and fame beyond the football pitch. From the time he arrived at Arsenal in 1929, James searched for ways to earn the extra money needed to finance his own 'taste for the good life' he had embraced on arriving in London from Preston North End. He obtained permission from manager Herbert Chapman to hold a well-paid job in Selfridges department store and had his own newspaper column. He was well aware that his name had a certain cash value but the commercial opportunities to exploit it were limited. Unfortunately, he had absolutely no head for business.

When he retired from the game in 1937, he quickly lost what money he had saved by investing in a football pools firm that went bust. He sold his memoirs to the Sunday newspapers, and lent his name to ghosted football match reports. By 1939, just two years after retiring from the game and declaring that he would never take a coaching job, he was forced to do just that. He went to Poland to coach the national side, a job for which he was ill-suited. His only stroke of luck was to escape internment, leaving on a tip-off just before the Germans invaded.

Sports Pictures

THE PAPER FOR ALL SPORTSMEN.

No. 280. [Registered at the G.P.O. as a Newspaper.] [For Week Ending] **SATURDAY, AUGUST 9, 1924.** [Phones:] [20 Pages.] Two Pence

FOOTBALLER AND ARTIST.

J. Seed, the Spurs' popular inside right, is as clever a caricaturist as he is a footballer, and all his chums and many of the club's officials and opponents are victims of his pen and pencil. Inset a sketch of Seed drawn by himself. *(Excl.)*

Ironically, he did own a sweet shop for a short time. Typically, he had bought it on a whim from a woman he met in a pub. He was forced to get rid of it when the local council insisted he install a toilet at the back for the one member of staff the tiny shop was able to accommodate.

James died virtually penniless soon after the Second World War, after being taken on by Arsenal to coach their second and third teams. His sad end was largely the result of his own poor judgement. He had never saved and hadn't invested in a house of his own. Herbert Chapman, his old manager, would have had no sympathy.

Billy Meredith, whose career had begun in 1894 and lasted until the mid-1920s, died in 1958. Just before his death, he was famously visited by Cliff Lloyd, the Players' Union secretary, when he held up his medals and declared that they were all he had after a lifetime in the game, the implication being that he deserved much more than he had received. Meredith, however, had been the proprietor of a prestigious sports goods shop in the early 1900s and had run two very successful public houses during the inter-war years following his retirement from the game in 1924. He'd starred in a feature film, made training films and appeared on stage to introduce them. He had invested in cinemas during the 1920s and had never been short of offers from newspapers keen to use his name above match reports. What's more, in 1912, he had received a record testimonial match pay-out while playing for Manchester United totalling almost £1,200, which was a vast sum of money then.

By the late 1930s, however, he was so deeply in debt that the Players' Union had to lend him money to pay it off. In 1947, yet another testimonial match was organised for him in Chirk, the village of his birth. He was buried in an unmarked grave in Southern Cemetery, Manchester.

In 1958, the same year that Meredith died, Fred Keenor, a Welsh hero with Cardiff City in the 1920s, and who led the 'Bluebirds' to two Cup Finals in 1925 and 1927, was discovered working as a builder's labourer in Cardiff. In 1937, just a year after hanging up his boots, he had spent some time in hospital with diabetes. With no visible means of support for his wife and children, an appeal had been launched, backed by the Football Association of Wales. By the time he died in 1972, however, he had been forgotten again, yet fifteen years later he was described in one of Cardiff City's official publications as 'quite simply the greatest Bluebird of all'.

Yet another Welsh legend, John Charles, also fell an awful long way before someone reached out to give him a hand. His initial fortune, earned in Italy in the 1950s, was largely lost in a failed restaurant venture. For a time, he ran a sports shop trading on his name in Cardiff, and after that he was a genial, but ultimately poor, publican. Charles had a mild brush with the law in 1976 when he was fined £25 for handling leather jackets, which turned out to be stolen. Later, in 1988, he spent a degrading evening in a police cell. He owed £943 in taxes on the pub, and three women magistrates in Huddersfield were not convinced by his plea that friends in football had promised a testimonial game that would pay off his debts. The magistrates sentenced him to sixty days' imprisonment. He served three hours before his second wife, Glenda, borrowed the money to bail him out. At the time they were existing on £70-a-week in social security benefit.

Wilf Mannion, Middlesborough's Golden Boy of the 1940s and 1950s, ended up as a tea-boy at ICI's factory near Middlesborough, and Tommy Lawton, after a great career with Everton, Arsenal, Chelsea and Notts County, was put on probation for three years in 1970 after various cheques bounced. The sad stories are legion. Whether they are indicative of anything is debatable, but they have often been used to suggest that footballers have been exploited and robbed and then thrown onto society's scrap heap. Yet all these men had earned far more money than their social peers and had been able, to a greater or lesser extent, to trade on their names. They had all either met with bad luck or shown poor judgement in preparing for their eventual retirement. They cannot be used as sticks with which to beat football authorities, however. What's more, in every case, it was football that came to their rescue, with the monies from testimonial matches putting them back on their feet, paying off debts, and securing them pensions.

Perhaps it was the sheer incongruity of their situations that upset football fans so much, the feeling that something else should have happened, and that these men could not be blamed for what had happened to them. They were household names, essential elements of a romantic history.

The story of Jack Slater, however, suggests that the average professional player, given some business acumen, some luck and a lot of ambition, was well placed to make a great deal more of his life after football than was commonly expected. In 1919, Slater told readers of the *Weekly News* how he had built up a considerable fortune from relatively modest beginnings.

'As a boy, football was my hobby and at the age of sixteen I was asked to sign as a full-back for Bolton Wanderers. A wage of £4 a week was too much of a temptation for a boy to resist and I signed.' He played for eight seasons, mainly in the Second Division, gaining promotion in 1909. After that, he was a reserve for three more seasons until August 1914, when he joined South Liverpool.

The son of a publican and living locally, he was in a position to save the money he earned as a footballer mainly because, having started work as a colliery clerk on leaving school, at the age of seventeen he was appointed managing salesman by Messrs Pearson and Knowles, a large Lancashire coal firm. 'After that,' he said, 'I never looked back.'

When he was nineteen he started on his own as a coal merchant, factor and exporter. By 1919, aged 30, and only five years after signing for South Liverpool, he owned nine collieries, an iron and steel works, blast furnaces, plus three ship-building yards. He was a Lloyds underwriter, had homes in Cheadle and London, had his own marine insurance corporation, his own life insurance company and, as if that wasn't enough, 'I own the second largest fishing fleet in the world'.

By 1932, according to the *Daily Mail*, he was the 'mystery man of millions', a man who 'uses aeroplanes like taxi-cabs'. He'd become involved in extensive City deals and acquired a controlling interest in Amalgamated Industrials Ltd, a deal that eventually lost him as many millions when Amalgamated went into liquidation. It hardly dented his fortunes. He was elected Conservative MP for the town but died suddenly of a heart attack in 1935, aged just 46.

Slater's incredible business success, though utterly untypical of players before the Second World War, was later emulated, if not in quite such a dramatic fashion, by Dave Whelan, the Blackburn Rovers full-back. Badly injured in the 1960 Cup Final against Wolverhampton Wanderers, he soon realised that he would never be the same again and that his promising career and England aspirations were over at 23 years of age. He made a comeback playing for Crewe, helping them get into the Third Division, but when he cracked a cheekbone he decided to retire and dedicate himself to running a market stall in Wigan. While playing for Blackburn Rovers, he'd apparently worked on Blackburn market where two traders taught him how to buy and sell toiletries. Now he put that experience to good use.

His Wigan stall was very successful: 'I used to sell patent medicines, toilet rolls, etc.' He even went to the High Court in London to do battle with the Pharmacists' Association for selling patent medicines such as aspirin and Beecham's Powders from a market stall. He won the case and, soon after, he purchased a small supermarket. He was an innovative salesman (he even sent his father round Wigan dressed in a suit of armour and carrying a placard advertising prices). He borrowed ideas that he'd seen in America while playing there, such as special sandwiches, and within a few years the single supermarket became ten. In 1978, he sold out for £1.5m. After a few days' rest, he bought a sports shop in Wigan called JJB Sports for £7,400, and introduced the self-service concept. He built up a multi-million pound empire of 450 stores with a £650m turnover. His personal fortune is said to be worth £300m.

Other enterprising players have since followed his example: Manchester City's Francis Lee making his millions from toilet paper; Chelsea's Ron 'Chopper' Harris becoming a multi-millionaire from building golf-courses. Recently, race-horse trainer and ex-Southampton winger Mick Channon paid £2m for a complete stable of horses. Johnny Haynes, famous for being the first £100-a-week player, established his financial security by going into partnership with a bookmaker called Tommy Benfield, a business they eventually sold to the Tote. Today he lives in Edinburgh, where he helps his wife run a dry-cleaning business.

Where Jack Slater is unique in British football history, however, was his entry into Parliament. Apart from a few local councillors, no ex-British footballer has made any sort of mark in public life that has not involved football in some way. In America, by contrast, 'legendary' professional sportsmen have regularly entered politics, some at the highest level. Jack Kemp, a great pro-football star with the Buffalo Bills, was a cabinet member and congressman as well being Senator Bob Dole's running mate in the

1996 presidential election. Tom Osborn, a famous football coach with Nabraska, entered the US House of Representatives, while Steve Largent, an All-Time Great footballer with the Seattle Seahawks became a congressman. Baseball pitchers Jim Bunning and Wilmer Mizell became a US senator and congressman respectively, while pro basketball star Tom McMahon was also a congressmen. To top it all, Byron (Whizzer) White, who won All-American honours and National Football League stardom just before the Second World War, was appointed one of the Supreme Court Justices in 1962 by President Kennedy.

In this country, other than Slater, the closest any soccer player has come to such significant public figures would be the late Sid Weighall, who was leader of the National Union of Railwaymen from 1975 to 1982. Weighall was a Sunderland reserve team player in October 1945. He was already working on the railway when he was offered £10 to sign on, £3 a match, plus travelling expenses. Though he travelled with the first team once or twice, covering for the regular inside-left, Raich Carter, he never seriously considered it as a career: 'I don't know how good I might have been; but even at the top of the profession you didn't go beyond thirty years of age and the pay then was nothing like as good as today's. The money from the football allowed me to buy the second-hand MG sports car, so comparatively speaking I was well off.'

English footballers who might have made a move into top politics had they been Americans would surely have been the World Cup winning 'Boys of '66'. Instead, they became after-dinner speakers, car insurance salesmen, ran family haulage and undertakers' businesses, managed football teams or dabbled in property. All received honours, but only one – Sir Bobby Charlton – has moved into anything approaching public life, as a roving ambassador for English football and Manchester United.

Why top soccer players have never made an impact outside the game is due to a combination of factors, primarily class, education and inclination. Where politics are concerned, the Conservatives would always have been too middle-class an organisation to have considered soccer players as parliamentary candidates (though a number of players in the 1930s did stand as local Conservative councillors.) The Labour Party has, until recently, refused to take football seriously, a reverse form of snobbery in which the greatest working-class spectator sports was considered a capitalist diversion. By contrast, the American political system has traditionally been more open to using popular personalities as figureheads.

Where education is concerned, many top professional American athletes have spent time at university on sporting scholarships – something completely unknown in this country – whereas the majority of British footballers have, until recently, shunned formal education almost completely. That, combined with the traditional studied indifference to anything beyond the confines of the football stadium, has left the soccer player an unlikely candidate for high office.

Also, again unlike the American experience, few British players have moved into show business in any significant way once their careers have ended. Billy Meredith was the first British footballer to star in a feature film as long ago as 1926, but as he was in his fifties by then, a career on the silver screen did not beckon. The 'Singing Footballer', George Mee, who was a regular performer on Blackpool Promenade in the 1930s, was never destined to become another George Formby, and though Sheffield Wednesday's Colin Grainger had a good enough crooner's voice to earn him regular guest appearances in variety theatres during the 1950s, he was never offered a recording contract. Hoddle and Waddle's 'Diamond Lights', though a hit record in the 1980s, was never seen as a career move for either of them. Ex-West Bromich Albion and England striker Jeff Astle did utilise a once fine voice to earn himself a short career doing skit songs on Skinner and Baddiel's *Fantasy Football League* television programme. Astle later toured the country in his own show in which he reminisced about his career – while dressed as Tina Turner.

One ex-British footballer who did make it into the big time as a performer was Charlie Williams, the Doncaster Rovers full-back, whose career was ended in 1960 by injury. Williams might have missed his opportunity had it not been for the fact that he was black. In 1962 he was offered a job as a player-coach by the Australian football team Auburn (near Sydney). He was guaranteed a house and £60–£70 a week, which was a lot of money in those days. 'But when the Australian immigration people saw from my passport that I were coloured, they decided I couldn't go,' a decision that the normally phlegmatic Williams admitted, 'hurt like hell at the time'. A campaign in British newspapers saw the decision rescinded, but Williams said no. ('To hell with that.')

However, he was equally unsuccessful at securing a job in early 1960s Britain, again due to his colour. Even that most traditional of footballers' standbys was never an option for him: 'I tried the breweries, to see if I could become landlord of a public house. But as soon as I turned up for the interview, that was it.'

He had won the occasional amateur talent competition and, 'as a footballer, I used to tell gags with the lads on the bus'. He turned his attention to building a career on the northern club and pub circuit, earning as little as £3 a gig in the early years. Being adept at handling hecklers and never afraid to use risqué, even racist, material, Williams gradually built himself a good solid working man's club career earning between £80 and £100 a week. He appeared on Yorkshire television telling jokes with Freddie Trueman, and in 1971 was offered the chance to appear on a national TV show called *The Comedians*.

It was crude, lewd, vulgar and wildly successful. With Ken Goodwin, Mike Reid, Bernard Manning and others, Charlie Williams became a household name. Within a couple of years, he moved on to compere *The Golden Shot* quiz show. He appeared in feature films such as *Man at the Top* and made some LPs. He was eventually the subject of the *This Is Your Life* programme.

Despite criticism of his blunt, head-on approach to race and a politically incorrect tendency to tell jokes against himself as a way of sending the whole 'race' issue up, Williams' achievements were remarkable and, until quite recently, there hasn't been another ex-pro footballer to match him in the field.

The Hollywood stardom that has recently come to Vinnie Jones, ex-Wimbledon and Sheffield United player, suggests that the British soccer player now moves in slightly more exalted circles than previously. Jones is, perhaps, a poor example, having built a reputation for gratuitous violence both on and off the football field, which he subsequently exploited in violent gangster movies. However, a football related movie, *The Mean Machine*, in which he plays a disgraced England captain, banned from the game for bribery and jailed for a drunken assault does approach some sort of sporting reality, being based on an old Bert Reynolds movie in which the hero was an American footballer, a sport renowned for physical violence. Jones didn't want to do the film originally: 'But when they explained it wasn't going to be like all those other naff [football] films, I agreed.' Sadly, the public disagreed…

The media success of ex-players like Gary Lineker, Alan Hansen and Mark Lawrenson, however, suggests something more substantial has happened in terms of post-football employment opportunities. The aforementioned trio sit at the peak of the new media world that has opened up for ex-footballers. Ex-professionals have gradually, from the mid-1970s, become a conduit through which we now view the game. They analyse it, discuss it, they present it and hand it back to us. Even though their objectivity is, at times, questionable, they are 'authentic' because they have played the game. The two major TV channels took twenty-five ex-players to the 2002 World Cup to act as pundits and commentators. The trained journalists may still write the copy, but on TV the ex-player is king.

It could be argued that this development is unrepresentative. There are only so many such jobs to go round, and they are dependent on the surge of TV money that flooded the game in the 1990s and which now looks like drying up. However, the TV 'boom' of the 1990s was based on significant, much broader changes in the way the game is now viewed and 'consumed' by fans, reflecting, in turn, changes that have occurred in the way the populace spends its leisure time.

Prior to the 1960s and 1970s, opportunities to remain in and around the professional game, unless you were a player, trainer or man-ager, were scarce. Today, however, football clubs, large and small, are more akin to social centres, offering many more job opportunities for players. They are now corporate entertainment venues, incorporating museums, restaurants and even shopping centres. They have become, to greater and lesser degrees, football 'experiences', offering a variety of in-club promotional jobs on club TV and radio stations, 'Football In The Community' schemes, ground tours, etc.

This leisure 'industry', of which football is a small but significant part, has transformed the lives of ex-athletes. Today, the fan can touch and talk to any number of local 'legends', who might once have dis-appeared into council-house penury: Charlie George and Nobby Stiles are just a couple of the more well-known. It's as if the old players, who once begged outside grounds for a few coppers, have now been invited inside to embroider and adorn the leisure moments of fans who wish to take a trip down their own special memory lane.

The vast changes in general leisure patterns have also provided opportunities for ex-players to move into jobs and careers that their special skills, experience and even image as footballers afford them entry to. Leisure centres, holiday cruises and villages, indeed, the leisure and fitness industry in general can use ex-sportsmen as coaches, fitness experts and games organisers.

The trend began a decade or so ago. In 1999, of the twenty-one members of the 1979 Manchester United team, fifteen were still in football and sport in some capacity. Some were club managers, scouts and coaches, one was a leisure centre manager; there was a School of Excellence coach and a PFA executive. Three were in television, two were in business, one was a sports agent, one had become a teacher, while four were in manual trades (two of the latter being players who had failed to establish themselves in the team and had drifted out of the game).

In 2002, Sports Workshop Promotions, a specialist sports agency based in London, outlined the potential for current and ex-pro players: 'Requests for both famous and non-famous players in all aspects of TV have been on the increase for some time. Partly because there are so many new TV channels with airtime to be filled and partly due to footballers themselves having broken new ground in TV. In printed media, the advertising agencies and photographers are finding that footballers make ideal models because of their well-conditioned physiques, good looks, natural co-ordination and, in many cases, flexible schedules, which are suited to filming.'

But it's not just leisure-related industries that ex-pros are making their mark in. Over the last couple of decades, the PFA has grown into an influential employment-cum-re-training agency for ex-players, helping its members into careers in all areas of life from fish farming to banking, the law, and small business. Grants are available for education as is a great deal of expert advice, the PFA being well supplied with money from TV to carry out such work. In fact, it was the struggle with the Premiership in 2001 over its share of TV monies that took the players' organisation to the brink of a strike.

Paul Lake, former Manchester City and England star, was tipped for stardom when he suffered a cruciate ligament injury in 1988. Eight years of struggle to regain fitness and make a comeback ended in 1996 with his retirement. With the help of the Professional Footballers' Association, he became a chartered physiotherapist and, together with a remedial masseur, Paul Webster, has opened a sports injury and therapy clinic in Northenden, Manchester, with the objective of keeping amateur sportsmen and women fit to play. 'There are probably hundreds of weekend athletes, amateur soccer players and runners who probably wouldn't know where to go for specialised treatment if they picked up an injury. Well, they can come along to our clinic in Northenden to get diagnosis and treatment, which will get them back on their feet quickly and back into their sport.'

The days when men such as Mannion, Lawton and James could find themselves drifting from poorly paid jobs to the dole office have probably ended. Individuals may still squander fortunes or drink themselves to death, but real opportunities are there. However, we are told by many ex-professionals that football is a drug and withdrawal symptoms can be lethal.

Lee Chapman's father was also a professional footballer and died of a heart attack when middle-aged: 'My father had paid the price. He had been out of professional football for about two years, unable to get another job in the game. He had only ever known the world of football, as a player, coach and manager over a period of thirty years. His time in the game had seen him earn very little money and in his need to pay the bills he had taken a job as a sports company representative. He had spent the majority of his time under great stress behind the wheel of his company car. After spending his life out in the open, he was now confined to a car for most of the week, and I have few doubts that this change in lifestyle resulted in his death. The mind is all powerful and my father had been desperately unhappy for quite some time.'

Nothing, it seems, can replace the excitement and the emotional highs that football brings. Andy Gray, the Sky TV expert commentator, when asked if commentating was better than playing, replied: 'Not at all. You can never replace playing the game. The adrenaline, the buzz, the excitement − live TV goes a little way to softening the blow of not playing by giving you a snapshot of those things.' Gary Lineker, with the BBC, agreed. 'I think it's difficult to replace football − the surge of adrenaline, the sense of being on the edge, slightly dangerous. And television does give you that edge.' Even film star Vinny Jones admitted that Hollywood stardom was just a substitute for playing: 'When I've got lines, and it's my scene, I still get the adrenaline rush I had when I was playing soccer.'

The adrenaline 'rush' and the security of that closed world of the team dressing room; the metronomic routine of training, relaxing, playing, training; the endless banter and laughter that accompanies the collective struggle; the magic carpet that whisks you from game to game with few of the day-to-day cares of the fans who watch and wish they were you; the loss of all these makes leaving the profession very difficult and coping with its loss extremely stressful. The long anticlimax of the rest of your life, as one ex-pro described it, must seem like an eternity. Some men find the experience too difficult.

The story is told of Archie Hunter, the old Aston Villa star of the 1880s who, close to death, asked that his bed be pushed to the window so that he could watch the crowds streaming towards Villa Park where he had once been their idol. In an interview in early 2000, a more contemporary ex-star, Alan Hudson, told commentator Brian Moore, 'If I wrote a book, I'd call it *They Don't Shoot Footballers, Do They?* Because they should. So many of us go down that horrible road. Terrible. It all happens so quickly and there's nothing there at the end of it for you. And it really is heart breaking, really.' Terry Butcher, ex-Ipswich and England star put it more simply: 'When you're a footballer you think you're going to live forever, play forever, the money's going to come in forever. It's a Walter Mitty world really.'

A world which even a real-life Walter Mitty, the rich and successful multi-millionaire JJB man, Dave Whelan, wished he had never been forced to leave. When asked if the injury that had ended his career was, in a perverse way, a stroke of luck, he replied: 'What I wanted to do was pull on a white shirt for England. I wanted it desperately, but when you're injured like that, you've had it, you can't do it. So was I lucky? No, I'd have sooner carried on with football. Football is the best profession to be in, always has been, always will be.'

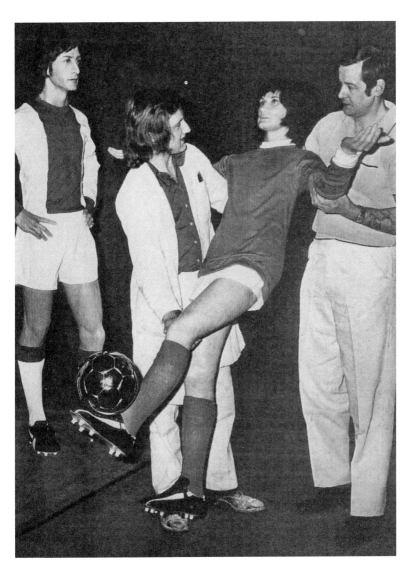

The end of the road:
George Best is
replaced by Johann
Cruyff at Madame
Tussauds in 1973.

Rules of the Trade

<u>Millwall Athletic and Football Club, Limited</u>

Rules to Players
1933

Players, except those in employment, are requested to attend at the ground (except when otherwise advised) each morning NOT LATER THAN 10 o'clock and in the afternoon NOT LATER THAN 2.30 o'clock for training purposes, and to obtain Manager's or Trainer's permission before leaving.

All players to sign the Training Book each morning and afternoon (when requested to attend) with the CORRECT time of their arrival.

No player during his engagement with this club – close and playing season – shall be allowed to ride on or drive a motor cycle and/or side car.

No player shall be permitted to reside in, or be engaged in any capacity on Licensed Premises.

Players in employment are likewise requested to attend at the Ground on Tuesday and Thursday Evenings, from 5 to 8pm for training, or such evenings as arranged with the Trainers.

ALL players must be indoors at their home or lodgings by 10pm on the evening preceding match days. Players on the sick or injured list must produce a Doctor's Certificate, and be indoors (home or lodgings) not later than 8pm.

Illness as an excuse for non-attendance to the provisions of this notice will not be accepted unless a Doctor's Certificate is produced.

Week-end leave not allowed except under very special circumstances.

All players will be supplied with their football outfit, and will be held responsible for the loss of same. All such outfits to be returned to the Trainer when requested.

Any case of infectious disease to be notified at once.

Anyone not complying with the above rules will be dealt with by the Directors.

NOTE. The above rules will be strictly enforced.

By Order of the Directors,

R. Hunter.

SPORTS PICTURES
and
FOOTBALL MIRROR

No. 286. | [Registered at the G.P.O. as a Newspaper.] | [For Week Ending] | SATURDAY, SEPT. 20, 1924. | [Phone: CENTRAL 5373.] | [20 Pages.] | Two Pence

THE FOOTBALLER'S DOLL'S HOUSE.

Sam Tonner, Clapton Orient's captain, can do other things well besides play football, as will be seen from our exclusive picture showing the doll's house which he is constructing for his bonny children. It is not quite as pretentious as the Queen's Doll's House at Wembley, of course, but it is a very excellent model all the same.

£200 FOR ONLY SIX AWAY. NO GOALS WANTED.

AND YOU CAN PICK WHERE YOU LIKE. *See page 19.*

Top players' earnings through the decades

1950s	1960s	1970s
Sir Stan Matthews **£12 a week**	**Bobby Moore** **£150 a week**	**Kevin Keegan** **£2,000 a week**
Barber's son from Stoke had a 33-year career with Blackpool, Stoke City and England (54 caps). Known as the 'Wizard of the Dribble'. Died in 2000.	Led England to famous 1966 World Cup victory. Pelé described him as 'the greatest defender I ever played against.' OBE. Died in 1993.	Miner's son from Doncaster made 230 League appearances and scored 68 goals for Liverpool. Moved to Hamburg for £500,000. 63 caps.
Highest earnings £650 a year.	**Highest Earnings** £7,800 a year at West Ham; £1,000 bonus for winning World Cup.	**Highest Earnings** £100,000 a year.
Other Income £20 a week for newspaper column plus £15 from Co-op.	**Other Income** £3,000 for Kellogg's ad in 1970. Total earnings that year were £22,000.	**Other Income** Various including Patrick boots. Total: £150,000 a year.
House Boarding house on Blackpool Prom.	**House** £100,000 'dream home' in Chigwell.	**House** Stud farm in Hampshire.
Car Ford Popular.	**Car** Basic Model Jaguar.	**Car** Range Rover.
Style Saved wisely to afford comfortable retirement in Stoke.	**Style** Gadget-packed home; hobbies included golf, cricket and tennis.	**Style** Invests wisely. Owns racehorses and a library of self-help books.
Family First wife was trainer's daughter Betty; two children. Second wife Milla, a Czech cultural attaché.	**Family** Married part-time model Tina in 1962; two children. Married second wife Stephanie in 1991.	**Family** Married childhood sweetheart Jean. Two daughters.
Holidays Golf in Scotland.	**Holidays** Barbados, Brazil, Italy.	**Holidays** Marbella.

1980s	1990s	2000s
John Barnes **£10,000 a week**	**Paul Gascoigne** **£25,000 a week**	**David Beckham** **£100,000+ a week**
One of world's best wingers in the 1980s. Born in Jamaica. Found fame with Watford, Liverpool and England. Footballer of the Year 1988.	Tears at 1990 World Cup; ushered in new period of football fashion. Life since blighted by scandals, injury and alcohol.	England Captain, who married Victoria Adams (Posh Spice) and whose World Cup exploits against Argentina in 1998 and 2000 captivated the nation.
Highest Earnings Best paid player in Britain at one time on £500,000 a year at Liverpool.	**Highest Earnings** £1.3m a year when he went to Rangers from Lazio. £1m signing-on fee.	**Highest Earnings** £75,000 a week plus £20,000 a week 'image' rights.
Other Income Substantial fees for Isotonic Lucozade Sport ad.	**Other Income** Walkers Crisps ads – £250,000; adidas deal – £150,000.	**Other Income** £1m sponsorship deals with Castrol, Marks & Spencer, Police sunglasses, Sony PlayStation and Golden Wonder crisps.
House Luxury home in Hemel Hempstead, Herts.	**House** £430,000 home in Kilbarchan, near Glasgow.	**House** £500,000 penthouse in Cheshire; £2.6m mansion in Herts (spent £3m doing it up).
Car Bespoke Ford Capri.	**Car** Usually chauffeur-driven.	**Cars** Porsche, Ferrari, Range Rover, TVR. £165,000 Bentley for his last birthday.
Style Committed family man. Sartorial tastes of the exotic kind.	**Style** Nights on town with mates are the stuff of front page scandal.	**Style** Designer everything; haircuts change regularly, setting trends for millions.
Family Married to Suzy; four children.	**Family** Married Sheryl in 1995 but marriage foundered. Son Regan.	**Family** Wife Victoria Adams, sons Brooklyn and Romeo.
Holidays Jamaica, Hong Kong.	**Holidays** Hawaii.	**Holidays** Elton John's Villa in the south of France.

Books:

Book of Football, Amalgamated Press, 1906.

Agnew, Paul, *Finney: A Football Legend*, Carnegie, 1989.

Allison, Malcolm, *Colours Of My Life*, Everest, 1975.

Astle, Jeff, *Striker!*, Pelham, 1970.

Barnes, Wally, *Captain of Wales*, Stanley Paul, 1953.

Bastin, Cliff and Glanville, Brian, *Cliff Bastin Remembers*, Ettrick, 1950.

Buchan, Charles, *A Lifetime In Football*, Phoenix House, 1955.

Bull, David, *Dell Diamond: Ted Bates' First 60 Years With The Saints*, Hagiography, 1998.

Cameron, John, *Association Football and How To Play It*, Health and Strength, 1906.

Campbell, Denis, May, Pete, Shields, Andrew, *The Lad Done Bad*, Penguin Books, 1996.

Carter, Raich, *Footballer's Progress*, Sporting Handbooks, 1950.

Cashmore, Ernest, *Black Sportsmen*, Routledge and Kegan Paul,1982.

Catton, Jimmy, *The Real Football*, Sands, 1900.

Chapman, Herbert, *Herbert Chapman on Football*, Garrick, 1934.

Chapman, Lee, *More Than a Match*, Stanley Paul, 1992.

Charlton, Jack, *The Autobiography*, Partridge, 1996.

Claridge, Steve with Ian Ridley, *Tales From The Boot Camps*, Gollantz, 1997.

Cullis, Stan, *All For The Wolves*, Rupert Hart Davis, 1960.

Dixon, Kerry, *The Autobiography*, McDonald, 1986.

Doherty, Peter, *Spotlight on Football,* Art and Educational Publishers, 1947.

Dougan, Derek, *The Sash He Never Wore*, Allison and Busby, 1972.

Dunphy, Eamon, *Only A Game*, Kestrel, 1976.

Eco, Umberto, *Travels in Hyper Reality*, Secker and Warburg, 1986.

Eyre, Fred, *Kicked Into Touch*, Fred Eyre, 1981.

Farmer, Ted, *The Heartache Game*, Hillburgh, 1987.

Finney, Tom, *Football Round The World*, Museum Press, 1953.

Firmani, Eddie, *Soccer With The Millionaires*, Stanley Paul, 1959.

Fishwick, Nick, *English, Football and Society 1910–1950*, Manchester University Press, 1989.

Ford, Trevor, *I Lead The Attack*, Stanley Paul, 1957.

Franklyn, Neil, *Soccer At Home and Abroad*, Stanley Paul, 1955.

Geldard, Albert and Rowlands, John K., *Albert Geldard*, Countryside, 1989

Gibson and Pickford, *Association Football and the Men Who Made It*, Caxton, 1906.

Glanville, Brian, *Soccer Nemesis*, Secker and Warburg, 1955.

Goodall, John, *Men Famous In Football*, 1905.

Guthrie, Jimmy, *Soccer Rebel*, Pentagon, 1976.

Hapgood, Eddie, *Football Ambassador, Sporting Handbooks*, 1944.

Harding, John, *Alex James*, Robson Books, 1988.

Harding, John, *For The Good of the Game*, Robson Books, 1991.

Harding, John, *Football Wizard*, Robson Books, 1998.

Hardwick, George, *Gentleman George*, Jupiter, 1998.

Holt, Richard, *Sport and the British*, Clarendon, 1990.

Hopcraft, Arthur, *The Football Man*, Collins, 1968.

Inglis, Simon, *Villa Park, 100 Years*, Sports Projects, 1997.

Jackson, N.L., *Association Football*, George Newnes, 1900.

Johnson, Frank, ed., *The Football Who's Who*, Associated and Sporting Press, 1935.

Kerrigan, Colm, *'Gatling Gun George' Hilsdon*, Football Lives, 1997.

Knighton, Leslie, *Behind the Scenes in Big Time Football*, Stanley Paul, 1948.

Lamming, Douglas, *An English Internationalist's Who's Who*, Hutton, 1990.

Lawton, Tommy, *Football Is My Business*, Sports Handbooks, 1946.

Lawton, Tommy, *When the Cheering Stopped*, Golden Eagle, 1973.

Mason, Tony, *Association Football and English Society 1963–1915*, Harvester, 1980.

Morris, Peter, *Aston Villa*, Naldrett Press, 1960.

Moynihan, John, *The Soccer Syndrome*, McGibbon and Kee, 1968.

Mullery, Alan, with Brian Woolnough, *An Autobiography*, Pelham, 1985.

Parkinson, Michael, *Best*, Hutchinson, 1975.

Sammels, Jon with Oxby, Robert, *Double Champions*, Arthur Barker, 1971.

Seed, Jimmy, *Soccer From The Inside*, Thorsons, 1947.

Seed, Jimmy, *The Jimmy Seed Story*, Phoenix Sports Books, 1957.

Shackleton, Len, *Clown Prince of Soccer*, Nicholas Kaye, 1956.

Sissons, Ric, *A Social History of Cricketers*, Kingswood, 1988.

Spalding's Football Guide, British Sports Publishing Company Ltd, 1906.

Stonewall, *Strong Enough To Survive*, 1994.

Swift, Frank, *Football From The Goalmouth*, Sporting Handbooks, 1949.

Taylor, Rogan and Ward, Andrew, *Kicking and Screaming*, Robson Books, 1995.

Tischler, Steve, *Footballers and Businessmen*, Holmes and Meier, 1981.

Tussaud, John Theodore, *The Romance of Madame Tussauds*, Odhams, 1920.

Upton, Gilbert, *Dixie Dean of Tranmere Rovers*, *1923–1925*, 1992.

Venables, Terry, and Hanson, Neil, *Venables, The Autobiography*, Michael Joseph, 1994.

Wagg, Stephen, *The Football World*, Harvester Press, 1984.

Ward, Andrew, and Alister Ian, *Barnsley: A Study in Football 1953–59*, Crowberry, 1981.

Ward, Andrew, *Armed With A Football*, Crowberry, 1994.

Weighall, Sid, *100 Years of Railway Weighalls*, Robson Books, 1984.

Whittaker, Tom, *Whittaker's Arsenal Story*, Sporting Handbooks, 1958.

Williams, Charlie, *Ee- I've Had Some Laughs*, Charlie Williams, 1973.

Young, Percy M., *A History of British Football*, Stanley Paul, 1968.

Journals and Dissertations:

'The Legalisation of the Professional Footballer Steve Redhead', PhD Thesis, 1984.

Manchester United F.C. 'An analysis of the youth policy 1950–1958', Tony Whelan: MA (dissertation): (Manchester Metropolitan University, 1999.)

Soccer and Society: 2001, Vol 2, No 3 (Autumn): Oyvind Larson: Charles Reep: A Major Influence on British and Norwegian Football

Matthew Taylor: Beyond the Maximum Wage: Earnings of Football Professionals In England 1900–39

Journal of Ageing Studies: 1999, Vol 13, No 1: Brian Gearing: More Than A Game

A Kick In The Right Direction: (PFA publication.)

Newspapers and Magazines:

Athletic News
C.B. Fry's Magazine
Charles Buchan's Football Monthly
Daily Mail
F.A. News
The Red Letter
Thomson's Weekly News
Topical Times
Player's Club (PFA)
Saturday Post
Shoot
Sports Budget
Sports Pictures
The People
Sunday Graphic
The 19th Century: (*The New Football Mania, Charles Edwardes, 1898*)
Windsor Magazine
The Footballer Players' Magazine 1914

Foot Ball Shin Guards

No. 1.
Leather with Elastic Fastenings.
Per pair, **2/6**

No. 2.
Gold Cape Straps, and Buckles.
Per pair, **2/9**

No. 3.
Leather Continuous Straps.
Per pair, **2/9**

No. 4.
Gold Cape Continuous Straps.
Per pair, **3/6**

No. 5.
Tan Leather and Ankle Guards.
Per pair, **4/6**

No. 6.
Gold Cape and Ankle Guards.
Per pair, **5/-**

A. G. SPALDING & BROS.
53, 54, and 55 Fetter Lane   LONDON, E. C.